West German Industrialists and the Making of the Economic Miracle

West German Industrialists and the Making of the Economic Miracle

A History of Mentality and Recovery

Armin Grünbacher

Bloomsbury Academic
An imprint of Bloomsbury Publishing Plc

B L O O M S B U R Y
LONDON • OXFORD • NEW YORK • NEW DELHI • SYDNEY

Bloomsbury Academic
An imprint of Bloomsbury Publishing Plc

50 Bedford Square
London
WC1B 3DP
UK

1385 Broadway
New York
NY 10018
USA

www.bloomsbury.com

BLOOMSBURY and the Diana logo are trademarks of Bloomsbury Publishing Plc

First published 2017

British Library Cataloguing-in-Publication Data
A catalogue record for this book is available from the British Library.

ISBN: HB: 978-1-4725-1050-1
ePDF: 978-1-4725-1128-7
eBook: 978-1-4725-1328-1

Library of Congress Cataloging-in-Publication Data
Names: Grèunbacher, Armin, 1962- author.
Title: West German industrialists and the making of the economic miracle : a history of mentality and recovery / Armin Grèunbacher.
Description: London ; New York, NY : Bloomsbury Academic, 2017. | Includes bibliographical references and index.
Identifiers: LCCN 2017000056| ISBN 9781472510501 (hb) | ISBN 9781472513281 (epub)
Subjects: LCSH: Economic development–Germany (West)–History. | Industries–Germany (West)–History. | Germany (West)–Economic conditions. | Germany (West)–Economic policy. | Germany (West)–History. | Germany–History–1945-1990.
Classification: LCC HC286.5 .G7195 2017 | DDC 338.0943–dc23 LC record available at https://lccn.loc.gov/2017000056

Cover image: The 'Miracle Makers' during a BDI members' meeting, 16.5.1957. From left to right: Minister for Economic Co-operation Franz Blücher, Economics Minister Ludwig Erhard, BDI President Fritz Berg, Robert Pferdmenges, BDI Chief Clerk Wilhelm Beutler (shaking hands with Erhard), at the far right Atomic Energy Minister Siegfried Balke. © Bundesverband der Deutschen Industrie, BDI Archiv SF 452 003.

Typeset by RefineCatch Limited, Bungay, Suffolk
Printed and bound in Great Britain

To find out more about our authors and books visit www.bloomsbury.com. Here you will find extracts, author interviews, details of forthcoming events and the option to sign up for our newsletters.

Contents

Illustrations

Tables

Abbreviations

ACDP	Archiv der Christlich-Demokratischen Politik
AKU	Algemene Kunstzijde Unie
ASU	Arbeitsgemeinschaft Selbstständiger Unternehmer
BBA	Bergbau Archiv
BBUG	Baden-Badener Unternehmergespräche
BDA	Bundesverband deutscher Arbeitgeberverbände
BDI	Bundesverband der deutschen Industrie
BMWi	Bundesministerium für Wirtschaft
BWA	Bezirkswirtschaftsamt
CBI	Confederation of British Industry
CDI	Centralverband der deutschen Industriellen
CDU	Christlich Demokratische Union
CoCom	Coordinating Committee (for multilateral export controls)
DA	Diskussionsabend
DAAD	Deutscher Akademischer Austausch Dienst
DAF	Deutsche Arbeitsfront
DDP	Deutsche Demokratische Partei
DEW	Deutsche Edelstahl Werke
DFG	Deutsche Forschungsgesellschaft
DGB	Deutscher Gewerkschaftsbund
DIHT	Deutscher Industrie- und Handelstag
DII	Deutsches Industrie Institut
DM	Deutschmark
DNVP	Deutschnationale Volkspartei
DP	Deutsche Partei

DVP	Deutsche Volkspartei
ECSC	European Coal and Steel Community
FDP	Freie Demokratische Partei
FRG	Federal Republic of Germany
GDP	Gross Domestic Product
GDR	German Democratic Republic
GFU	Gesellschaft zur Förderung des Unternehmernachwuchses
GHH	Gutehoffnungshütte
HGF	Hauptgeschäftsführer
HOAG	Hüttenwerk Oberhausen AG
IHG	Investitionshilfe Gesetz
IHK	Industrie- und Handelskammer(n)
JEIA	Joint Export and Import Agency
KADI	Kriegsausschuß der deutschen Industrie
KPD	Kommunistische Partei Deutschlands
MBA	Master of Business Administration
MP	Member of Parliament
NAM	National Association of Manufacturers
NPC	National Productivity Centres
ÖTV	(Gewerkschaft) Öffentliche Dienste, Transport und Verkehr
POW	Prisoner of War
PR	Public Relations
RDI	Reichsverband der deutschen Industrie
RKW	Rationalisierungskuratorium der Wirtschaft
RM	Reichsmark
RWWA	Rheinisch-Westfälisches Wirtschaftsarchiv
SME	Small and Medium Enterprises
SPD	Sozialdemokratische Partei Deutschlands
TKA	Thyssen-Krupp Archiv
USTAP	United States Technical Assistance and Productivity Program

UVR	Unternehmerverband Ruhrbergbau
VDEh	Verein deutscher Eisenhüttenleute
VFKK	Vereinigung der Freunde von Kunst und Kultur im Bergbau
VGF	Vereinigte Glanzstoff Fabriken
VIHK	Vereinigung der Industrie- und Handelskammern (in der Britischen Besatzungszone)
VW	Volkswagen
Wiwi	Wirtschaftswissenschaften
WMF	Württembergische Metallwaren Fabrik
WVES	Wirtschaftsvereinigung Eisen und Stahl
ZAG	Zentralarbeitsgemeinschaft

Acknowledgements

This book has been a long time in the making. The initial idea for a *Mentalitätsgeschichte* of German industrialists developed after I had finished my book on West German reconstruction finance; further ideas came after reading Jonathan Wiesen's *West German Industry and the Challenges of the Nazi Past*, which provided me with a steady beacon of reference in regards to the scholarship on West German industrialists. The work on the book then suffered a delay because of another book project, which then also changed the original concept.

I would like to thank the staff of the various archives that I have visited during my research for their invaluable support, advice and assistance. Without their help this book would still not be finished. They include the ever-helpful staff at the Bundesarchiv Koblenz; the Bergbau Archiv Bochum; The Historisches Archiv des Bundesverbandes der deutschen Industrie, Berlin, which allowed me very generous use of their photocopiers; and of the Wirtschaftsvereinigung Stahl, Düsseldorf. I am also grateful to the staff at the Archiv für Christlich-Demokratische Politik (ACDP), Sankt Augustin, as well as the staff of the Library of the Institut der Wirtschaft, Cologne (formerly Deutsches Industrie Institut) and here in particular Herrn Norbert Uersfeld (now retired) for allowing me 'short loan borrowing rights'. While I cannot list all of the archivists who were helpful to the project, I do have to mention by name Dr Christian Hillen, Dr Jürgen Weise and Manfred Greitens of Stiftung Rheinisch-Westfälisches Wirtschaftsarchiv zu Köln. Their expert knowledge of the *Industrie- und Handelskammern*, the Reusch papers or aspects of the personal histories of Otto Wolff von Amerongen and their constant willingness to discuss particular details of my research was greatly appreciated. Thanks too to the RWWA's Frau Dorothee Gräfrath. Her enduringly warm welcome to the archive made me always look forward to my visits to Cologne. At the Thyssen-Krupp Archiv, Duisburg, I was well supported by Andreas Zilt and Professor Manfred Rasch, who, together with their team, were always very generous with their time in discussing aspects of company history one would not easily find in the sources, or in accommodating special requests from the 'foreign' scholar. I am grateful to them too for their steady supply of tea during hot (and not so hot) summer days.

Special thanks have to go to Manfred Greitens (RWWA), Susanne Witschaß-Beyer at the BDI archive and Dr Gabriele Teichmann at Sal. Oppenheim, as well as the marketing team at Die Familienunternehmer (formerly *Arbeitsgemeinschaft Selbstständige Unternehmer*, ASU) for their kind help and support in providing me with the portrait photos in this book and the cover photo.

Among the academic colleagues I have to thank for their comments and feedback, Sabine Lee has (once again!) been outstanding and I am very much obliged for the manner in which she gave her support.

Finally, I must thank my wife, Juliane Schwarz, for her patience during the summers when I disappeared into the archives for weeks and the weekends when I was not available because I tried to get the book into shape. For her the process must have dragged on even longer than for me – and nevertheless she volunteered to read and comment on drafts. I know that I have to make up a lot to her.

Parts of the research were supported by grants from the British Academy (no. SG36018) and a Small Travel Grant from the Economic History Society which I both gladly acknowledge.

Introduction

Werner Abelshauser stated controversially – but not altogether without reason – that the history of the Federal Republic of Germany (before the reunification of 1989/90) was first and foremost an economic history and that the so-called 'economic miracle' of the 1950s had become West Germany's founding myth. In actual fact, West Germany's economic outlook was not as bleak as its then devastated cities suggested. Neither the damage of industrial infrastructure caused by Allied bombing nor the dismantling of the late 1940s were as bad as contemporaries had perceived them. Because of the influx of refugees, the overall demographic situation was not as parlous as one might have assumed it to be in the face of millions of war dead; and these refugees, usually well trained, young and mobile, would provide the reserve labour force required once reconstruction began.[1] The 'economic miracle', together with the Cold War (which had in the first place facilitated the emergence of the 'miracle' so quickly after the Second World War), became West Germany's indulgence from the crimes committed under the Nazis and allowed the Germans 'to be somebody again'.

There was one group in German society which was particularly interested in spreading the story of this miraculous recovery: industrialists. During the 'miracle years' of the 1950s and 60s, reports and articles on German industrialists were commonplace, with Germany's leading newsmagazine *Der Spiegel* reporting frequently on captains of industry and economic developments. Interest in the 'German miracle' spread further afield. Even *Time* magazine wrote lead articles on German businessmen, while *Wohlstand für Alle*, a book written by Minister for Economics Ludwig Erhard, made it into an English translation (*Prosperity Through Competition*).[2] In the late 1960s, when the 'miracle' came to an end and West Germany had to cope with much more modest growth rates and economic problems similar to most other Western countries, this interest abated. Furthermore, the impact of the 1966–67 mini recession and the 1968 student protests meant that hagiographic biographies of businessmen fell out of fashion in Germany. What was left were commissioned histories to celebrate company anniversaries, such as Wilhelm Treue's two-volume oeuvre on Thyssen, whose uncritical gaze ignored the company's involvement with National Socialism.[3] It was only in the 1980s when Daimler-Benz AG commissioned a study into its history under the Nazis, and subsequently the 1995 publication of Deutsche Bank's 125th anniversary history, that this amnesia fell away and a full account and examination of organizations' history, especially under the Nazis, began to emerge.[4]

Thirty years ago, Volker Berghahn opened a new debate about German industrialists when he argued that during the 1950s and 60s, they had adopted American management methods.[5] Around the turn of the millennium, German historians began to look afresh at, and renewed their interest in, post-war industrialists, first as part of studies into elite circles and networks and then as an investigation into *Bürgertum*, Germany's particular brand of bourgeoisie, which many historians and sociologists had claimed had disappeared due to the two world wars. The new millennium saw also a renewed interest in industrialists' links with Nazism. The outstanding English language study on this topic is arguably Jonathan Wiesen's monograph, while the German field is led by Norbert Frei.[6] Those studies have, by their very nature, a strong backward-looking approach. By contrast, the aim of this study is not to explore industrialists' common memory, as Wiesen has done, but rather to explain the mentality of the 'miracle makers'. It will follow Peter Burke's suggestion that mentality is formed to a large part through collective, not individual, attitudes.[7] This means finding out what common outlooks and ideas drove them during the years of the economic reconstruction and how they saw themselves in, and reacted to, the process of modernization that was going on in 1950s and 60s Germany. Since most leaders of Germany's industry regarded themselves as *staatstragend* (crucial to the maintenance of the state), they saw their activities to save and then revive the country's economic fortune not at all as self-serving even though these actions allowed their companies to survive; they rather confirmed to them their own claim to work for the common good and endorsed their assertion for an elite status in society.

The book is divided into three parts which blend a chronological with a thematic approach. Part I explores how, from the very first day of Allied occupation – i.e. in many cases even before the war had ended – industrialists began to work on rehabilitating their public image. In the absence of industrial associations, which had traditionally dealt with political demands and public relations matters, but which had been dissolved by the Allies and needed time to re-establish themselves, this task fell to the *Industrie- und Handelskammern* (IHK, Chambers of Industry and Commerce). Thus the IHK became the 'missing link' in industrial organisation, in particular in the British zone of occupation where, due to the nature of British occupation policy, conflicts between capital and labour were most intense. Chambers of Industry and Commerce are not usually at the top of the list of exciting or 'sexy' topics of economic and business history, but the role they played between early 1945 and mid 1948 has made them a crucial piece of Germany's post-war economic survival. This was particularly the case in 1945–46, the IHK not only helped to prevent economic life from collapsing, but more importantly also defended the existing model of capitalism against trade union demands for workers' participation in business associations, and furthermore guaranteed its survival when it was under severe pressure. Notwithstanding this vital role, literature on post-war IHK is sparse and written mainly from the perspective of institutional history. Only Rainer Schulze partially addresses some of the political motives of those chamber officials and entrepreneurs, but he fails to explain why it was the usually hard-line conservative industrialists at Rhine and Ruhr who were prepared to accept union participation, and even parity, within the Chambers.[8] The chapter will give an explanation of why trade union inclusion was fought tooth and nail, and eventually successfully, by industrialists in northern Germany. It thus gives us a first insight into the mentality of businessmen as a group.

Chapter 2 addresses what are arguably the three most important factors for industrialists' redemption from their involvement with the Nazi regime: these were first and foremost a massive public relations campaign both in Germany and in the US, which reached its first peak at the time of the Nuremberg industrialists' trials and lasted well into the 1950s. Tellingly, denying any complicity whatsoever with Nazism was the only way industrialists as a group (and also overwhelmingly as individuals) confronted their past. Second, and emerging from this campaign, was the creation and work of the Deutsches Industrie Institut (DII) as an industry mouthpiece and anti-union propaganda instrument.

The third factor, and again one that is almost forgotten although (or because!) it signified the return of heavy industry's associations to their old influence, is the *Investitionshilfe Gesetz* (IHG, Auxiliary Investment Law). This episode of post-war economic history demonstrates in an exemplary way how industrialists adapted to political situations. Within a few days they turned from total opposition and hostility to such a bill to public approval and then, in the process, managed to portray themselves as the saviours of German basic industry who selflessly provided reconstruction funds out of their own pocket.

The four chapters of the book's second part deal with distinct topics and issues which were at the heart of industrialists' self-perception during Germany's fifteen-to-twenty-year reconstruction period. Chapter 3 addresses an aspect which has developed out of Berghahn's seminal study, namely whether or not German industrialists changed their mentality, and if so, when. I argue that despite Allied internment, there was a distinct continuity in senior management and company leadership, in particular once the internment had ended. Continuity in personnel meant a very strong continuity in mentality. In my opinion it was more due to newcomers and *Querdenker* (lateral thinkers, men able to think outside the traditional box) arriving in top positions that a 'new' entrepreneur did indeed emerge well before the late 1960s, whereas Berghahn argues that this transformation in mentality happened due to a generational change. There is, however, a certain paradox in entrepreneurs' behaviour, because despite the new thinking, some traditional attitudes continued even with, and amongst, the new men. One of those was the claim for an elite status within society which survived at least well into the 1970s.

The degree to which traditional and new thinking became increasingly intertwined, at least for some time, becomes very clear in Chapter 4, which addresses the question of 'Americanization' in leadership and management training. Business historians, most notably Robert Locke, Matthias Kipping and Christian Kleinschmidt, have challenged Berghahn's assumption about 'Americanization'. By looking at what were arguably Germany's three most prominent training institutions – the *Baden-Badener Unternehmergespräche* for top management training, the C. Rudolf Poensgen Stiftung as a mainly regional institute for small and medium-sized businesses leadership training, and the eventually infamous Bad Harzburger Akademie für Führungskräfte der Wirtschaft, which offered mainly middle and lower management courses – the chapter argues that German managers did indeed go their own way. This 'special path' and belief in entrepreneurial exceptionalism at the top management level had a significant impact on the selection of successors. I argue that at mid and lower levels of management training it was, ironically, the work of the socially conservative Harzburger Akademie, whose customer base stemmed primarily from companies with a more traditional outlook, that ultimately led to a more modern approach to personnel management and to the acceptance of international management methods they had disliked. The Harzburger Akademie's special approach unintentionally paved the way to modernize German human resource management.

Chapter 5 looks at traditional attributes of German *Bürgerlichkeit*, culture and codes of honour, and how those were applied differently depending on whether or not one was a newcomer or part of the established elite. Research into the German bourgeoisie originally had focussed on the pre-First World War period as the zenith of this social phenomenon. Only during the last two decades has the focus shifted to the interwar and post-Second World War era, resulting in (amongst others) a number of studies in the *Wirtschaftsbürgertum*, Germany's economic bourgeoisie and their influence in society and the economy. The chapter argues that the bourgeoisie did indeed survive war and economic chaos: bourgeois attitudes were too deeply rooted in the mentality of the business elite who had survived the war to just fade away or to be easily dropped. Bourgeois values were rather seen as stabilizing social factors in the uncertainty of the post-war period and therefore industrialists picked up on traditional bourgeois patronage of arts and culture. This was done not least because it had the additional benefit of improving the public image of the industrial elites. At the same time, these elitist cultural activities confirmed and reinforced the claim for elite status.

Part II's final chapter addresses another research desideratum, namely the influence businessmen had over politics and the role of German industrial association in the post-war period. Although there exist some very good contemporary studies by US scholars on German businessmen's attitudes to politics and associations, as well as Braunthal's monograph on the Federation of German Industry, the scope of these studies, in particular on the associations, remains limited and needs updating. Associations had been at the heart of German economic life at least since the latter part of the industrial revolution but after the Second World War their influence reached new heights which brought significant political influence for industry. Despite their political influence, the associations' main role, apart from lobbying, was the reconciliation of interests within specific associations or between different branches of industry. Their success in keeping their quarrels almost always behind closed doors contributed to the image of almighty and politically powerful industrialists, despite their claim to the contrary. Neither the lamentation by contemporary US commentators about the lack of political involvement of German industrialists nor their hesitant membership in political parties mean that they were apolitical – on the contrary. The chapter highlights that industrialists' political involvement was not dependent on party membership but on perceived business interests. I demonstrate that the overall political influence of business was actually quite significant, either because of the large donations they provided to the right-of-centre political parties or because they were able to place MPs (often association functionaries) in crucial parliamentary committees. Business's influence found its limits only when it interfered with Chancellor Adenauer's (foreign) policy aims.

The book's third part, and its last two chapters, takes a close look at business conduct. Chapter 7 shows how industrialists handled the increased influence of the trade unions. This did not only concern the coal and steel industry where, as a result of German legislation which codified British military government rulings, the unions had gained equal representation on the supervisory boards, and, worse from a management point of view, also had a representative on the managing boards in those industries. In particular these so-called *Arbeitsdirektoren* were despised even by those entrepreneurs who were not affected by the 1951 co-determination law, as in their eyes 'only management can manage'. The ongoing and virulent hostility towards labour representatives on the management boards in particular and co-determination in general were therefore first and foremost an expression of feeling threatened by the trade unions. Union bashing, despite successful co-operation on the boards, would continue well into the 1970s when a Social Democrat-led government eventually expanded co-determination into other industries. The final chapter shows the sharp contrast between businesses' loathing of trade unions and their almost paranoid fear of communism within West Germany: this was industrialists' desire to conduct business with Eastern Europe and the Soviet Union. In this section I argue that this wish to trade with communists was because of the positive experiences gained in German–Soviet trade in the interwar period. After the 1929 Wall Street Crash many German companies had to rely on trade with the Soviet Union to survive the Depression and found the Soviets tough but reliable business partners. Trade with the East eventually became the area where German businessmen began to challenge the previously unquestioned supremacy of politics over economics, although they challenged only where they found political reasoning and demands as being no longer in sync with reality and therefore unreasonable. As industrialists' attitudes towards Adenauer's *Westintegration* and European integration have already received much attention and were, overall, much less contentious, Eastern trade is the only example in this book where industry's foreign policy considerations are discussed.

German industrialists during the post-war reconstruction period were a very heterogeneous group. Geographical location (including originally which occupation zone they were located in), industrial sector and company size, but also an individual's personality and background, all played a role in their mentality. The main focus of this study is on the entrepreneurs and managers of the Ruhr's big businesses of the iron and machine manufacturing sectors, due to their economic significance at the time but also because of their revival as economic and political payers. However, considerable attention will be given to the leadership of small and medium-sized enterprises (SME), through the activities of the *Arbeitsgemeinschaft Selbstständiger Unternehmer* (ASU, association of independent entrepreneurs), since they were (and still are) the real backbone of the German economy. Despite their significance, they have been long neglected by historians and research into this group has begun only recently but because of their disparate nature, general conclusions can be even less expected than those from 'big' industrialists. As independent entrepreneurs liked to point out, they were the 'real' entrepreneurs, in contrast to the salaried managers, for which ASU member Josef Winschuh had coined the term *beauftragter Unternhemer* (authorized entrepreneur)[9] so that he could avoid the term 'manager', which was still frowned upon by German businessmen until the mid-1960s. The common ground and the growing divisions between 'real' and 'authorized' entrepreneurs will feature throughout this study. Although the terms 'industrialist', 'manager' and 'entrepreneur' are used almost synonymously in this book, at the time the German words had significantly different meanings, which tend to get lost in translation.[10] It is nevertheless hoped that the reader will understand the fine nuances of the terminology.

Part I

From War Criminals to Captains of Industry

Whenever a man is suitably qualified, then there is most certainly a stain on his papers which relates to his activities in the NSDAP.[1]

1

The 'Missing Link': The Role of the Chambers of Industry and Commerce in Entrepreneurial Self-perception in the Immediate Post-war Period

Industrie- und Handelskammern (IHK, Chambers of Industry and Commerce) played a crucial role in Germany's economic and business history. The Chambers had been introduced in Germany, initially in Prussia, in the aftermath of the French Revolution and Napoleonic occupation of the Rhine provinces. From the late 1840s onward, they were entrusted with state authority and administrative duties (*Hoheitsaufgaben*) and all businesses within industry and commerce became compulsory Chamber members; the companies involved in the trades (*Handwerk*) were organized similarly in *Handwerkskammern*. After Bismarck's unification of the Reich, this Prussian model of the IHK was adopted in those parts of the Reich where it had not already been in place. In contrast to industrial and employer associations, which are voluntary associations under private law with the explicit purpose of representing particular interests, the IHK were supposed to represent the interests of all non-trades enterprises in their district, regardless of sector or size.[2] By having been given administrative duties, the Chambers took on their distinctive German form, evolving into what Wolfram Fischer has described as legal entities with a 'dual character' of auxiliary authority (*Hilfsbehörde*) and interest representation, the latter of which they carried out together with the employer associations and sectoral industry associations.[3]

When the Nazis came to power in 1933, they made sure that the 'right' (or at least not the 'wrong') kind of people were heading the Chambers of Industry and Commerce. As a result, Jewish or democratically minded presidents and/or chief clerks (*Geschäftsführer*)[4] lost their posts; now Chamber presidents were appointed by the Reich Economics Ministry instead of being elected democratically by the Chamber membership. Many Chamber officials joined the party, either out of conviction, opportunism or fear for their jobs. Under the regime's onslaught, the Chambers lost – or rather gave up – a good deal of their previous independence, although Schulze has argued that this did not change their character or purpose. In 1942/3 the IHK came nominally to an end when the Nazis merged them with the *Handwerkskammern* into new agencies, the *Gauwirtschaftskammern*, to better utilize them for the war economy. In this context they played a significant role in the allocation of labour and raw materials to local companies. In contrast to the personnel changes that happened after 1933, the restructuring into the *Gauwirtschaftskammern* occurred with an almost complete transfer of staff which, significantly, helped to safeguard the continuation of IHK traditions and mentality.[5]

When the Allies advanced into Nazi Germany in the spring of 1945, German civil administrative structures disappeared temporarily. Men who had held public offices under the Nazis such as mayors and district leaders (not to mention the infamous *Gauleiter*) left their posts fearing arrest by the Allies due to their association with Nazism. The local military governments the Allies installed in every town usually sacked anyone who had not stepped down voluntarily as part of their attempt to denazify German society. The absence of a functional elite on local level, either because they had left or had been removed from their posts, combined with the turmoil of the war's end brought widespread chaos to Germany. The *Industrie- und Handelskammern* were one of the few institutions which did not follow this trend when they reconstituted themselves out of the *Gauwirtschaftskammern* either just before, or immediately after the Allied occupation. Almost all Chambers acted like the IHK Hannover, where the chief clerks had decided in their final meeting on 3 April 1945 to disobey the order given by the Nazis to break contact with the enemy and withdraw because, as they said, 'in times of crisis the Chamber belongs with its companies'.[6] In contrast to the industrial associations which the Nazis had reorganized without any resistance from the industrialists to better serve the war economy, the IHK were not regarded by the Allies as part of the Nazi war economy and thus were spared instant disbandment on Allied orders.[7]

Soon after the Nazis had been ousted from towns and cities, entrepreneurs and the re-established IHK were faced with challenges from anti-fascist groups and committees, usually consisting of trade unionists, social democrats and communists. Their aim was to purge Nazis, active or nominal, from political and economic life and to influence political events and decisions towards a more democratic direction. In Bremen, *the Kampfgemeinschaft gegen Faschismus* (Combat Alliance against Fascism) tried to sway the appointment of new IHK members, as did the *Ausschuß für Wiederaufbau* (Committee for Reconstruction) in Hannover. However, in particular the American officers of the combat units that had liberated the towns were suspicious of the anti-fascist activities, which they suspected of being part of a communist attempt to gain power.[8] Without any political backing either from the Allies or from the newly appointed German administrations, their attempts very quickly failed. The re-established IHK did their part to stop the anti-fascist committees. Thanks to their ability to rely on most of their old staff, they had a vastly superior knowledge in economic matters; furthermore, they could depend on traditional networks of influence, and so it was easy for them to survive this first tilt at the existing economic order. Allied actions played their part too. As early as 1 June 1945, the British Military Government proscribed the activities of the anti-fascist groups and thus ended the German grassroot attempt at denazification.[9]

For a number of reasons, the Chambers of Industry and Commerce were not just saved from dissolution but actually re-established themselves quickly once a town had been taken by the Allies and as soon as hostilities had ceased in an area, even before the war itself had come to an end. In some cases the Nazi name *Gauwirtschaftskammer* had been dropped before the Allies had moved in, or it was done straight afterwards.

Instead the old names, either *Wirtschaftkammer* (with inclusion of the *Handwerk*) or *Industrie- und Handelskammer*, and *Handwerkskammer* respectively, in cases where they split again, were adopted once more. Referring to themselves again as *Industrie- und Handelskammer* happened sometimes out of the expectation that the traditional name had an international recognition and would not be associated with Nazism,[10] irrespective of the difference between German IHK and their Anglo-Saxon namesakes. In the majority of cases the renaming happened on the initiative of IHK staff or men who had lost their position within the Chambers in 1933 or had been demoted by the Nazis but who now became 'reactivated'. These men were usually supported by the newly appointed German civil administration but also asked for and received the blessing of industrial elites.[11] Rainer Schulze emphasizes that the support from the civil administration was given for two reasons in particular. First, the new administrators, men who very often had held public office before 1933, remembered and could relate to the position the IHK held pre-1933 as bodies with auxiliary state authority.[12] The second reason was rather more pragmatic: the IHK were indeed one of the few remaining administrative bodies left in Germany, and they had an outstanding knowledge in economic matters, not only on a local basis. Alongside the renaming, and usually in co-operation with the newly installed mayor, the Chambers underwent a rudimentary process of 'self-denazification', in which outspoken Nazi supporters within the Chambers were removed from their posts if they had not already disappeared to avoid arrest. This 'self-denazification' was, however, only skin-deep since in many cases only the most ardent Nazis and those deemed 'unpleasant' were removed, but otherwise the 'postponement of the Pg [*Parteigenosse*, party membership] question until calmer times' was advised.[13] Thus high-ranking Chamber officials who were classed as being only nominal party members usually remained in their posts until late 1945, when the Allies insisted on more stringent vetting, because their knowledge and expertise was desperately needed. The involvement of local industrial elites in the Chambers' (re)creation, however, is also very significant.[14] With the exception of Heinrich Kost, none of the leading Ruhr industrialists took centre-stage in this process, but their presence behind the scenes was always felt. The appointment of Düsseldorf's new senior chief clerk in April 1945 was sanctioned by an 'informal gathering of business representatives' which 'met regularly on the orders (*auf Anordnung*) of Herr Sohl'.[15] These kinds of arrangements and influences allowed the industrial elites significant influence in the IHK, and the spirit of this influence continued after their arrests later that year.

While they always had the final say on the matter, in the early weeks of the occupation, the Allies allowed and even encouraged the work of the IHK, quite in contrast to their attitude to the industrial associations, which had been suspended because of their links with Nazism. In a complete misunderstanding of the political situation, many leading German industrialists had expected to continue in their posts because they believed that the Allies would need their skills and experience to rebuild the German economy.[16] This was true only during the first weeks of the occupation, when utterly unprepared front-line officers had to set up rudimentary civil administrations. For this they needed, and were grateful for, German support.[17] German misperception about the new political realities combined with old attitudes showed itself in the correspondence IHK Cologne had early on with the Military Government. The Chamber declared itself 'will[ing to] work in close co-operation ... and with the Military Government Cologne' and promised that the Military Government regulations on firm licensing 'will be respected'; furthermore, the Chamber was willing to forward all permits to the Military Government for final approval.[18] The language used in the document was certainly not one of the vanquished but rather shows an ongoing feeling of superiority, and well in line with thoughts and expectations industrialists had about their future before the occupation began, which they saw 'not as desperate in any way'.[19]

Irrespective of the actual differences the Americans and the British viewed the IHK as apolitical as they referred to their own national experiences; furthermore, the Chambers and even the *Gauwirtschaftskammern* had always been local in character and were not regarded as likely centres of anti-Allied and pro-Nazi activities. In the absence of almost any other working civilian administration in the occupied areas, the Allied military commanders, like the German administrators they had appointed, had to rely on the IHK for the maintenance of basic supplies for the local population. Both the Americans, and from June 1945 onward the British – who replaced them as occupying powers in northern Germany – used the Chambers as their link to local businesses for the economic sustainability of their occupation zones.[20] This meant, for example, that the IHK were given the responsibility for the provision of labour for clear-up work and the allocation of raw materials. They were also given the authority to issue permits of operations for small companies of up to twenty-five men, which included the vetting of company owners for Nazi activities. In many cases the issuing of permits would take as much as two years to be completed.[21] Although the British had allowed a restricted operation of economic association by late July 1945,[22] their influence remained limited for some time, not least because many of the top industrialists who led the associations were arrested later that year.

In the autumn of 1945, the British Military Government ordered the IHK in its occupation zone to begin with a more thorough screening for Nazis, both within the IHK and company ownership or management. Within the Chambers, denazification was seen as nonsensical and unpleasant, a task so sensitive that it should be left to the British themselves to carry it out; it was called a 'disguised class warfare' and was often carried out with considerable leniency, so much so that the Cologne Chamber had to warn their staff that they would be dismissed by the British if standards did not improve. In many ways the IHK reacted to denazification as most Germans did, but they furthermore denounced it as an attack against *privat-kapitalistische Unternehmerwirtschaft* (entrepreneurial private capitalism).[23] Their existing group loyalty allowed them to make a clear distinction between what they saw as only 'nominal' or even 'forced' party membership (so as to 'protect' a company), or more forthright Nazi activities.

Unsurprisingly, the continuity of personnel within the IHK was high. For his investigation into the North-Rhine Westphalian Chambers, Jürgen Weise claims that the Chambers' internal continuity came first and foremost through the stability in personnel, but he rejects Diethelm Prowe's theory that this meant a continuation of Nazi sympathies within the IHK. Indeed, only five of the twenty *Hauptgeschäftsführer* (senior chief clerks) in North-Rhine-Westphalia's IHK remained in their post after the ousting of the Nazis, but half of their replacements had held executive functions within IHK or business associations before the Nazi era. Weise therefore speaks of a continuation of a pre-1933 mentality.[24] Exemplary for these cases was the senior chief clerk of IHK Düsseldorf, Josef Wilden, who held the job since 1920. Seen off into early retirement without termination of his contract on the orders of the *Gauleiter* in 1938, he was asked in April 1945 by the acting mayor if he would resume the role of *Hauptgeschäftsführer* and in 1946 he became Chamber president. The influence of the pre-1933 faction within the IHK is also demonstrated by the fact that they did not introduce new statutes for Chamber elections, but, in a clear sign of continuity, decided to reactivate those which had been in place before 1933.[25] Weise highlights another line of personnel continuity: almost all Chambers staff who had lost their jobs for political reasons because of Allied vetting were back in post after 1949/50. This is not a Chamber-specific development, but one indicative of wider German continuity lines and Allied inability (and sometimes unwillingness) to carry out unpopular policies against German wishes, as John Gimbel has convincingly shown.[26] Posts that had become vacant because of staff being killed during bombing raids or denazification dismissals were filled by politically untainted IHK staff who had fled from the Soviet-occupied part of Germany; their expert knowledge of Chamber business, but also their similar mentality, provided further continuity to the Chambers' work and outlook.[27] A slight deviation in this development is visible only with the position of the Chamber presidents.

In contrast to the chief clerks who were salaried employees (*hauptamtlich*), the Chamber presidency had been an honorary position (*ehrenamtlich*) to which the post holder was elected by the Chamber Assembly (*Vollversammlung*), which in turn had been elected by the Chamber's member companies.[28] The president was usually a very prominent man: in Cologne, for example, the role was occupied by the banker Louis Hagen (1915–31), Paul Silverberg (1931–33), and under the Nazis Baron von Schröder (1933–45); C. Rudolf Poensgen (1908–33) held the position in Düsseldorf; and in Duisburg it was mining manager Heinrich Kost who held the post 1944–47 and again in 1954–64.[29] For a good number of years after the war, however, the positions were filled with lower profile and more local businessmen, many of them managers or owners of small and medium-sized enterprises. The reasons for this are manifold: many of the leading industrialists had been arrested and interned by the Allies so that they were not available for the position, and after their release from internment their first priority was the reconstruction of their own companies. Another significant reason was one of image: industrialists were fully aware that managers of big industry were mistrusted both by the Military Government and the German public alike, with the mistrust of the latter 'reaching even far into the ranks of the *Mittelstand*' because of their espousal of Nazism.[30] With even parts of the economically active bourgeoisie being so critical, it appeared to be the right strategy to put forward less well known and therefore less exposed figures for these prominent posts. The exception to the rule was the renowned banker Robert Pferdmenges, who became president of the Cologne IHK in 1945. A man of the highest integrity, Pferdmenges had been a partner in the banking house of Sal. Oppenheim which he took over in 1938 in a staged

Aryanization to prevent it from falling into Nazi hands. Being close to the 'Confessing Church', he had never made a secret to his opposition to National Socialism and was briefly arrested after the 20 July bomb plot against Hitler, subsequently spending the rest of the war under house arrest. Pferdmenges, who had seen himself as a mere trustee for the Oppenheim bank, returned it to the owner family in 1947. As the dominant character amongst his fellow Chamber presidents, he became chairman of the association of Rhenish IHK and a leading proponent of change until he was removed from office by the British Military Government in September 1946 after he was denounced anonymously with false claims about his Nazi past.[31] Pferdmenges went on to become a Member of Parliament after 1949 and a very influential link between industry and politics. A member of the supervisory board of Vereinigte Stahlwerke, he took charge of the company and managing board after the arrest of its appointed members in late 1945. By the end of the 1950s, Pferdmenges held twenty-two supervisory board memberships of top German companies, eleven of which were chair positions and three more deputy chairs.[32] While Pferdmenges was one of two prominent Chamber presidents (Heinrich Kost being the other), Schulze has pointed out that even in this office there was a significant level of continuity. Seven out of ten

Figure 1.1 Robert Pferdmenges (1880–1962), Cologne banker and pivotal link between the business fraternity and politics. Made honorary president of IHK Cologne in recognition of his services after his dismissal by the British, Pferdmenges gained his influence from being a close confidante to Adenauer and holding almost two dozen supervisory board posts. Conservative to the core, but moderate in his views, his influence amongst industrialists can hardly be overestimated. © Historisches Archiv Bankhaus Sal. Oppenheim.

Chamber presidents in Lower Saxony had held higher offices in Chambers or business associations before 1945, so that in these positions, too, the Chambers provided a high level of continuity.[33]

The operation of the Chambers of Industry and Commerce suffered only a few days of interruption at the most once the war ended.[34] The self-interest of the first wave of Allied occupation officers allowed the Chambers to continue their work almost immediately, in contrast to the fate of the industrial associations, which had to reconstitute themselves in a much slower and lengthier process. It was during this time that the IHK became the voice of businesses and industry and the champion for the continuation of the traditional capitalist order which was severely threatened by the trade unions, often with support from German politicians. In the aftermath of businesses' involvement with the Nazis, trade union leaders tried to seize the opportunity for expanding economic democracy (*Wirtschaftsdemokratie*) by demanding equal workers' representation in all Chamber bodies.[35] Such a demand would have totally changed the self-perception and self-image, but also the traditional role, of the IHK as self-administrative bodies of industry. From this resulted a long and fierce debate about the trade union demands and how to reply to them. Somewhat surprisingly, the entrepreneurs' response was far from unanimous and at times very angry disputes developed. In the American occupation zone, as in the British, German politicians of almost all parties supported union participation.[36] However, in American tradition, Chambers of Industry and Commerce had always been private associations without compulsory membership and state authority, and the Americans introduced this voluntary model in their zones as well. Initially German entrepreneurs resisted the establishment of private Chambers along these lines but soon realized that this was a way to prevent trade union participation in the Chambers. As purely private organizations, they could determine structure and membership without interference from the outside. By late 1946, possibly under the influence of hardliners such as the Augsburg Chamber President Otto Vogel, the Bavarian Chambers were prepared to sacrifice the traditional administrative duties and compulsory membership as a way to prevent trade union participation.[37] Only after the establishment of the Federal Republic and the passing of a federal law in 1956 did the IHK in the American occupation zone regain their traditional roles and powers.[38]

The remainder of this chapter will focus on developments in the British occupation zone because of the significance of the Rhine–Ruhr area as West Germany's economic heartland. The Chambers of Industry and Commerce in the British zone faced a bigger challenge and more threats to their self-concept and to their entrepreneurial image than those in the US zone. This was in part a consequence of British policies to nationalize industries, which gave support to the trade unions' claim for wider economic democracy. The different responses to these challenges taken by business leaders at different times and in different regions display, in spite of the variety of opinions, an underlying common mentality of industrialists and entrepreneurs. It was in the British occupation zone that, in the absence of strong business and employers' associations, the IHK turned into the defenders of entrepreneurial mentality and self-perception.

British policies towards the Chambers of Industry and Commerce as expressed in the 21st Army Group's Technical Directive no. 49 were initially similarly restrictive to

US directives. It was for practical reasons that they soon allowed the continuation of a system of compulsory Chamber membership which also entailed the Chambers to keep their rights as *öffentlich-rechtliche* agencies, which meant that they could continue to carry out state administrative duties.[39] In contrast to the Chambers of Industry and Commerce, which had continued their work more or less uninterrupted, trade unions in the British zone were allowed to re-form, step-by-step from the bottom up, only in the autumn of 1945. This put them at a clear disadvantage for the coming contest for workers' participation within the IHK who could build on their old networks and personnel. Notably in Cologne, there had been contacts between industrialists and trade unionists during meetings of the anti-Hitler resistance movement. One of their discussion topics had been about the filling of Chamber jobs on a parity basis.[40] Once re-established, the trade unions wanted to expand their say (*Mitbestimmung*) in the economy, not least because of their experiences under the Nazis into areas above and beyond company level.[41] In this area they had had some experiences with economic democracy in the wake of the Stinnes–Legien agreement of 1918, which had given them the right to have works councils. The unions eventually proposed a three-tier model of economic chambers (*Wirtschaftskammern*) at district, state and national levels, made up of equal numbers of representatives from employer organizations and unions.[42] In other words, the district level IHK were supposed to open their doors to the same number of trade union representatives as there were industrialists.

The Chambers' reaction to these demands was not unanimous and at least until late 1947 the different factions amongst the IHK in the British zone fought each other as least as hard as some of them fought the unions' demands. A 'West-versus-North' division emerged. The Rhenish Chambers (Cologne, Bonn, Aachen, Duisburg, Essen, Düsseldorf, Krefeld, Mönchengladbach, Neuss, Remscheid, Solingen and Wuppertal) and the Westphalian Chamber at Dortmund were very much in favour of some form of trade union participation. The Chambers in Lower Saxony, Bremen, Hamburg and Schleswig-Holstein, on the other hand, were strongly opposed to worker representation. The exception to this rule was the Braunschweig Chamber which was the only one in Lower Saxony that favoured – and actually practised – trade-union participation, due to historical circumstances. Before 1933 Braunschweig had been one of the sixteen states of the Weimar Republic. Small in size, from the mid-1920s onward the state had always had a strong Social Democrat vote. Within its borders was Europe's largest steel plant, the Nazis' Herman Göring plant at Salzgitter, as well as Ilselder Hütte steel plant at Peine and Germany's Wattensted iron ore fields. Schulze sees the appointment of a Social Democrat and two trade union representatives to the Braunschweig Chamber *Präsidium* (board), which also had the explicit support of the British Military Government, as politically motivated. It was an attempt to protect the Chamber's work against wider political interference from the city's mayor and the state's minister president, who were both Social Democrats. At least one of these three appointees continued as a board member until the late 1950s. It remains open to question whether admitting these 'outsiders' to the Chamber's highest body showed a genuine willingness to include all sides in the reconstruction effort or if it was merely an attempt to 'prevent worse'.[43]

The Rhenish Chambers had traditionally been dominated by the big iron and steel, coal and manufacturing companies. These companies had had some experience with worker representation since the 1918 Stinnes–Legien agreement had introduced works councils, and despite the fact that the management had remained reluctant, if not outright hostile, to the councils, they had learned to live with them. Ironically, the *Betriebsgemeinschaft* (factory community) imposed by the Nazis seemed to have eased some of the tensions between workers and management, in particular during the time of the Allied bombing campaign. Further cooperation between workers and managers developed (as will be shown in Chapter 7) in the wake of the British dismantling plans in an attempt to save the plants and workplaces. The strongest advocate for trade union participation in the Rhineland Chambers was Robert Pferdmenges. In line with his more compromising approach, but also typical of underlying conservatism, was IHK Duisburg president Heinrich Kost. At a meeting of the Rhineland Chamber presidents in January 1946, when labour's participation in management was discussed, he emphasized that a trusting collaboration with the workers existed. They should be given 'so much influence in a company's operations that was equal to their abilities to work for the benefit of the company'. Workers should not be left 'on the side lines without influence. It was the duty of the entrepreneur to educate their workforce in such a way that they with their resources and connection could be utilised fruitfully in the reconstruction process.'[44] Kost's paternalism, which was similar on the question of labour representation at the IHK, stopped, of course, at the question of workers' inclusion on a company board, since they supposedly lacked the ability a board member needed; instead they should deal with social issues within companies and training young blood (*Nachwuchsfragen*).

There were two interlinked reasons why the 'northern' Chambers, in particular those in Lower Saxony, were so vehemently opposed to union participation. Lower Saxony had only a very small number of large firms which could have dominated the business environment; instead the region's economy was characterized by small and medium-sized industrial enterprises, wholesale and retail companies and external trade businesses. This set-up meant that these type of companies, usually run by the owner-entrepreneurs, had a considerably larger influence in the IHK than in the Rhine–Ruhr area.[45] As these companies had not had experience with labour representations under the Stinnes-Legien agreement, they were even more rooted in the traditional *Herr-im-Haus* ('master in the house') mentality. The second reason derived in part from the first one: because Lower Saxony was much more rural than North-Rhine Westphalia, the mentality of its population (and business community) was also much more conservative, and in some instances even parochial. This can be seen in the fact that the Deutsche Partei (German Party, DP), a national-conservative party to the right of Adenauer's Christian Democratic Union (CDU), had its heartland in Lower Saxony; a considerable number of IHK members or staff were actively involved in DP politics.[46]

In spring of 1946, the British allowed the IHK in their occupation zone to set up a coordinating body on a zonal level. However, with the establishment of the Association of IHK in the British Occupation Zone (*Vereinigung der Industrie- und Handelskammern in der Britischen Besatzungszone*, VIHK) under the chairmanship of Pferdmenges, the difference in opinion between the northern and western Chambers of Industry and Commerce on how to deal with the trade unions only intensified.[47] On 18 July 1946 association representatives met in preparation for a meeting with Viktor Agartz, the chairman of the *Zentralamt für Wirtschaft* (Central Economic Office), a German agency the British had created to organize and plan the running of the economy in their zone. As a trade unionist, Agartz had been a strong supporter of union parity in the Chambers. The outcome of the preparatory meeting, the so-called '*Ölkrug* resolution' (named after the restaurant it took place in) was the first joint strategy statement by the Chambers and a victory for the hardliners. It stipulated that while workers should have a say in economic policy decision-making, this should not take place within the IHK, but at a higher level. The association also rejected the call for a new law to regulate the Chambers of Industry and Commerce on the grounds that there was no freely elected parliament to pass such a law.[48] The latter has to be seen as a purely tactical statement to play for time and delay union representation in the Chambers, but it had far wider significance. Weise has pointed out that the *Ölkrug* resolution was not just a rebuff of trade union demands, as they were basically being fobbed off with a rather vague commitment to a talking shop outside the Chambers. When the entrepreneurs claimed that the 'new' economic order should not be decided by non-elected bodies (i.e. the *Zentralamt*, which was dominated by Social Democratic advocates of economic planning) or even the Military Government, they were not merely playing for time. The *Ölkrug* resolution was, in actual fact, a statement by the entrepreneurs on the economic constitution of the British occupation zone as a whole, a statement which called for the preservation of the existing capitalist order, at a time when socialization of industries was a real threat to this order.[49]

The *Ölkrug* meeting did not end the dispute within the IHK about union membership – in fact it did not even pre-determine the outcome of the debate – but it did set the direction the developments would eventually take. For the time being, the Rhenish Chambers, who had lost their dominant figure after Pferdmenges had to step down as president of the Cologne Chamber, continued to be in favour of filling Chamber positions and bodies on the basis of parity. But even here the meaning of the term 'parity' seemed to have changed increasingly towards one of 'participation' or to 'parity in a body outside the Chambers', something the trade unions rejected as insufficient.[50] Weise states that there is no evidence for any particular reason why Pferdmenges had supported Chamber parity, something he did up to the early 1950s.[51] This is different in the case of the western Chambers in general, which had strong reasons for union participation: On 16 March 1946, the Allies had announced their first Industrial Plan for Germany, according to which Germany's industrial production would be reduced to 75 per cent of the 1936 level, requiring some 1,800 industrial plants to be destroyed, dismantled or used for reparations.[52] In this situation the managers on the Rhine and the Ruhr were dependent on the support of the trade unions, who for their part fought for the maintenance of those plants because their loss would have meant widespread unemployment. The Chamber at Aachen, furthermore, saw itself confronted with Dutch territorial claims which would have affected their district and which they thought could only be averted with the political help from the trade unions. Unwilling or unable to understand, the northern Chambers called the Aachen approach 'grotesque' and accused that Chamber of being the 'Wild West'. This inflammatory language by some northern senior chief clerks was used only after

Robert Pferdmenges had resigned his post after unproven allegations against him, but at a time when the resistance against parity had been crumbling. Pferdmenges' replacement as chairman of the VIHK BBZ was Hannover president Christian Kuhlemann, who, together with his senior chief clerk, Hans-Joachim Fricke, had been at the centre of northern resistance to any form of trade union participation.[53] The northern IHK were the driving forces for the retention of the traditional 'master in the house' attitude adopted by most entrepreneurs, especially those in small and medium-sized companies. The approach of the western Chambers, which by late 1946 or early 1947 had also become the first line of defence against British dismantling plans due to the absence of powerful industrial associations, was driven by political need.[54] Once this need for trade union support had disappeared, the western Chambers withdrew their willingness to allow trade union participation, although they had acknowledged it in principle in December 1946 in an internal document.[55]

It was a two-fold shift in policy that came to the entrepreneurs' rescue. In the first instance, a change in Allied policy helped the IHK to retain their status as a purely entrepreneurial body. Although the British Government, inspired by their own policy of nationalizing key industries at home, had been trying to implement a policy of socializing the coal and steel industries of the Ruhr, Britain's economic weakness and Cold War policies prevented the implementation of these plans. The growing British dependency on the US, which culminated in the Bevin–Byrnes Agreement of 2 December 1946 and the establishment of the 'Combined Economic Area' (or Bizone for short) on 1 January 1947, meant that British nationalization policies were scaled back gradually in the second half of 1946. The visible expression of the British retreat was the 'Friedmann Ordinance' of 11 November 1947, which had confirmed almost all the traditional Chamber functions, in particular compulsory membership.[56] The ordinance was seen by the entrepreneurs as a further signal to play for time. With increased American influence on economic policy matters in the British zone, the prospects of trade union participation in the Chambers of Industry and Commerce declined more and more and even the Rhenish Chambers now turned away from the idea. Bernhard Hilgermann, senior chief clerk at the IHK Cologne, told a colleague at the Chamber Koblenz in the French occupation zone that the Rhenish Chambers never intended to have full parity of workers' representatives in any Chamber body. In actual fact, they had always rejected this, but they had been prepared to allow some representatives to participate in committee work.[57] After lengthy negotiations between trade unionists and Chamber representatives during a meeting in Wuppertal in mid-February 1947, the entrepreneurs achieved a 'unique triumph' (Prowe), when the unions acknowledged and accepted the traditional set-up and role of the Chambers. By March, the trade unions had retreated so far that they were prepared to accept *Wirtschaftskammern* (economic chambers) on a parity basis outside the IHK.[58] This was nothing less than a full retreat from their economic demands to a talking shop.

The second political shift that happened was on the German side. With the trade unions moving their focus of attention away from Chamber parity towards the co-determination question in industry, it was the state parliaments in North-Rhine Westphalia and Lower Saxony which from 1947 onward tried to pass legislation enshrining labour representation within the IHK. Without the threat of direct Allied intervention and trade union influence that has passed its peak, this was a challenge the entrepreneurs could deal with much more easily thanks to their old and re-established networks and connections within the state administrations and bureaucracy.[59] In Lower Saxony, a bill to restructure the IKH was introduced to parliament in spring of 1947, where it was defeated on 25 March with the votes of the non-left parties.[60] In North-Rhine Westphalia, where a minority of Chambers were still prepared to accept labour representatives, parliamentary debates went on for fifteen months throughout 1948–49. When the law was eventually passed in July, it was the British military government which vetoed it on 4 October 1949, weeks after the creation of the Federal Republic of Germany, on the grounds that the issue had to be settled by German federal law, not state legislation. Weise argues convincingly that the British decision was driven by political motives and in consideration of American anti-socialist policies.[61] The year 1947 was important for the IHK not just because of the Lower Saxony vote. It was the time when the Chambers became key players in the re-establishing of industrial and employers' associations. In addition they became increasingly and actively involved in local and regional politics when ever more leading IHK figures joined political parties and entered legislative bodies. They gained further influence through the political donations they made to bourgeois parties. It was during this period of the post-war years that the entrepreneurs' self-portrayal as 'unpolitical', a claim they had invented to deflect from their involvement with the Nazis, was exposed as nothing more than fiction.[62]

Their definition of 'unpolitical' was very narrowly defined. Representative of this claim is Hans-Günther Sohl, former deputy chairman of Vereinigte Stahlwerke, and during the 1950s and 1960s managing director of Thyssen Steel and the dominant personality of German heavy industry. In his autobiography he stated that after their bad experience with the Nazis – by which he meant the internment by the Allies and the denazification process – many entrepreneurs decided to remain unpolitical.[63] However, in reality 'unpolitical' meant only a decision not to join a political party. Amongst most industrialists who held an *Ehrenamt* within a Chamber of Commerce, but even more so amongst the chief clerks, the attitude was very different. They had realized that they had to act and get politically involved in order to protect their vested interests. Consequently, Chamber members participated actively in the establishment of the bourgeois parties, often on the pretext of 'fighting the socialist threat'. None went as far as the IHK Bremen, which in the autumn of 1947 passed a resolution that selected Chamber members should join designated political parties in order to influence their decision-making.[64] How far the actual political involvement had developed by May 1949 is highlighted by the working committee of IHK in the Joint Economic Area. It listed Chamber members who held high political office: besides Hans-Christoph Seebohm, president of IHK Braunschweig, who sat on the Parliamentary Council, there were eleven members of the Economic Council (*Wirtschaftsrat*) and forty-two Chamber representatives who had seats in state parliaments. In addition, fifty-seven Chamber officials held high-ranking posts in economic associations.[65]

The political, but perhaps even more the ideological, impact the Chambers had in the early post-war years is visible from mid-1946 onward. This was the time when the

British tried to shift the economic distribution role the Chambers had held for almost a year away to the *Bezirkswirtschaftsämter* (BWA, District Economic Offices) to implement better economic control and planning. While the Chambers protested vigorously against the increased bureaucratization this move towards 'economic planning' would bring, the BWAs lacked sufficient and sufficiently qualified personnel to master the task. The British attempt backfired and strengthened the IHK's position, not to mention their self-confidence. Since the BWA's untrained personnel were unable to distribute and allocate resources adequately, they had to rely increasingly on IHK advice and knowledge. This was taken by the Chambers as proof that only businessmen, but not bureaucrats, were able to run an economy successfully. In Lower Saxony the BWA eventually lost its influence when in June 1948 Otto Fricke, Vice President of IHK Braunschweig, became the state's Economics Minister, just at the time when Ludwig Erhard abolished economic controls in the wake of the currency reform.[66] Chamber representatives were not shy to claim the credit for the following improvement in the supply situation.

The claim that the Chambers of Industry and Commerce were 'the missing link' in West Germany's post-war economic history is true on several levels. In the first instance, they kept the economy going during the last days of the war and in its immediate aftermath, often with express consent from occupying authorities. On the one hand they knew the rationing and allocation system and understood how to work with state authorities on different levels, including the re-emerging ministerial bureaucracy. On the other hand they were trusted by, and had the confidence of, businesses. In Cologne, for example, this trust was expressed through hundreds of letters of inquiry sent by companies in the first couple of days and weeks after the war to the Chamber, in which it was asked for advice on anything from where and how to get permits and raw materials to more organizational questions of who was to represent their interests.[67] At a time when the traditional industrial associations were unable to function properly, it was the Chambers of Industry and Commerce that stepped into the breach to represent entrepreneurial interests. It was in this role that the IHK became the defender not just of the 'master in the house' attitude of many small and medium-sized business leaders, even despite some tactical and temporary concessions they made at Rhine and Ruhr. The successful resistance, especially of the northern IHK, against trade union participation in the Chambers has to be understood as a very significant contribution to the retention of the economic policy status quo at a time when there was a real possibility that it could change towards a more socialist model. Had the trade unions been successful in achieving their model of economic democracy in the British occupation zone, it would have been very difficult to reverse this change, even for the American Military Government, which gained ever greater prominence in the running of the Bizone. There is one more, again often forgotten, reason why the IHK have to be seen as 'the missing link' in West Germany's reconstruction process. It was they who in the late 1940s re-established foreign trade relations with Germany's western neighbours.[68] Considering that Germany's 'economic miracle' was export-driven, these early post-war contacts can hardly be overestimated in their importance.

At the time the entrepreneurs were defending their traditional economic model, they also began to create the legend that businesses and entrepreneurs found themselves in complete fragmentation after the Nazi capitulation and under pressure from both the Allies and the all-powerful trade unions. The reality was very different. Because in spring 1945 the IHK had been allowed to continue their work, they had, first of all, a head-start vis-à-vis the labour movement and the trade unions. Furthermore, they could build on a very strong personnel continuity and benefited from their previous experiences as statutory bodies. Their invaluable experience and professional expertise combined with practical knowledge of administering economic affairs afforded them a very strong position against the occupying forces who were struggling with the prevailing economic chaos and, as long as they stood together and spoke with one voice, against any political claims from trade unions. Last but not least, they could rely on pre-1945 (or pre-1933) networks.[69] With their traditional and conservative stance on social and economic policy matters, the IHK contributed to the recruitment and reconstruction of the German bourgeoisie, the *Bürgertum*. They were certainly successful in applying a new tactic, namely selling their own interests as public interests by twisting the facts and creating a 'we' against 'them' attitude, especially against labour representatives and left of centre politicians.[70] This tactic would be used by entrepreneurs and especially by the re-established industrial associations throughout the reconstruction period whenever they were faced with 'unappealing' trade union demands.

2

Ways of 'Redemption': Public Relations, the IHG and the DII

German industrialists had begun their planning for the post-war and post-Nazi years in secret as early as 1943 when the events of the war had made it obvious that the German Reich could not possibly win the war.[1] Although the Nazis had prohibited any such planning as *Wehrkraftzersetzung* (sabotage of military strengths and morale), which was punishable by death, the planning intensified the closer the war's end came. The industrialists' thinking had revolved around the fact that the victorious Allies would need their expertise to rebuild Germany's shattered economy and infrastructure as soon as the war had ended. Yet this belief displayed a good level of naivety, even incomprehension, about their position and status on the one hand and Allied war aims, perhaps best summarized by the title of General Eisenhower's post-war memoirs, *Crusade in Europe*, on the other.[2] In particular the Americans were convinced that businessmen and industrialists, in part through their conservative thinking and in part through the cartelized organization of German capitalism, had been responsible to a considerable degree for the rise of the Nazis. They were certainly responsible for keeping the German war economy going, and therefore guilty of sustaining the regime and prolonging the war; thus they had to be removed from their positions of influence.[3] Except for some very prominent figures such as Alfried Krupp von Bohlen und Halbach, who was taken into custody in place of his father Gustav who suffered from dementia, it took the Allies about eight months from their occupation of the Ruhr to arrest leading industrialists in November and December 1945. That the arrests were made after such a long delay caused considerable surprise, consternation and even bitterness amongst the industrialists and came as a severe shock to them, although some claimed in their memoirs that they had been awaiting the arrest 'with their rucksacks ready'.[4] A further blow to the industrialists' self-regard was the fact that it was not only the Allies who saw them as heavily involved with the Nazis: large parts of the German population did so, too.[5] Their sense of disbelief and upset increased further once it became clear that the Americans would put on trial for alleged war crimes at Nuremberg certain industrialists who they regarded as key protagonists. However, at least in relation to German public opinion, the Nuremberg industrialists' trials mark a watershed as they were seen, not without reason, as 'victors' justice', even more so when the verdicts were announced in 1948. By that time, the industrialists had been busy mobilizing public opinion in both Germany and the US, and had staged a vigorous defence of the accused. German entrepreneurs and industrialists, especially those from the Ruhr, had regarded themselves as pillars of state and society at least since the founding of the German Reich in 1871. The incarceration of themselves or their peers, and being 'chained together like robbers and murderers', as Günther Henle recalled in his memoirs, was a very humiliating experience for them as a group.[6]

The following chapter will show how entrepreneurs and businessmen began to use 'public relations' as their new miracle weapon in the fight in an attempt to redeem their tarnished reputation in the eyes of the public on both sides of the Atlantic. After the release of most industrialists from internment and after the Nuremberg industrialists' verdict, they were able to make considerable progress on their own in this public 'rebranding', culminating in the creation and work of the *Deutsches Industrie Institut* (DII, German Industry Institute). It was, however, changing Cold War policies and especially the outbreak of the Korean War which really boosted this image transformation. The Korean War stimulated West Germany's economy – which had been struggling with deflation and high unemployment at the turn of 1949–50 – and proved to be the priming of the 'economic miracle'.[7] It was the industrialists' claim that the economic success of the 'Korea boom' was of their making that helped significantly to turn their public image from that of Nazi stooges and war criminals towards one of being the facilitators of West Germany's economic recovery. It will be shown that the 1952 *Investitionshilfe Gesetz* (IHG, Auxiliary Investment Law), initially born out of industrialists' desperation to prevent the re-introduction of economic controls during the so-called 'Korean Crisis' of early 1951, helped to change the public image of industrialists in general but also helped to return heavy industrialists to their previous dominant position in the German economy.

The entanglements of German companies and their managers with the Nazis were extensive and ran deep. Paul Reusch, the creator of the Gutehoffnungshütte (GHH) conglomerate, said as much in a letter to his son Hermann in March 1946, when he stated in regards to the denazification questionnaire that 'nobody in industry has a clear *Fragebogen*'.[8] Reusch Senior's comment, even though it had been made in private, is unusual and may have resulted from his bitterness about having not received any support from fellow Ruhr industrialists when the Nazis had pushed him out of his post in 1942 after more than thirty years of GHH chairmanship, but it also contained more than a grain of truth.[9] Only a very small number of individual managers and entrepreneurs were prepared to look honestly at their action over the previous twelve years. Instead, companies began to look for ways in which they could exculpate themselves from any accusations of wrongdoing, especially in regard to their use of slave labour.[10] The 'restoration' of industry's reputation would be played out in stages, the first of which would be on an individual basis. Initially, like the rest of the population, business and industry provided *Persilscheine*[11] for each other, usually in the form of a declaration in lieu of oath, in which they confirmed that a person, although having nominally been a party member, had never been an active Nazi. Even those few industrialists who had been opposed to the Nazis participated in this closing of ranks. Representative here is Herman Reusch. Because he had left GHH together with his father, he was seen as above reproach and in late 1945 the British allowed him to become acting chairman of GHH before he took full chairmanship in 1947. In October

1946, Reusch provided a declaration in lieu of oath for Wolfgang Pohle, general plenipotentiary of Mannesmann and a Nazi party member since early 1933. Reusch stated that in confidential talks during the war Pohle, 'who had joined the party only to protect his livelihood', had admitted to fighting, in open and clandestine ways, for the interests of the mining industry against the party and the German Labour Front.[12] In other words, Reusch implied that Pohl had been a resistance fighter. This strategy of self-exculpation by turning others or themselves into resistance fighters was almost standard and used even by men who were far more than simply Nazi fellow travellers (*Mitläufer*). One example of this is Walter Rohland, who, before he became chairman of Vereinigte Stahlwerke, had been chairman of the tank production committee from 1940 to 1943. He declared himself a resistance man because he did not carry out Hitler's infamous *Nerobefehl* (Nero Order), which had demanded the destruction of the Ruhr area's infrastructure in the last days of the war, a claim other industrialists could make for themselves with much more justification.[13]

There were very few cases where industrialists did not participate in the closing of ranks, and these men suffered the consequences. Ewald Löser, finance director at Krupp until he left the company in 1943, stated in his defence during the Nuremberg industrialists' trials that he left the company so that he would not be responsible for the use of slave labour. In so doing, however, he shifted the blame for this malfeasance onto his fellow directors and indeed Alfried Krupp himself. Consequently his fellow industrialists deprived Löser of any group support; despite his attempted cooperation with the prosecution, he would be the last industrialist to be released from Landsberg Prison in 1951. He also suffered the wrath of his former colleagues for breaking solidarity: he was the only industrialist convicted at Nuremberg who would not return to a big company directorship and was excluded even from supervisory board positions.[14]

The next step on the way to the restoration of industrialists' reputation came almost in parallel to the provision of character statements and was aimed not so much at individuals but rather at industry and industrial associations as a whole. The first of these appalling attempts was undertaken in February 1945, even before the war had ended. The infamous Poensgen Memorandum, entitled 'Hitler and the Ruhr industrialists. A retrospective by Ernst Poensgen' and distributed to a small circle of friends, was the first attempt to whitewash heavy industry.[15] A follower of Chancellor Brüning during the late Weimar years, Poensgen had been chairman of Vereinigte Stahlwerke from 1935 to 1943 and, until 1942, when the Nazis pushed him out of office, chairman of the Iron and Steel Association. Poensgen claimed in the memorandum that steel industrialists (except for Fritz Thyssen, who, Poensgen emphasized, ended up in a concentration camp and for the coal industrialist Emil Kirdorf, who had died in 1938), had no sympathies with the Nazis. He evidenced this with the claim that they had no Hitler portrait in their assembly room, but one of Kaiser Wilhelm. Steel industrialists had joined the Nazi industrial organizations only 'to prevent worse from happening instead of standing idly by', which had also been the reason why some of them may have joined the party. Not intended for public circulation, Poensgen's whining article had little impact, but it did display the industrialists' distorted view of reality and the place they thought they had in it.[16] More waves were made by August Heinrichsbauer's

1948 political booklet *Schwerindustrie und Politik*, however, which was another blatant attempt to exculpate the steel industrialists.[17] A rather sweeping declaration in lieu of oath was made by the senior chief clerk of the Iron and Steel Association, Wilhelm Salewski, which was to be used for the defence of industrialists at the Nuremberg tribunals. Euphemistically entitled '*Arbeitseinsatz*' (deployment of labour), it completely misrepresented heavy industry's use of slave labour. Salewski had written his tract in an attempt to pre-empt a potentially much more damaging statement by a colleague, which had been compiled 'from memory only' and he strongly criticized what he viewed as unhelpful and thoughtless behaviour. Salewski's report, which he calls in his covering letter to Hermann Reusch '*als meine Anstandspflicht*' ('my duty of integrity') was, to say the least, very economical with the truth, if not outright perjury, and contained appalling national stereotypes about the foreign workers. He claimed that neither the Iron and Steel Association nor individual companies had any influence on the allocation of labour, for which 'Berlin authorities' were solely responsible and, as far as he could remember, the foreign workers' daily food rations were equivalent to those of German workers. However, the 'Italian workers' could not cope with the provision of cabbage and swedes which were supplied as vegetables.[18] The content of Salewski's declaration and the explanation he gave for industry's behaviour under the Nazis was typical of the time.[19] The covering letter to Reusch, however, reveals even more about the prevailing mentality. Salewski felt that his integrity would be in danger if he did not unflinchingly support the reputation of his association and its member companies and managers. We can again see that industry leaders' unquestioning loyalty to 'their own' took priority; those who did not follow this creed were inevitably criticized and ostracized.

Salewski's remarks were surpassed by those of his then boss at the Iron and Steel Association, Hermann Reusch, just weeks after Reusch had stepped down as association chairman in protest against British decartelization policies.[20] In his declaration in lieu of oath on the political attitude of industry, Reusch sugar-coated his remarks in defence of industry by pointing to its political heterogeneity. This diversity, he claimed, had made it impossible for them to resist the Nazis. If business leaders had been able to agree on a clear 'No' towards him, then Hitler would have faced real problems, but because of their political plurality, the industrialists could not have stopped him. Reusch went on to argue that it was actually the trade unions who had failed to halt Hitler by not calling a general strike on 2 May 1933, after the Nazis had seized trade union offices.[21] In response to, and in protest at, Reusch's very divisive remarks, the trade unions called a general strike in the British occupation zone. Even amongst his peers Reusch was seen as a hardliner but the comments were, nevertheless, not unique in pushing the blame away from industry onto other sectors of society. This was irrespective of the role heavy industrialists, and in particular Hermann Reusch's father, Paul, had played if not in the rise of the Nazis, then at least in the fall of the Weimar Republic.

The three major trials of prominent industrialists and managers from the IG Farben conglomerate, the Krupp company and the Flick trusts at Nuremberg were intended by the Americans as a symbol of the indictment of the German functional elite. The resulting verdicts deeply shocked German businessmen, especially the verdict against

Krupp, who received the highest prison tariff and who suffered the confiscation of his private assets, which industrialists called an attack on private property. However, the trials also became a turning point for the public perception of industrialists' trials. In marked contrast to the trials against the leading Nazis a year earlier, the public began to regard these trials as 'victors' justice'.[22] Encouraged not least by industrialists' propaganda, a growing segment of the public began to see industrialists no longer as Nazi agents but as victims of Allied revenge on Germany. This turnabout had several reasons. After the conviction and execution in 1946 of the major war criminals, the German people, who at the time were struggling first and foremost with everyday survival, were no longer interested in what was seen as Americans pursuing 'collective guilt' when they themselves wanted a return to 'normality'. Another reason was the perceived arbitrariness with which the accused had been chosen, in particular in the case of Krupp and eleven of his co-accused top managers. Considering overall company size, Krupp's company was not even the most important armaments firm in Germany, but it was certainly the most famous one. Because the company's reputation had been built on the manufacture of big artillery guns, it represented Germany's industrial militarism. In contrast, the reputation Friedrich Flick had acquired even amongst his fellow industrialists was considerably worse than Krupp's, so far that some of the men from the Ruhr were hesitant to extend group solidarity to Flick and provide any support to him at all.[23] Finally, a combination of the industrialists' defence strategy in which they described themselves as victims of the Nazi system and ongoing lobbying by their peers outside began to have an impact, and calls for their early release and rehabilitation grew ever louder.[24]

August Heinrichsbauer's already mentioned apologetic *Schwerindustrie und Politik* had been initiated and supported by Herman Reusch. The booklet's aim was 'to inform those who had to know', but it was not addressed to the general public. The work received a mixed reception from industrialists, not least because it fostered the paradox of the non-political industrialist who resisted the Nazis on ideological grounds. Heinrichsbauer was also one of three co-authors who drafted another booklet, *Warum wurde Krupp verurteilt?* (*Why was Krupp sentenced?*), which used much sharper language and accused the Allies of a 'war of annihilation' against German industry. The book was published in 1950 under the name of Krupp's brother-in-law, Tilo von Wilmowsky, presumably to take advantage of his involvement in, and arrest after, the 20 July plot against Hitler, which would have reduced suspicions of him being an apologist.[25] Subsequently, in 1949, Heinrichsbauer became the first head of the press department of the newly founded *Bundesverband der Deutschen Industrie* (BDI, Federation of German Industry), where he tried to promote and improve industry's public relations.[26]

Since the late nineteenth century individual companies in Germany had fed carefully selected information to the public in order to create a certain company image. This overall hesitant approach to public relations changed significantly after the Second World War when, under the influence of the US and lessons the first German PR men had learned from the Americans, German industrialists began to use *Öffentlichkeitsarbeit*, as PR was still often called, in a much more proactive and broader way.[27] Although the American intention to symbolically indict German industry altogether through the selected three companies at the Nuremberg trials backfired, German industrialists realized that they had to do much more to restore their reputation. Industry-wide reaction and attendant PR measures were called for and during a steel managers' meeting in June 1949, it was decided to provide much more money for PR and especially so in English.[28] For the first time, German companies and business associations hired public relations managers and lobbyists, usually from the United States, though evidence suggests that in many cases the initiative for the cooperation came from those American PR companies themselves.[29] The first use of US lobbying by German managers concerned the *Neuordnung* (reordering) of the Ruhr industries. *Neuordnung* meant the horizontal and vertical break-up of the heavy industry conglomerates into smaller companies, as the Allies had decreed in their Military Government Laws 75 and 27.[30] Initially there seemed to have been hesitation on the part of the managers to commit to what was for them a new form of communicating their notions to the public and American authorities. The steel association's newly founded committee on the reordering (*Arbeitskreis für Fragen der Neuordnung*) limited their mandate to the US lawyer Raul E. Desvernine and his German associate, Wilhlem Beutner, initially for two months. Desvernine, a conservative Republican and staunch opponent of Roosevelt's New Deal, received for his services in the fourth quarter of 1949 a total of DM 187,000 (or $44,500), which were paid not by the Iron and Steel Association, but by the individual companies affected by the reordering.[31] Although at one stage even the Federal Government approached Desvernine to support an official German delegation to Washington, and despite the original contract being extended twice until December 1950, the Iron and Steel Association's willingness to use Desvernine's services gradually declined, as evinced by a drop in fees with every extension. The companies eventually decided that, since the problems were political and not legal in nature, the use of lobbyists would not really help their cause. The last time the contract was extended, it was done as a defensive move on the part of German industrialists. They had decided to use US law firms to make their claims against *Neuordnung* in the United States but feared that Desvernine would see this as an unfriendly act and make unfavourable remarks about them.[32] At a time when large parts of US public opinion were still critical of German big business, such a risk could not be taken.

Although Desvernine's activities were relatively short-lived, and despite initial scepticism amongst some managers about the use of public relations, its importance became more and more apparent. When Krupp director Carl Hundhausen, who would become the founding father of German PR, delivered a field report on the topic to the Iron and Steel Association board, it was received 'with strong applause'.[33] The responses to Hundhausen's talk are twofold: first, it shows that industrialists had realized the importance of better outward representation; but, secondly, it also showed that if the claim was made by 'one of them', industrialists were more inclined to take the lessons on board. Public relations was one of the first modern management tools German industry adapted from the US and some American PR companies would have a big impact on this development and go on to operate successfully in the Federal Republic, most notably Julius Klein Public Relations, Chicago. Wiesen argues convincingly that the motivation for the American PR men was not commercial, but political in the first instance. Their belief that German industrialists were the West's best hope to prevent the spread of communism in Germany and Europe was the reason why they got involved with tainted industrialists. Klein, who was of German Jewish descent, had risen to the rank of Major General in the US Army during the war; he had understood that West Germany's (and especially West German industrialists') attempts to rely on its economic success for the country's moral renewal were double-edged. On the one hand, Germany's recovery was admired; on the other, there remained a link in people's minds between the Nazis and the industrialists.[34] After having taken the credit for the initial success of the economic recovery, some German managers seemed to have forgotten that they were still perceived with some suspicion, especially in the US. When Klein approached the Iron and Steel Association in 1955 to offer his services and pointed out that the association was still regarded as 'a symbol of war-mongering fanatics', Hans-Günter Sohl, the association chairman, annotated this passage with a question mark in the margin, indicating some bewilderment about such an accusation.[35] Nevertheless, one month later the association decided to sponsor a book which questioned the Nuremberg industrialists' trials' legitimacy for $2,500 so as to give it wider prominence in the USA.[36] In contrast, if there were publications unfavourable to their view, leading industrialists tried to pull strings to prevent their publication, at least in Germany.[37] To further their cause at home, they set up the Association of Friends of Albert Vögler (*Freundeskreis Albert Vögler*), named after the former Vereinigte Stahlwerke chairman who had committed suicide during his arrest by the Americans in 1945. The main purpose of the association was the publication of hagiographic biographies of German industrialists or companies. Many of those were penned by Gert von Klass, who wrote no fewer than three books on the Krupp company or family as well as biographies of Hugo Stinnes and Albert Vögler. For the latter Klass was heavily criticized by his industrial masters since, in their opinion, it contained too many references to the Nazis and any such link was seen as highly inopportune.[38] Other laudatory collections which focussed on the 'new men' of the Ruhr and their achievements in the economic miracle included Karl Heinrich Herdenröder's *Neue Männer an der Ruhr*, to which one of the Ruhr grandees, Wilhelm Zangen, former chairman of Reichsgruppe Industrie and supervisory board chairman of Mannesmann, provided industrialists' blessing in the form of the introduction.[39] With a barrage of pro-business publication in magazines and newspapers, usually in support of Ludwig Erhard's 'Social Market Economy', this PR offensive had considerable success. Wiesen concludes in his seminal study that with the help of mass media, businessmen were able to create the image of a new industrialist, one untainted by the Nazi past and dedicated to the public good, as the next chapter will show. Although by the mid-1950s there were warnings that PR was losing its shine in the United States, and that a backlash was under way which would soon affect Germany as well, this did not in fact happen. On the contrary, by the end of the 1950s a conference called 'Public Relations as duty of industry' (*als Aufgabe der Industrie*) showed that industrialists had now fully embraced what had been seen before the war as very much an 'American' concept.[40]

This form of 'soft' public relations, born out of the attempt to disassociate from the Nazi past and in response to the Nuremberg industrialists' trials, was accompanied by less subtle means. With the establishment of the *Deutsches Industrie Institut* on 16 January 1951, businesses, and as will be shown, heavy industry, created themselves a very powerful *Kampfinstitut* (institute for industrial conflict). At the time when management felt threatened by co-determination, it was directed in particular against trade unions. At the same time the DII was intended to raise entrepreneurial spirit and self-confidence by declaring them as the new social elite and defender of western values. Volker Muthesius, an influential economics journalist, wrote to Hermann Reusch in June 1949 to inform him that a group of industrialists had met on 18 May and 10 June and decided on the establishment of a *Gesellschaft für wirtschaftliche Meinungspflege* (Society for Economic Public Relations). In February 1950, Reusch received a thirteen-page memorandum from Heinrichsbauer which set out the organization and task of industrial public relations. In the paper Heinrichsbauer emphasized the need for businesses to influence proactively democratic opinion-making.[41] With the outbreak of the Korean War and against the backdrop of the ongoing debate about co-determination in German basic industries, industrialists' efforts to get an institute up and running intensified. The driving force for the establishment of the society, now already renamed the *Deutsches Industrie Institut*, was once more Hermann Reusch, though as a DII publication later phrased it apologetically, 'progressive' managers participated in the Institute's founding as well.[42] In December 1950 Reusch wrote to the designated chairman, textile industrialist and vice president of the BDI, Carl Neumann, and explained that the creation of the Institute should happen before Christmas, with the initial set-up costs of DM 500,000 being shared equally between the BDI and the Federation of German Employer Organizations (*Bundesverband deutscher Arbeitgeberverbände*, BDA).[43] Fritz Hellwig, the Institute's chief clerk (*Geschäftsführer*), would become its rhetorically most eloquent rabble-rouser and most active asset and propagandist for the 'new' entrepreneur. Between April and December 1951 alone he delivered more than sixty presentations and lectures on behalf of the DII and another twenty-five for 'others', mainly for the CDU's economic association.[44] Under his leadership the DII would eventually produce three regular publications: the *Unternehmerbrief* (literally: *Entrepreneur's Letter*); the *Schnelldienst* (*Express Service*) and the *Vortragsreihe des Deutschen Industrie-Instituts* (*DII Lecture series*). They all have to be seen as part of the wider, usually very aggressive, public relations campaign and an attempt to increase entrepreneurs' self-image and confidence.[45]

This uncompromising nature was visible as early as the DII's first publication, authored by Hellwig and his fellow chief clerk Otto Mejer and dated 30 April 1951. In it they outlined the reasons for the establishment of the DII and its intended tasks in stark and revealing language. The article explained that German entrepreneurship had been pushed into a minority position in political discussions; and that entrepreneurs were threatened by further exclusion from the ongoing societal, economic and political debate about the reordering of Germany. Hellwig and Mejer bemoaned that entrepreneurs were regarded as outlaws (*vogelfrei*) and scapegoats who could be insulted in the daily political business. 'The company community (*betriebliche Gemeinschaft*) which had developed between entrepreneurs and their co-workers in the years of decline and downfall' was now threatened again by a revival of class struggle, by which they meant co-determination. Because of this antagonism, the DII had been set up since the existing industrial and social policy associations were unable

Figure 2.1 Hermann Reusch (1896–1971), Director General of the Gutehoffnungshütte conglomerate. As a *Bergassessor* Reusch was one of the most hard-line conservative Ruhr industrialists and crucial in the re-establishment of associations and the BDI. Unwilling or unable to adapt his views to the times, by the 1960s he was regarded as an anachronism even by many of his peers. In contrast to his political conservatism, he was one of West Germany's great sponsors of modern arts. © Rheinisch-Westfälisches Wirtschaftsarchiv Köln RWWA 130-45000/67.

to counter any of those challenges, due to their heavy workload of everyday business. In an attempt to reassure businessmen, the two authors stressed what the DII did not want to become: it was neither a super-association nor an economic research institute, nor a bloated, top-heavy bureaucracy – and certainly not an 'institute for class struggle'. Instead the key foci of the Institute would be an emphasis on the work and role of entrepreneurs, including their social and political responsibility within society, and an end to the distorted image industrialists had to suffer in the public's eye.[46]

Presenting entrepreneurs to the outside world as being victims of Allied injustice who were also disregarded by the political class and threatened in their existence by trade union pressure and talk of industrial socialization was typical at the time, but it hardly matched reality. It showed, nevertheless, the level of insecurity and bourgeois *Angst* which prevailed after Allied attempts to denazify the German economy, which in some cases had prevented company owners from entering their firms until as late as 1949.[47] The prevalent feeling amongst industrialists and the resulting public claim of being politically disregarded, however, implied to a degree that they *had* had political influence earlier, either before 1945 or before 1933, or both. This assertion therefore directly contradicted their argument that they had been 'unpolitical' entrepreneurs. Feeling disregarded was rather an expression of what they feared might happen to their bourgeois and upper bourgeois position and influence within society and politics. The sharp rhetoric the DII used when entrepreneurs saw the company community threatened by the return of the trade unions who wanted to revive class struggle also belied reality. After all, industry had welcomed the crushing of the trade unions by the Nazis in 1933 and the subsequent introduction of the leadership principle in the companies, along with the 'proper' terminology of *Betriebsführer* (factory leader) and *Gefolgschaft* (retinue), which had ended the unloved co-operation with (or rather tolerance of) trade unions and labour representatives. It is indicative that at least some employers continued the use of the terminology of *Gefolgschaft* and *Betriebsappell* (factory roll call) at least into the early 1950s.[48] Furthermore, nobody in industry had spoken about class struggle during the 1946–9 period when industrialists had been more than happy about the co-operation and support they received from trade unions when factories were facing dismantling.[49]

The claim that the DII was not to be intended as an instrument for class struggle belied reality to a significant extent also. In a letter to their mentor Reusch in December 1951, the DII was very pleased about an article the previous month in the SPD paper *Neuer Vorwärts,* in which it had been called the 'propaganda department of entrepreneurs' and employers' associations' and accused of polemic reporting. This judgement was shared by neutral contemporary observers as well. Writing for the RAND Corporation in 1957, Gabriel Almond saw the research and publication of the DII as 'primarily polemic in nature'.[50] Not every manager was happy with this aggressive form of public relations, though. At the DII's first members' meeting in 1952, Ernst Falkenheim, board member of Deutsche Shell and later BDI executive committee member, criticized and demanded an end to the 'well aimed mud-slinging at the trade unions', but he was a lone voice. Josef Winschuh of the *Arbeitsgemeinschaft Selbstständiger Unternehmer* rather called the DII 'the entrepreneurs' general staff in a fight for life and death'.[51] Over the next year or so, the DII saw an internal fight for its direction. More moderate managers saw the DII's role as a professional and advisory body (*Fach- und Beratungsorgan*); the hardliners wanted it to be a means for 'mass psychology' which could 'influence the mass of the electorate'. By early 1953 the hardliners had won and it had been decided that the Institute would focus its work much more on mass psychology by providing appropriate news stories to journalists and newspapers for wider dissemination. The additional advantage of this new way of operation was that the DII would be less visible as a propaganda machine. However, its very aggressive tone against trade unions and Social Democrats did not cease and the Institute saw itself faced with a number of law suits from the SPD and the public workers' union ÖTV for libel and slander.[52] The DII more than once managed to inflame situations with its polemics too, and perhaps the most striking example came in 1955. In a public speech in January of that year, Herman Reusch had turned facts upside down when he declared that the 1951 co-determination law in the coal, iron and steel industries had come about only because the trade unions had blackmailed the state at a time when the government had been weak. While there was condemnation for Reusch's inflammatory remarks behind closed doors from other industrialists, outwardly they closed ranks following the trade union's announcement of a twenty-four-hour general strike at the Hüttenwerk Oberhausen AG (HOAG) steel plant. The strike at HOAG was highly symbolic as it had been the core steel plant of Reusch's Gutehoffnungshütte conglomerate before it was split from GHH by the British as part of the post-war *Entflechtung* (breaking-up of companies). The DII then poured oil on the flames by calling the strike unlawful, which only caused it to spread across the whole of the Ruhr. For their statement the DII was heavily rebuked by the press. In an act of entrepreneurial solidarity, at its next executive committee meeting, the BDI declared its solidarity with Reusch and the affected companies. Although the BDI board conceded that the co-determination law should not be directly challenged for political reasons, the DII was asked to prepare countermeasures through a new media campaign.[53]

Around the mid-1950s, the first internal tensions began to emerge within and around the DII that would eventually erupt due to the wider conflict of 'big' versus small and medium industry. Those tensions came to the fore because of the way the DII was funded. The BDI had established a formula according to which its member associations had to contribute to the DII's maintenance. By 1954, the clothing industry association had accumulated funding arrears of more than DM 240,000. The following year, the BDI announced that a 'special contribution for non-metal industries' would be levied. The way the BDI letter was phrased suggests that struggling industries such as clothing were allowed an overall reduction to their contribution. However, as the shortfall was covered by heavy industry and because there were other thriving non-metal industries, in particular chemicals, the contributions of which were not raised, the bulk of the DII funding would have come from metal-working associations and heavy industry, a regulation which was officially confirmed in 1962.[54] In other words, DII funding came from more influential industrial associations which themselves were carried by big companies who obviously expected that their interests would take priority over those of lesser contributors. As a result the Institute got caught up in the ongoing dispute between large and small companies and was accused of only representing big business.[55] This came at a time after Fritz Hellwig had taken a new job at the High Authority of the European Coal and Steel Community, starting in 1960.[56] With his transfer, the DII did not just lose its biggest rhetorical and propaganda asset but also a man who, in his articles and speeches, had been able to bridge the gap between big industries and their salaried managers on the one side and small and medium companies with their independent owner-entrepreneurs on the other.

Hellwig's move, together with the changing social and political atmosphere in the Federal Republic of the late 1960s, heralded a change in the DII's mission and approach which showed itself tentatively in the Institute's fifteenth anniversary publication in 1966. On the one hand, the DII was proud to have organized the joint BDI and BDA 'Aktion 65', a large-scale newspaper advertisement campaign against trade union demands. In the *Arbeitskreis Mitbestimmung* (working party co-determination) of the same year the Institute had also stated that because of '*wirtschaftsdemokratische Mitbestimmung der Gewerkschaften wird aus der Sozialen Marktwirtschaft eine sozialistische Wirtschaftsform*' ('through the trade unions' co-determined economic democracy, the social market economy is turned into a form of socialist economy'), there were nevertheless signs of changes.[57] Fritz Arlt, the DII's education and training expert, in his contribution to the anniversary publication highlighted industry's obligations in this field and how these supported the market economy; in Heinrich Schreiner's contribution on the Institute's role in the social policy discussion, the DII was no longer the *Kampfinstitut* but a service provider for industry in all matters concerning economic policy.[58] This transformation process found its provisional conclusion in 1973, when the DII was renamed *Institut der deutschen Wirtschaft* (German Economic Institute). While it is still representing business interests, it does so no longer as a traditional lobby and public relations institution but rather as a service provider and an economic policy think tank for all sectors of the economy, not just the manufacturing industry.

The last example of events or actions which heavy industrialists used to redeem themselves, the 1952 *Investitionshilfe Gesetz* (IHG), was unpopular when it was proposed. Initially they actually opposed it outright, but under pressure from unfolding events, they seized the initiative and turned it into a public relations success and political triumph. Once the Allies had changed their economic policy in occupied Germany in 1947 from one of punitive restrictions to careful reconstruction, they placed their main emphasis on the recovery of basic industries – coal, iron and steel – which revived production in the sector. After the currency reform of 20 June 1948 and the subsequent economic reforms introduced by Ludwig Erhard, the future economics minister of West Germany, the emphasis shifted decisively towards consumer goods. Partly for ideological reasons, partly for his dislike of heavy industries and their cartel tradition in general, Erhard preferred the consumer goods industries, 'even if Germany's reconstruction would take five to ten years longer' as he infamously explained in February 1948.[59] Heiner Adamsen quite rightly points out that Erhard's consumption-driven policy completely lacked any strategy for capital formation.[60] As it turned out, from the summer of 1950 onward this was a very dangerous policy, considering Germany's dire economic situation and the challenges of reconstruction. The outbreak of the Korean War on 25 June 1950 had several negative effects on the West German economy. With raw material prices globally rising on average by 25 per cent and the German export industry still struggling on the world markets, by late 1950 the country was faced with a balance of payment deficit of critical proportion. Erhard had to suspend a number of import liberalizations he had introduced and the Central Bank, the *Bank deutscher Länder*, severely tightened its monetary policy. What was worse was that the Americans threatened to suspend vital Marshall Plan deliveries if West Germany was not to change its economic policy away from consumption towards a contribution to the 'defence of the West'.[61]

The payments deficit could be turned around in early 1951 due to an export boom based on a huge influx of foreign orders, which marked the beginning of West Germany's export miracle. As the only country in the West with spare industrial capacity, both for consumer and investment goods, including steel, western countries, which had switched their economies back to war production, needed German finished and semi-finished goods to cover their domestic shortfall. However, because of Erhard's investment priorities, German heavy industry, especially the coal industry, could not deliver the output needed to sustain the boom. Some Ruhr steel companies had to agree barter trade with American companies, trading German steel for American coal so that they could continue their production. Even more embarrassing for Ludwig Erhard was the fact that the coal supply from the Ruhr (which was still handicapped by forced coal exports) for a brief time was not even sufficient to cover the basic needs for the electrical industry's power plants. With the resulting power cuts emerged simultaneously a black market for coal which was more or less sanctioned (or at least tolerated) by the government. A humiliated Ludwig Erhard had to announce the appointment of a *Rohstoffbeauftragter* (raw materials commissioner) in order to prevent the full-blown reintroduction of government controls in the basic industries. The man chosen for the job was Otto A. Friedrich of the Hamburg rubber company Phoenix.[62] While Friedrich held the post more as a token gesture and did not implement any real measures of control, he was one of the few big-name industrialists at the time who stood wholeheartedly behind Erhard's concept of a market economy; the large majority of industrialists remained ambivalent or even outright hostile. Although they liked the idea of a free market economy as advocated by Erhard, 'free' for them meant free of all state interference, in particular the freedom to re-establish cartels and a lifting of all remaining price controls.[63]

What became apparent very quickly was that the imposition of a rather inactive raw materials commissioner did not change the underlying issues of the coal industry, namely the lack of investment, even from Marshall Plan counterpart funds.[64] By the end of March 1951, any 'market conforming' solutions were off the table and the government began to put pressure on the industrial associations to contribute to a solution.[65] When the BDI executive committee discussed investment aid during their meeting on 27 March, there were strong objections to a plan by the banker Hermann Josef Abs, who called for a re-direction of tax depreciation, while a proposal by Marshall Plan Minister Franz Blücher, who had suggested that industry was to raise a DM 1.2 billion loan themselves, was called unrealizable.[66] However, a meeting at the Chancellery on 8–9 April would be significant. When BDI president Fritz Berg reported back about the meeting to the executive committee, his tune had completely changed, not least because industry would be allowed to determine the distribution of the raised funds to basic industries. Furthermore, Berg pointed out, the alternative would be a 'stringent government bill from the Left'. The main problem with the plan lay in convincing companies in non-heavy industry to participate, as the strong resistance to the proposal by Otto Vogel, the Bavarian textile industrialist, indicated.[67]

Eventually, it was the BDI legal department that wrote the first draft bill. It was rushed through Parliament and came on the statute book on 7 January 1952. The bill was an almost complete success for the BDI and heavy industry although neither coal nor iron and steel were by this time member associations. All commercial businesses (*Gewerbetreibende*) above a certain size had to contribute to the raising of the funds in proportion to their tax revenue. For this reason state tax authorities had to get involved in the process of collecting the funds. The money that was raised had to be paid into a special account (*Sondervermögen Investitionshilfe*) held at the Industriekreditbank, a bank which had been set up by industry in 1949 to provide credit for medium-sized enterprises. In this way, the funds were kept out of the government's hands. A board of trustees (*Kuratorium*) decided on how funds were to be distributed. On the board a president appointed from industry together with five industrial and three trade union representatives had voting rights, clearly favouring industrial interests. In terms of propaganda, the best part for the industrialists was that they were able to present to large parts of the population their DM 1.2 billion contribution as a 'donation'. This sleight of hand, together with the impact of an economy that was reviving fast due to international demand, helped to style businessmen as saviours of the economy. The reality was quite different: for any payment to the fund, companies received tradable and interest-bearing bonds, so all businesses *did* eventually make some profit out of the scheme. Furthermore, and more importantly, the law contained a clause which allowed heavy industry in particular a 50 per cent tax depreciation over a two-year period on all new investments. Ludwig Erhard also managed to insert a clause into the law which would allow him to raise prices of basic commodities without having to rely on Parliament's consent, although he rarely used this power.[68]

The IHG demonstrates the early influence of business associations, in particular the BDI and the Iron and Steel Association, but also how quickly they could change their position, in this case from outright opposition to providing the early draft of the bill. There had been strong and ongoing opposition to the bill, from outside heavy industry, in particular from small and medium-sized companies opposed to the special treatment heavy industry received. Their lawsuit had eventually to be decided by the Constitutional Court, which in 1954 dismissed the claim and ruled that the law did not violate private property rights as enshrined in the Federal Republic's Basic Law.[69] Fears that existed during the bill's parliamentary proceedings that the iron industry may not benefit at all from the law were unfounded. Direct lobbying by Berg and Friedrich, as well as intervention by CDU and FDP deputies close to industry, made sure that funding would be available. When the board of the Iron and Steel Association met again in December 1951 to comment on the passing of the bill, the minutes spoke of a

Table 2.1 Proposed and final distribution of loans under the IHG (in million DM)

	Original *Kuratorium* proposal	**Erhard's proposal on 24.9.51**	**Decision by BMWi**	**Means agreed by the *Kuratorium***
Coal mining	300	260	234	228.2
Electrical power	300	380*	252	241.8
Gas supply	–	–	126	106.1
Iron & steel	300	260	278	296.5
Rail freight cars	–	50	50	50
Water supply	100**	10	60	77.4
Others	–	40	–	–
Total	1,000	1,000	1,000	1,000

*Including funds for gas supply.
**Including money for other projects.
Source: Adamsen, *Investitionshilfe für die Ruhr*, p. 264

'formidable success' and pointed to the depreciation clause and price clause as particularly 'favourable conditions'.[70] How favourable the iron and steel industry fared from the IHG in terms of investment funds is obvious from Table 2.1, which shows it eventually as the single biggest beneficiary of a law that was initially designed to help the coal industry.

As it had caused significant friction within the business community and also had shown the flaws of Erhard's economic policies, all sides were happy to forget the episode as quickly as possible. This is the most likely reason why the IHG is often overlooked by historians, despite its impact and importance. Even at the time it was criticized by the eminent economics professor Franz Böhm as the first sign of a *Verbände Staat* (association state), where the associations usurp functions which should remain with the state. And indeed, regardless of the embarrassment it had caused to the Economics Minister and to industry, the IHG nevertheless signified a return of association powers, a fact Erhard had to tolerate. The IHG symbolized in particular an increase in power for heavy industry, with the steel industry regaining most of their lost influence 'under the special conditions of the 1950s, until the steel crisis of the 1960s terminated this renaissance for good'.[71] With some justification Abelshauser called it a return to the corporatist model.[72] Most importantly, the IHG helped to restore the reputation of West German entrepreneurs, if only indirectly. The law was a direct result of the 'Korean crisis' of late 1950 and early 1951, which then turned into the 'Korea boom' which was the trigger point for Germany's astounding economic recovery. As such, the IHG and Korea boom were at least in part at the root of the mentality which many German entrepreneurs displayed during the 1950s. Not least because of new public relations methods and especially the work of the DII, the recovery became closely linked not just to Erhard but to the *Unternehmer*, or entrepreneurs (as businessmen now preferred to be called in all walks of the economy) as well. Germany's working public, which in February 1950 had faced up to two million unemployed, or 12 per cent of the workforce, hardly questioned the industrialists' claim that the quick economic upturn after 1952/3 was caused by entrepreneurial prowess and not as a result of an export boom. The IHG thus can be seen as the last of three steps of entrepreneurial (self) rehabilitation, which were closely intertwined and linked together by extensive and ongoing public relations exercises. These had started out with portrayals of themselves as victims of victors' justice in the wake of the Nuremberg industrialists' trials, and were followed by the creation and early propagandistic activities of the DII, which then could almost seamlessly move on to lead the propaganda for the IHG. That the law coincided so closely with the economic upswing made this task so much easier. Any criticism of entrepreneurs or associations, such as that from Böhm or the political left, could have easily been brushed aside by pointing to the now booming economy.

Part II

The Miracle Makers: Industrialists and their Self-perception in the 'Economic Miracle' Period

'The modern industrial society needs a stratum of responsible men, an elite, which, out of national-political (staatspolitischem) sense of responsibility, dedicate themselves to public affairs with the same passion as they carry out their business.'[1]

3

The New 'Entrepreneur'

Ever since the publication of Volker Berghahn's seminal book *Unternehmer und Politik in der Bundesrepublik* in 1985,[2] there has been an ongoing debate amongst historians about whether or not the mentality and attitude of German industrialists changed after the Second World War. Berghahn claims that a change did come about, but only towards the end of the 1960s, when a new generation of managers took over the reins of companies. In contrast, Alexander von Plato argues that, although there was a considerable continuity in the leadership personnel in industrial associations, a shift in mentality took place as early as the 1950s.[3] Stefan Unger, in a short study on heavy industry, supports von Plato's theory but argues that it was due to a change in personnel, which came about largely because of the Allied denazification policy.[4] A much more provocative stance is taken by Paul Erker, who sees a very strong continuation in mentality, which was carried not least by the industrial associations (that is, by the associations' chief clerks), despite the changes in company leadership.[5] The studies by Hervé Joly and Michael Hartmann, finally, discount the discontinuity theory and argue strongly that there was a continuity of industrial leadership personnel.[6]

The picture is more complex, though, and depended on what lessons the industrialists had learned (or not) from the Nazi *Volks-* and *Betriebsgemeinschaft*, from the war and the subsequent experience of occupation. However, Erker sees industrialists' thinking as being much more rooted in the experiences of the First World War than in those of the Nazi period.[7] While this may be true for those industrialists who did experience military service between 1914 and 1918 and/or subsequent fighting in the Freikorps in 1919, this claim is difficult to explain for those managers born after 1900, men like Hans-Günther Sohl, Ernst-Wolff Mommsen or Berthold Beitz; it is certainly not true for newcomers like Willy Schlieker. There were simply too many different industrial branches and sizes of companies to consider, and, of course, the individual mentality of each manager or entrepreneur. A case in point here are the attitudes of Sohl, Hermann Reusch and Günter Henle. All three men headed a big iron and steel company, but each had a different approach. Henle, for example, a former diplomat, was one of the strongest advocates of the Schuman Plan and Franco-German reconciliation and he was in favour of trade union participation in the Chambers of Industry and Commerce. At the other end of the spectrum Reusch, the quintessential *Bergassessor*, viewed Adenauer's European policy as a sell-out of German industrial interests, and trade unions as a hindrance and nuisance to the running of his company.[8]

Despite some differences, there was important common ground that industrialists shared and propagated throughout the 1950s. Perhaps the most important to mention here, and one from which other idiosyncrasies developed, is the claim of elite status that spread during the early 1950s and which has to be understood as part of West Germany's myth of the 'economic miracle'. It arose in the context of the early reconstruction period, i.e. from 1948 onwards. Germany's long-established elites – Prussia's landed aristocracy and its military class – had lost their traditional powerbase, their estates, either because of the Potsdam Treaty and the ceding of German territory east of the River Oder, or because the Soviets expropriated them in the territory that made up the GDR. The officer class and its attendant traditional German militarism was utterly discredited after the Second World War; the nature and scale of the defeat made it impossible for them to blame another 1918-style 'stab-in-the-back' conspiracy.[9] The third historical pillar of the German state, the senior civil servants or *Beamtenschaft*, had been significantly tainted by their close cooperation with the NS regime and, following Allied purges, could return to their old posts only gradually. As mentioned above, the industrial elites, on the other hand, were able to use their old networks and influence to portray themselves as victims of Allied 'victors' justice', in particular after the Nuremberg industrialists' trials. Their fight against the dismantling of industrial plants was their first step towards rehabilitation, and in most cases this was led by the *Bergassessoren* of the Ruhr. Not least because of their training, which had been carried out and overseen by the Prussian state, and their time as Prussian *Beamte*, they too had seen themselves traditionally as part of the *staatstragende* (state-supporting) establishment, outside of, but parallel to, state authorities.[10] Even if this attitude was no longer as strongly pronounced amongst the post-war generation as it had been in the Wilhelmine era, they had still been exposed to and nourished by this mentality, which described *Bergassessoren* as 'more arrogant, conceited and more aware of their power than even the officer caste'.[11]

From at least the middle of 1947 onward, it had become obvious that American policy towards Germany was changing because of the Cold War situation; economic reconstruction was on the cards again, which meant the knowledge and expertise of the managers was once more needed. When the economic recovery got under way, industrialists not only claimed credit for it, but they claimed *sole* credit and were eager to defend 'their' achievement at all costs. When in 1952 Christian Fette, the chairman of the *Deutsche Gewerkschaftsbund* (DGB, German Trade Union Federation) claimed that the merit for the reconstruction lay with the workers, Fritz Berg replied to these almost blasphemous remarks in an open letter that he regarded this as an '*unmittlebare Verunglimpfung*' (direct denigration) of entrepreneurs' achievements.[12] In other words, entrepreneurs claimed that they alone were responsible for the reconstruction boom. Since the 'economic miracle' was the Federal Republic's 'founding myth', they therefore laid claim to a leading role in the state as well.[13] They could make this claim because the demise of the old elites and the slow reformation of a political class had created a social vacuum which they could now easily fill. In particular the owners and managers of small and medium-sized firms saw companies, regardless of size, as stabilising social factors during the upheaval of the post-war years. Because they provided a fixed reference point for many workers, companies and with them the *Betriebsgemeinschaft* became 'more important than housing'.[14] The responsibility for the firm and the continuing availability of these jobs lay with the entrepreneurs. Traditionally they had based their claim for leadership on three pillars: the ownership of the company (or at least proxy ownership in the case of the salaried managers); what they termed '*die Berufung*' (the calling) to be an entrepreneur; and finally their elite status.[15]

Initial attempts made by German industrialists to prevent dismantling of plants, including ideas of offering shares to foreign companies if they were prepared to offer reciprocal treatment, had no success.[16] It was only the political concessions made by the Allies (as in the (second) revised industry plan of August 1947) and subsequently negotiations conducted by Chancellor Adenauer, especially those leading to the Petersberg Protocol in November 1949, which reduced the number of plants that were to be dismantled.[17] Notwithstanding their inability to prevent dismantling themselves, by late 1949, due to the changed political situation which went hand in hand with improving economic conditions, most industrialists had regained their old self-confidence. During his introductory speech to the founding meeting of the BDI, Hermann Reusch emphasized that the *produzierende Wirtschaft* (manufacturing industry) was the bedrock of the economy altogether.[18] Although the economic situation in the Federal Republic after the currency reform of 20 June 1948 did improve for businesses, the overall economic performance was mixed at best. A profit inflation which had immediately followed the currency reform had turned into a deflation by early 1949 and unemployment was rising, peaking at a record 2 million, or 12 per cent of the workforce, by February 1950.[19] Notwithstanding the economy's ability to provide work, in a speech in April 1950 to young entrepreneurs Josef Winschuh of the *Arbeitsgemeinschaft Selbstständiger Unternehmer* declared the industrialists to be an elite group in the country.[20] At this stage, Winschuh's claim would have been very much based on the *Selbstverständnis*, the entrepreneurs' self-image, as men who were active and creative, not just for their company but, as they claimed, for the common good. Because an entrepreneur, and in particular the owner of a small or medium-sized company '*haftet mit Kopf und Kragen*' (was liable with his blood and his bones), he had to be universally trained (*universell vorgebildet*) to fulfil his task properly. In contrast to a politician, he had to know and really understand his business.[21] Winschuh's statement gives an insight into and provided the seed for a division in the industrialists' camp which would eventually turn into open conflict. This was the differentiation between the *Unternehmer* and the 'manager', a word that was widely despised in the German business community well into the 1960s. In contrast to the *Unternehmer* who looked after the long-term interest of his company and his workforce as well as fostering a wider social responsibility, a 'manager' was seen as nothing more than a soulless man in a grey suit. His only interest was, at best, a short-termist profit maximization after which he would move on to another company; in his worst incarnation, he was regarded as nothing more than a capitalist functionary. If applied strictly, this definition would of course have excluded the managers of the big companies from being entrepreneurs, an exclusion they would have rejected outright. It was the creation of the term *beauftragter Unternehmer* (authorized entrepreneur) which kept the salaried managers a part of the 'family' at a time when industrialists were faced with Allied dismantling and trade union demands for participation in decision-making. Wiesen

Figure 3.1 Josef Winschuh (1897–1970), co-owner of a textile company, one of the most effective advocates for small- and medium-sized enterprises and bustling representative of the *Arbeitsgemeinschaft Selbstständiger Unternehmer*. He invented the term '*beauftragter Unternehmer*', which distinguised between owner-entrepreneurs and salaried managers, but crucially allowed both groups to carry the term 'entrepreneur'. © Die Familienunternehmer.

sees this change in terminology as part of the industrialists' rhetoric attempt to rehabilitate themselves. In contrast to the term '*Fabrikbesitzer*' (factory owner), which was close to 'capitalist' and thus linguistically linked to 'big capitalist', i.e. one of the people who were associated with bringing the Nazis to power, an *Unternehmer* was someone who worked hard, created jobs and employment and enterprisingly used his own property and wealth for the good of the company so that it could benefit his workforce and through it the population in general.[22]

As will be shown in the following chapters, this artificial brace disappeared towards the end of the 1950s and led to significant disputes amongst the two groups.

Obviously, not only the ASU and independent entrepreneurs regarded themselves as 'elite'; following the example of the *Bergassesoren*, top industry leaders were also very liable to do so. In 1955, Ernst Wolf Mommsen edited a book called *Elitenbildung in der Wirtschaft* (*Elite Forming in the Economy*) in which contemporary writers, both active business leaders from Germany as well as prominent men from abroad, analysed training methods for leadership cadres.[23] In his introduction, Mommsen first of all distanced himself from the Nazi period and how the term 'elite' had been misused by the Nazis. He explained that for him elite meant 'the determination of leadership qualities in all walks of public and private life.' This was best summarized by 'the model of the manager who came to the top through courage and willingness to accept responsibility'. He concluded with the statement that: 'elite was not a choice through which the chosen became the "elected"; being elite rather meant to provide the best in performance, ability, willingness and knowledge.'[24] The book's message was quite clear: the elite role of management bestowed on them not just the task, but the *obligation*, to look for and develop the next generation of top leaders.

Inevitably, this claim for elite status led to political demands. It was once again Josef Winschuh who, in a speech on (or rather, against) economic democracy, criticized the political establishment in Bonn and called for the creation of a second chamber that was composed '*von einer arbeitsfähigen Elite aus allen Ständen*' (of an elite willing to work and drawn from all estates).[25] Winschuh may have phrased this much more starkly and bluntly than many other industrialists, but he was certainly not alone in asserting a claim for industry's political involvement or even a claim for leadership by the economy over politics. Heidrun Abromeit's detailed research on business leaders' claims for leadership during the periods 1965–68 and 1972–75 confirms this.[26] Although her second investigation period is outside the scope of this study and the first one very much at its end, the findings (especially for the 1965–68 period) can still be regarded as representative of industrialists' mentality during the reconstruction era. Their claim for an overall responsibility of business stemmed from two assertions. First, because in their view they were the ones responsible for the nation's prosperity, and this had been achieved through the competitiveness of each individual business, businesses were therefore not an end in themselves but rather crucial for the benefit of the whole nation.[27] Their second assertion arose because, in particular during the late 1940s and early 1950s, industrialists had managed to claim that their interests were identical to those of the general population. They justified both claims with the idea of '*Sachzwänge*' (inherent necessities), which only they, and not elected politicians, could really tackle. As Abromeit points out, however, this argument is not necessarily compatible with democratic principles.[28]

The industrialists' public claim for political leadership had been made as early as 1954 by the BDI chief clerk Gustav Stein, when he edited a book entitled *Unternehmer in der Politik* (*Entrepreneurs in Politics*).[29] Actually written by Herbert Gross, the business journalist and co-founder of the influential *Handelsblatt* newspaper, the book implicitly criticizes representative democracy and ultimately called for the creation of a new elite, the main task of which was to act in global responsibility for all. This then would lead to a society and economy which would be approved by all: 'The better this [new society] would work, the less likely was the voter to seek out the state.'[30] In a review at the time, the book was understood as industry's claim to be the new 'aristocracy of merit'. It was the entrepreneur who, based on his expert knowledge, made decisions for the common good. Morten Reitmayer's study actually misses the point when he states that the elite image of the entrepreneur had the disadvantage that it called for 'lonely decisions' and excluded the possibility of delegating decision-making authority.[31] It was the industrialists' claim of being able to make those 'lonely decisions' which set the entrepreneur apart from the rest of the population, and was in fact the only legitimation for their claim to elite status and leadership.

With the demand for elite status and an elevated position came, almost by default, the separation between the ingenious individual and what entrepreneurs called – and constantly warned against – 'the masses' and the 'massification' of society. Typical of this thinking is a speech by Hermann Reusch at the Bad Mergentheim Rotary Club. He lamented that the modern world had become a '*Massewelt*' (a world of the masses), driven by short-lived fashion fads, the driving force of which had been National Socialism and Communism. The German economy, in contrast, did not achieve its 'miracle' because of the masses but because of the person who did not fall prey to *Vermassung* (massification) but remained an individual even in a big company.[32] For ASU representatives, *Vermassung* took place in society in the form of urban conurbations, but also in the economy, through 'oversizing' – in the form of ever larger companies – and also through the 'collecting of supervisory board membership', which was increasingly seen as a problem.[33] Within the business community, Winschuh's warning about excessive concentration of supervisory board memberships would have been rather a particular ASU concern about the growth in size of big industry; his warning about massification, though, had the same origins as those made by Reusch and other top managers. A social aspect of this underlying fear of the rise of the masses is evident in a letter by Hermann Kost. Otherwise not known to hold socially reactionary views, he complained that young unmarried coal miners who lived in miners' hostels had 'too many motorbikes and big radio sets'. While his call for the swift introduction of a 'bachelor tax' may sound a bit like a joke today,[34] it was hard for the industrial elite to accept the ongoing democratization of society, which accompanied a growing accessibility of consumer goods that had hitherto been available only to the better off. The process found its entry into the post-war German vocabulary under the term '*nivillierte Mittelstandsgesellschaft*' (levelled middle-class society), which had been coined by the conservative sociologist Helmut Schelsky. His theory, which remained valid in West Germany until the 1980s, argued Germany was losing its class antagonism and rigid social stratification. The social and economic decline the traditional elites experienced in the aftermath of the war on the one hand, and the socially upward mobility enjoyed by large segments of the working class due to the growing consumerism that the 'economic miracle' had created on the other, meant that in Germany society came together in the form of a new and expanded *Mittelschicht*.[35] The idea that the masses of ordinary people were now increasingly demanding equal treatment from their supposed betters was a direct threat to the idea of an elite. It is therefore not a surprise that many industrialists, and once again first amongst them Hermann Reusch, were followers of the Spanish philosopher José Ortega y Gasset and his reactionary anti-democratic world view. Presumably at Reusch's invitation, he attended the BDI's 1953 *Kulturkreis Tagung* as guest of honour.[36]

The industrialists' claim for elite status also had an important political side to it, something that showed quite often in their speeches and in the attitudes of those managers who went into politics: it was the implicit belief that democracy should not mean the rule of the masses, but that of a responsible elite. This meant, by their own definition, that they saw themselves as the ones who created the national welfare. Gerard Braunthal points to this very potent mix of 'irrational belief in the managerial superiority, in charismatic leadership, based on the "calling"' as the source of this elite attitude.[37] In the years of the so-called economic miracle with its almost unbelievable growth rates, even mediocre businessmen could be successful and claim their share of the achievement, thereby boosting their self-confidence. It would take some spectacular company collapses during the first half of the 1960s, most notably the collapse of the car manufacturer Borgward or the Schlieker shipyard, before the business community became aware of the limits of growth – and their own abilities. Hermann Reusch commented very pessimistically – and prematurely – after the collapse of Schlieker's company that the time of the economic miracle was now over and the fight for economic survival in times of normality had begun, and he repeated such claims after the 1966 mini-recession.[38]

The flip-side of the entrepreneurs' claim for elite status was their feeling of responsibility, even if it arose out of an old-fashioned and traditional paternalism for their workers. Here too, however, things were changing. In a booklet entitled *Das Leitbild des Unternehers wandelt sich* (*The Concept of the Entrepreneur Is Changing*), Otto A. Friedrich, director-general of the Hamburg rubber manufacturer Phoenix, saw the responsibility of entrepreneurs as no longer limited just to their company and workforce, but now also extending towards the consumer, the state and public opinion and even towards their competitors (the latter in the form of opposition to anti-competitive practices and as guarantors of free enterprise). An entrepreneur's whole socio-political reputation depended on how he handled these responsibilities.[39] Friedrich was one of the men who from the mid-1950s helped to shape the concept of the entrepreneur which then in turn became part of business associations' official language.[40] This new image took the entrepreneur and manager away from a definition which was based on the traditional attributes of being *arbeitsam, fleißig, ehrgeizig, zielbewußt* (hard-working, assiduous, ambitious, purposeful), which were used time and again in the hagiographical portrayal of industrialists during the 1950s.[41] However, these attributes, and the way in which they were presented, made the men appear almost as economic superheroes but reduced the companies they ran to mere accessories of their will and personality. In 1973, when Rainer Koehne carried out the research for a sociological study into entrepreneurial self-perception, he found that there were significant differences between older and younger entrepreneurs' attitudes. Although there was still a very high belief in functional legitimacy – some 90 per cent believed that entrepreneurs were crucial in the reconstruction of the country and carried big responsibilities – 'traditional' values, including responsibility for the firm and even more for its workforce, were much more pronounced amongst the older entrepreneurs, i.e. those who had been active in their managerial roles at least since the post-war reconstruction period but possibly as far back as the 1930s.[42] Younger entrepreneurs saw their position as less positive and had a significantly lower job satisfaction rate than their older peers. Almost 50 per cent of the younger entrepreneurs believed that entrepreneurs were losing their place in society, either because of a victory of socialism (4 per cent) or a convergence of the social systems (43 per cent).[43] Those doubts simply did not exist in the 1950s.

Koehne's figures very clearly show a change in outlook and expectations, at least amongst the younger entrepreneurs. While the older generation had used extremely stinging rhetoric against the trade unions and co-determination up to the mid-1950s, and often portrayed themselves as helpless victims of a socialist onslaught, this changed in the wake of the 'Korean boom', when they began to stylize themselves as the makers of the economic miracle and the creators of the nation's prosperity. Social and political changes, in particular the student movement which is commonly summarized under the term '68' and, in 1969, the change from a conservative government to one led by Social Democrats, together with the mini-recession of 1966–67 would have contributed to this change in perspective. Christian Kleinschmidt has called it 'the managers' 1968'. However, although he claims that 'the managers' '68' did indeed happen, he locates it not in a single date but into a development which began well before that year. It was a gradual process that had often been initiated by managers themselves, through their reading about, and reacting towards, developments in US management theory way back in the late 1950s.[44]

Koehne's findings highlight not just a generational shift but a trend Hartmut Berghoff has called the '*Abschied vom klassichen Mittelstand*', a farewell to the traditional *Mittlestand* that had been made up of family-run businesses, which he argues, began as of the early 1970s due to a number of factors. Following the retirement of those entrepreneurs who had run the family business during the war and post-war years, businesses were taken over by a generation which no longer followed family tradition unquestioningly (which certainly explains in part the dissatisfaction Koehne had found amongst younger entrepreneurs). The growing need for academic training in order to lead small or medium-sized businesses effectively gave entrepreneurs' sons a wider perspective and opportunities to look for careers beyond the family firm. Berghoff's figures on the declining capital ratio of SMEs, however, are at their highest for the period 1950–65, when the capital ratio fell from about 57 per cent to 30 per cent; during the remainder of the twentieth century, it fell only another 10 per cent. This means that during this period SMEs had to rely increasingly on outside capital, and thus the family influence on companies declined overall.[45] Although this generational change had a significant influence on the *Mittelstand* companies and SMEs simply because of their prevalence, Berghoff also points out that the generational change was a problem for big family companies, too: in 1967, 107 of Germany's 300 biggest companies were still in family hands.[46] However, for them it was easier to hire managers from the outside to run the business on their behalf.

During the 1950s, one result of entrepreneurs' changing outlook was how they shifted their interpretation of the 'social market economy' and perceived Ludwig Erhard and his anti-cartel policies. Industry was very pleased when, after years of economic controls and restrictions, both under the Nazi war economy and the post-war *Trümmerwirtschaft* (rubble economy), the currency reform launched on 20 June 1948 was followed by Ludwig Erhard's *Leitsätze Gesetz*, which abolished almost all rationing and price controls. They were even more delighted about the DM Opening Balance law (*Eröffnungsbilanz Gesetz*). It allowed companies to revalue their old assets, especially those which had been written down due to tax depreciation, and allowed the firms considerable tax savings on their actual profits because they could again depreciate their revalued assets.[47] At a time when most of the western world followed Keynesian economic principles, and thus needed some degree of governmental economic planning, Erhard's idea and understanding of a free market economy, based on non-state intervention, was much more to the liking of German industrialists. However, during 1949/50, it became increasingly obvious that Erhard's definition of a free market economy and that of industry differed widely. For industry, and in particular for heavy industry and small and medium-sized companies in the consumer goods sector, a 'free' market economy meant first and foremost free from government interference, and in particular the freedom to establish cartels. Erhard saw in any form of cartel, be it a price, quota or market area cartel, a limitation of competition. Anti-cartel rules were therefore one of the very few occasions he thought state intervention in the economy was justified. Industrialists' desire to return to cartels is easily understood in the light of the fact that there had been about 3,000 industrial cartels in Germany in 1930.[48] Large parts of industry and at its forefront Fritz Berg, who became the most outspoken opponent to an anti-cartel law, saw cartels as essential to the prevention of a ruinous competition between companies which they thought would arise automatically out of a 'free' market. Although there had been Allied demands for a cartel ban as a precondition to the creation of the Federal Republic, industry was able to prevent the passing of a German anti-cartel law in 1952. They achieved another victory by delaying the passing of a bill for a further five years and when it eventually made it on the statute books in 1957, it was in a much watered-down version. This outcome demonstrates that industrial lobbying had been able to push back the much tougher regulations originally intended by the US occupiers.[49]

Although not necessarily always visible to the public, by this time there was little love lost between Erhard on the one side and Berg and heavy industry on the other. An Economics Ministry report on the BDI's 1957 annual meeting and Berg's speech summarized it as 'showing little sense of responsibility for the national economy … full of contradictions … shallow statements and blunt misjudgements'.[50] The Iron and Steel Association, for their part, speculated in October 1957 whether Adenauer would become Federal President 'if a suitable successor for the chancellorship had been found by then'.[51] At this time Erhard was seen by most people and politicians to be Adenauer's natural successor. Questioning whether he was suitable to succeed the Chancellor shows how little interest heavy industry had in such an outcome, not least because Erhard had just publicly clashed with coal mining representatives about an increase in the price of coal they had implemented the day after the 1957 federal election.[52] When in 1959 Erhard was suddenly mentioned publicly as a candidate for the federal presidency, suspicion was quickly voiced that it had been Fritz Berg or, on his behalf, the BDI, who had leaked this idea to the press in order to prevent Erhard's chancellorship by 'kicking him upstairs'. Berg had to send a telex to the Economics Minister in which he reassured him that neither he personally nor the BDI had anything to do with the press report and had to repeat the statement in front of the BDI board.[53] Sometime before this, in 1954, Erhard had been publicly attacked by the textile industrialist and BDI board member Carl Neumann, first in the DII's *Unternehmerbrief* and then in an article in *Die Welt* newspaper, for his lack of action in protecting the German textile industry from increasing imports from the Far East. The criticism in the *Unternehmerbrief* in particular was so severe that the BDI *Präsidium* had to discuss the matter. Neumann was not rebuked for the content of his articles, he was merely criticized for the way he had chosen to air it, as it created the impression that he had been speaking for the whole of the BDI, as well as for his timing. Indeed, the BDI stated that as the textile association's president, he even had the duty to speak out against Erhard's unlimited trade liberalization which had begun to impact badly on Germany's textile industry.[54] At the time of the presidential crisis in 1959, the situation had changed and Erhard received considerable support from the textile industry association's new president, Curt Becker, who was also a CDU MP. Eventually Becker was one of only thirteen CDU parliamentary group members who signed a letter asking Erhard to remain in post after he had once again been publicly embarrassed by Adenauer.[55]

Ludwig Erhard's liberal policy did slowly but surely change German industrialists' thinking, especially about cartels. During the Schuman Plan negotiations, the French High Commissioner André François-Poncet had criticized German industrialists as 'having too little fantasy and therefore having to struggle to understand a system which deviated from what they had known since childhood', but more and more of them became converted to Erhard's philosophy.[56] One of the earliest and leading converts was Otto A. Friedrich. Probably influenced by his brother Carl Joachim Friedrich, a Harvard professor and then advisor to the US Military Government, by 1948 Otto A. Friedrich had drifted into Erhard's anti-cartel camp. But even he called some early statements made by Erhard in late 1949 to implement the anti-cartel laws regardless of industry's objections as 'megalomania à la Hitler'.[57] Ultimately, there were two very significant reasons why German industrialists turned away from cartels. First, the economic interests of the trading nation West Germany were better served by a liberal system compared to any form of market limitation.[58] Second was the influence of industrial entrepreneurs who could be classed as 'outsiders', either because they were newcomers or because they had been able to overcome traditional thinking. These were men like Berthold Beitz at Krupp; Heinrich Nordhoff at VW; Max Grundig in the electric entertainment industry; or Alfons Müller-Wipperführt in the textile industry; not to mention the mail-order business of Josef Neckermann, Gustav Schickedanz and Werner Otto. What they all had in common was that they did not believe in, or adhere to, traditional (i.e. cartelistic) ways of doing business. Grundig, 'the nobody from Fürth', regarded the committee of the electro-entertainment business association which was supposed to set production quotas simply as 'a debating club'. He was heavily criticized by other electro-entertainment companies for completely ignoring agreed quotas, not to mention fixed prices.[59] Müller-Wipperführt actually had lost out on an early post-war contract due to cartel agreements, a setback he had not forgotten.[60] Neckermann, Schickedanz and Otto and their respective catalogue businesses were significant in bringing down prices of a wide range of consumer goods,[61] which then forced traditional retail businesses to improve their competitiveness. Cartels in consumer goods began to lose their attraction and this trend spread to other sectors. Although in February 1959, eleven German steel companies were each fined DM 10,000 by the European High Authority for Coal and Steel because of price fixing, the will for the creation of official cartels had all but disappeared.[62] By the mid-1960s, when the traditionally cartelistic oriented steel industry was badly hit by global overcapacity, there were very few voices who called for the establishment of traditional cartels; instead they set up regional *Verkaufskontore*, or sales offices. The fact that both the German government and the High Authority allowed them to operate shows that they were not seen as traditional monopolistic cartels but rather as an emergency measure to stabilize the market. In the late 1970s, it was the German chemical industry which prevented the establishment of a European plastics cartel when that sector was hit hard by increased competition from Eastern Europe. This was despite calls from France and Italy for a cartel, as had happened previously with another cartel for artificial fibre.[63] German industrialists had learned that despite all temporary difficulties, they would fare better in a market that was not bound by any collusions. The occasional cases that came to light afterwards rather confirm this rule.

There is one particular attribute of West German entrepreneurs which is linked to their elite status and which made them stand out even amongst their international peers, namely their work ethic and the hours they worked. Contemporary observers were already commenting on the significant number of hours managers spent in their firm. Gabriel Almond quotes an unnamed leading figure of a business association who called them 'factory functionaries' and 'industrial fanatics' and added, 'Did you ever think what it would be like to spend your whole life in Oberhausen?'[64] That remark was most likely a potshot directed against Hermann Reusch, who lived throughout his years as Gutehoffnungshütte chairman in a rather spartan and uninviting dwelling in the factory grounds, directly next to the steel plant, with hardly any space for societal representation or social entertainment.[65] Reusch's housing situation in this regard was unique; most top managers lived either in the Ruhr's rural outskirts or at least in neighbourhoods of more 'appropriate' villas, indicative of their social status. Even at the time Oberhausen was well behind other Ruhr cities such as Essen and even Duisburg, not to mention Düsseldorf, all of which had much larger and more sophisticated cultural scenes. Reusch's choice may have had to do with Schloss Katharinenhof. Reusch Senior had bought this former royal hunting lodge near Stuttgart in 1916, and it was seen as the family home. Living close to the factory certainly had the advantage that Reusch did not have to waste any time on the daily commute. Fritz Berg, for example, was driven every morning at precisely 6.30 from the apartment he had in Cologne to his factory in Altena or the offices of the IHK Hagen; after lunch, he took the one-hour trip back to Cologne for his work and commitments as BDI president.[66] At the time it was standard practice for all managers to work on Saturdays and even on Sundays, which made family life rather thin on the ground; in the Reusch household, family occasions were therefore almost formally celebrated as a form of compensation.[67]

The reason for the long working hours came not only from the need to physically rebuild the companies and re-establish old markets and networks, as most of these processes had been completed by the mid-1950s. Contemporary analysts saw the economic activity and the resulting reconstruction as a way of redeeming involvement in the Nazi system and the devastation of the war. The speedy economic reconstruction after 1948 and the economic boom after 1950 helped to restore businessmen's reputation.[68] The public use and constant repetition, not least in the commissioned publication at the time, of words describing the traditional bourgeois values and 'German *Primärtugenden*' (primary virtues) of *Fleiß* and *Arbeitsamkeit* (hard work and industriousness) did pay off.[69] Established entrepreneurs but also social climbers very much defined themselves, even in retrospect, through their '*Fleiß*, perseverance and *Fleiß* again'.[70] Koehne's study has shown that the West German public recognized the special status of, and the work done by, entrepreneurs during the reconstruction period, despite seeing them still as 'secretive', 'anti-trade union' and with 'rude manners'.[71]

Managers in big industry gained their self-perceived elite status either from (and through) their company's history and reputation or, in the case of heavy industry, through their even more prestigious and elitist title of *Bergassessor*. For the owner-entrepreneurs of SME businesses, it was the combination of the traditional company values of quality production and the feeling of 'responsibility in a socio-cultural system', and the experience and mentality of the economic miracle period which created a new *Mittelstandsmentalität* which celebrated SMEs.[72] In 1950, there were only 719 'big' companies in West Germany, i.e. those with more than 1,000 workers; by 1960, the number had risen to 1,331, which was still only 0.1 per cent of all companies. In 1950, those companies employed 12.7 per cent of the total workforce, rising to 15.9 per cent in 1960. The sheer number of companies with fewer than 1,000 workers (about 11.8 million in 1950 and 19.2 million in 1961) gives extra weight to this *Mittlestand* and their self-perception.[73] Not least because of their prevalence, these companies and their owner-entrepreneurs have to be understood as a crucial part of Germany's industrial foundation and success.[74] Although there was no clear definition of what constituted a SME in terms of workforce or turnover, the contemporary cut-off point for a 'large' company was usually seen to be the 1,000-employee mark. However, the growth and concentration process during the 1950s and 1960s had an impact on companies' categorization. Significantly, as the examples of BDI president Fritz Berg and ASU chairman Alfred Flender show, *Mittelstand* had a different meaning than just 'SME', as their companies employed 1,500 and 1,800 people respectively.[75]

Although both the managers of big companies and the owner-entrepreneurs felt accredited in their elite status by their apparent success in Germany's 'economic miracle', the latter felt much closer to their company and their life's work than most managers who retired when they reached pensionable age. Although some chairmen of boards of managers, perhaps most famously Thyssen's Hans-Günther Sohl, Krupp's Berthold Beitz and in the banking sector, Hermann Josef Abs, moved on to the supervisory board chairmanship of their businesses and continued to influence day-to-day businesses, most managers retired gracefully; after all, they were 'only' salaried employees themselves. This was much less the case with the owners of SMEs. Many independent businessmen of the generation born between 1890 and 1910 found it hard to let go and hand over business to their heirs. Steeped in their family tradition, having worked twelve to fourteen hours a day or more during the 1950s and having seen their companies grow and prosper in the reconstruction period, their business had been their life's purpose; even if they officially had stepped down from their official positions, many still interfered in decision-making. Numerous companies went out of business in the late 1960s and 1970s because those men, stuck in their traditions, were unable to adapt to a changing economic situation.[76]

Without a doubt, both the big companies' salaried managers and the owner-entrepreneurs of small and medium-sized companies lived for their companies and the company had priority over everything else, to a degree which may be difficult to understand in the context of the early twenty-first-century work–life balance debate. Being *arbeitsam, fleißig zielbewusst* and *verantwortlich* (hardworking, industrious, purposeful and responsible) were the attributes they would have applied to themselves and liked to see in any description of themselves. Ambition was seen as good and important but it had to be measured, not exaggerated, and for the benefit of the company. This is well expressed in Ludwig Vaubel's diary entry of 24 March 1949. There was a level of shock in Vaubel's notes when he wrote about a discussion he had with a colleague who accused him of 'ruthlessly chasing after a board membership and because of this being no longer loyal to the company' and Vaubel realized that he 'had to take this accusation seriously'.[77]

After the Second World War, industrialists were more conscious than ever of their own importance in state and society, be that real or perceived. In contrast to their pre-World War peers, this importance and the social status that went with it were no longer displayed in the same swanky way: on the contrary. A very striking example of this change is the *Stahlhof*, the original administrative building of the Iron and Steel Association, built in 1906–08. It had never been designed to be just an administrative office building, but rather as a visible statement of political and economic power and influence. After the Second World War, the British Military Government used it intentionally as one of their administrative centres to demonstrate who was now in charge. When it was released from military use, the re-established Iron and Steel Association did not return to the ostentatious building, however. Instead they settled for the much more modest and functional *Neuer Stahlhof*, a 1930 high-rise building just down the road which they bought and repaired for a total of DM 3.3 million. This building was an expression of the association's new mode of functionality and practicality.[78] The new architectural modesty was in no way caused by self-doubt, but after the Nazi experience, leadership and elite status were being expressed less pretentiously. However, this was a change in style, not substance.

This chapter has shown the continuity lines in German industrialists' mentality. Neither the Nazi capitulation nor industrialists being called to account for their involvement in Nazi crimes, either through Allied internment or the Nuremberg industrialists' trials, caused a general change. A 'new' entrepreneur in Germany did not emerge quickly after 1945; in fact, as Erker has argued, the old mentality persisted for years, even decades. Nevertheless, change did begin in the 1950s, gradually at first, but picking up speed as the decade progressed and accelerating in the 1960s after Adenauer's resignation. The following chapters will show how and in which areas of management new ways of thinking developed. It was not only technological and societal change which contributed to this process, which has to be understood as one of modernization. A shifting bourgeois *habitus* played a role in this slow metamorphosis as well, but what is important to note is that significant changes were under way well before the late 1960s, where Berghahn had located a generational change and thus a change in mentality.

Figure 3.2 *Der Stahlhof.* An ostentatious building commissioned by the North-Western Group of the Association of the German Iron and Steel Industrialists between 1906 and 1908 to demonstrate their power. After 1945 it was used by the British Military Government as their regional headquarters. Its grandiosity meant that it was not used again by industry and is now home to the Düsseldorf administrative court. Author's photograph.

Figure 3.3 *Neuer Stahlhof*. Built during the 1920s, the *Neuer Stahlhof* became the home of the WVES from 1951 onward. Although located right next to *Der Stahlhof*, this building symbolized the much more functional and less 'assertive' approach that characterized post-war presentation and representation by industry. Author's photograph.

4

'Americanization'? Leadership Recruitment and Training

The topic of the 'Americanization' of western countries and societies since the Second World War has attracted a huge amount of attention, both from observers at the time and since about the 1980s from historians. While 'Americanization' affected all areas of society, its impact on the economy has been especially hotly debated.[1] Arguably, within the economic field, leadership training and leadership recruitment are the areas in which West German industry experienced the biggest change in the post-war years. There has been a fierce debate amongst historians and business historians about whether this change constituted a wholesale 'Americanization' (Berghahn) of German management or whether it was only a societal 'modernisation and westernisation' (Doering-Manteuffel) which in turn had an impact on prevailing German leadership and management methods.[2] Robert Locke argues that German entrepreneurs' views on their leadership style, which they regarded as superior, were, despite the lost war, so deeply ingrained in their psyche that they remained convinced that their approach to running a company was better than American 'managerialism'.[3] This belief would only be strengthened further once the so-called economic miracle got under way, as it seemed to confirm the entrepreneurs' achievements and performance. German company leaders continued to frown upon the term 'manager' until the mid to late 1960s. Werner Abelshauser, one of the fiercest critics of 'Americanization' goes so far as to call the adaptation and assimilation process of management techniques in Germany that intensified after the Second World War a *Kulturkampf*, a cultural struggle.[4]

The root of German management training's development was linked to the Cold War. Once the Americans began to see the Soviet Union as the new global threat, they began to 'make Europe safe for Democracy', with economic recovery and prosperity lying at the heart of this endeavour. American experts identified Europe's (and in particular Germany's) lower productivity as the biggest hindrance to increased prosperity. To their surprise they found that Germany's poorer productivity was usually not because of inferior technology, but rather due to local customs, social and cultural traditions and, most importantly, due to labour–management relations.[5] To close the productivity gap, in 1949 the United States had created the 'United States Technical Assistance and Productivity Program' (USTAP) as part of the Marshall Plan. USTAP tried to address the management issue by setting up joint US–European top management seminars and discussions, for which they enlisted the help of the US

National Association of Manufacturers (NAM), and required the creation of National Productivity Centres (NPC) in Marshall Plan countries.[6] A further measure introduced early on by USTAP were study trips for European entrepreneurs to the US, where they visited factories and had informational meetings with American managers and trade union representatives. After their return, the participating businessmen had to write reports on their experience and disseminate them amongst their colleagues, which was seen as a good way to spread American management lessons. Hanns Voith, head of one of Germany's largest family-owned manufacturing and engineering companies, was one of two German entrepreneurs who, in the summer of 1949, went on such a sixty-day study trip. In his thirty-two-page report Voith expressed great surprise at US managements' close co-operation with trade unions and the ongoing communication and talks between management and labour, which was seen by both sides as *überlebenswichtig* (vital) for the company's survival. Voith stressed that: 'what we can learn from the Americans is the tone within a company; and it will be dangerous to disregard any attempts in this direction by creating the principle that within a company the tone has to be rough!'[7] He also expressed a good deal of excitement about the Industrial Relations departments at American universities and their scientific analysis of company procedures. He was even more surprised to see that the universities also offered training courses for managers of up to fourteen weeks' duration: and in contrast to Germany, 'management' in the US included the foreman, the equivalent to the German *Meister*, another point Voith emphasized in his report.

Being the owner-entrepreneur of a family run-business, Voith's opinion would certainly not be representative of German heavy industry, in particular with regard to the trade unions. It is therefore unsurprising that the judgements of other visitors under the USTAP and similar successor programmes were quite varied and not always so positive.[8] In particular 'Operation Impact', another US attempt to convince European managers to convert to the American management style, proved less successful for various reasons. For one, in contrast to USTAP, which had been paid for from Marshall Plan funds, participants had to pay for their own Atlantic crossings as well as cover all expenses incurred by their accompanying wives.[9] At a conference of BDI chief clerks in May 1950, it was noted that because of the high costs but also because of 'hypertensive and almost defamatory requirements concerning the political past', US study travel had almost ceased.[10] Five months later, BDI President Fritz Berg officially complained to Chancellor Adenauer about the fact that the US had imposed stricter visa regulations which made it almost impossible for former members of the Nazi party to visit the US.[11]

Matthias Kipping speculates that there may have been a longer term diffusion process of US management style and education in Germany resulting from USTAP and Operation Impact, despite the latter's failure.[12] However, due to costs and visa restrictions, American and German authorities realized that the programme would attract only a limited number of participating businessmen. Thus in August 1951, the Americans initiated the first of a series of *Betriebsführergespräche* (business leaders' talks) which were to run throughout the 1950s. They were held in co-operation with the *Rationalisierungskuratorium der deutschen Wirtschaft* (RKW, Rationalization Committee of the German Economy), which had been set up in the 1920s to help rationalize German small and medium-sized enterprises. Up to 150 German businessmen discussed in seminar-style talks their approach to questions of productivity, human relations, sales and marketing and general management with American entrepreneurs and academics. The week-long talks cost about DM 200 per head, plus another DM 80–100 for accommodation. The cost and time frame meant entrepreneurs from small and medium-sized enterprises, usually the companies' owners, could afford to attend.[13] It has to be assumed that the *Betriebsführergespräche* had an impact on the modernization of German management style and culture throughout the 1950s, even if it will be very difficult to quantify this.

In 1952 Germany's management training was greatly influenced by the publication of a groundbreaking book by Ludwig Vaubel, the rising star of artificial fibre company Vereinigte Glanzstoff Fabriken (VGF). *Unternehmer gehen zur Schule* (*Managers Go to School*) was Vaubel's filed report of attending Harvard University's thirteen-week Advanced Management Program[14] in 1950, the first German ever to do so. Although he had nominally been a member of the Nazi party, his exemplary conduct at the VGF partner company AKU in the Netherlands during the war provided him with outstanding character references from the Dutch chief executive, which would have helped to meet the stricter US visa regulations.[15] In the book, Vaubel reflected on his experience at Harvard and the idea that managers, and even top executives, were attending *Weiterbildungs* (continuing training) seminars, an idea which was rather outlandish in Germany in the early 1950s. Although full of praise for the Harvard system, Vaubel nevertheless warned against blindly aping the American model and reminded his readers of German traditions and the different situation German managers found themselves in.[16] Subsequently German entrepreneurs would develop their own specific path in management training.

In December 1952, the BDI established a small working party to investigate how to best promote 'entrepreneurial young blood' in industry. The committee was chaired by Wolf-Dietrich von Witzleben, deputy chairman of the Siemens supervisory board. Committee members were – apart from Ludwig Vaubel, with his first-hand experience of the Harvard programme – the textile industrialist Carl Neumann, and for the *Arbeitsgemeinschaft Selbstständiger Unternehmer* Josef Winschuh, the bustling advocate of the owner-entrepreneur.[17] The report they presented to the BDI board a year later made grim reading. The problem German companies faced was not the ageing of the company and supervisory boards as Kipping and Kleinschmidt have argued; this was only a symptom of, and consequence from, the war years. The actual challenge was demographic: Germany's birth deficit caused by the First World War had been massively exacerbated by the huge loss of life during the Second World War. As a result, whole year groups had been reduced to half or less of their pre-First World War size. This shortfall would affect company leadership down the line in ten to fifteen years' time in the form of insufficient numbers of suitably qualified men. (Company leadership by women in the 1950s was rather unusual, to say the least.) Many of the men who had survived the war and would normally have been qualified for leadership positions now lacked experience due to their lengthy military service, captivity as POWs or simply because the upheaval of the war and its aftermath meant that they had not been able to keep up their practical experience or theoretical knowledge.[18] Von Witzleben's committee concluded that German industry as a whole had to provide additional training for promising candidates in order to counter the expected shortfall of suitable personnel, otherwise they would suffer in the long run because of a dearth of qualified leadership candidates.

The report not only highlights the acute problems German companies were potentially facing from the late 1950s onwards, though; it is also very revealing in regard to the underlying mentality that persisted amongst the majority of industrial leaders. The committee rejected the notion of solving the looming leadership crisis by setting up a US-style management academy or a school. Von Witzleben's claim that following the Nazis' attempt at 'schooling the Nation', the Germans had had enough of 'schooling' must be seen as a poor excuse. His real motivation can be found in the sentence 'eine schulmäßige Ausbildung zu einem "fertigen" Unternehmer *gibt es nicht*.'[19] ('Schooling to produce a "completed" entrepreneur *does not exist*', emphasis in the original.) The implication of the statement is clear: entrepreneurs are born, not made; leading a business, the report stated, depended first and foremost on an individual's personality, which was determined not by a one-dimensional strength but by inner balance, inner wealth and openness of character. The real task German industry was facing was not the schooling or training of candidates but selecting the right ones for the leadership post. In line with German tradition, which had produced significant numbers of non-academically trained business leaders, the report accepted that university training was not an obligatory precondition for a leadership role. However, it expected that the majority of candidates would be university educated, as this training would allow them to address complex matters more easily.[20] The report's other striking statement was that special care and attention had to be given to cover the needs of young entrepreneurs, entrepreneurs' sons and junior partners – *Weiterbildung* was not limited to the potential leadership of big companies but explicitly had to include SME and family-firm leadership as well. While it can be assumed that Josef Winschuh had some influence in the inclusion of this passage, this preferential treatment signifies the claim of the salaried managers, or *Beauftragte Unternehmer* (authorized entrepreneurs) as Winschuh used to call them, that they too were true entrepreneurs. This claim was made time and again during the early 1950s, both by salaried managers and independent owner-entrepreneurs. Kipping and Kleinschmidt argue that although the US had become a 'reference society' for West German businesses, even strong advocates of US methods such as Vaubel emphasized that blind copying of US practices should be avoided in favour of selective adaptation.[21] The *Baden-Badener Unternehmergespräche* (BBUG, Baden-Baden entrepreneurs' talks), which were launched by the BDI with two trial sessions on 13 June 1954 and 17 March 1955 as a direct result of von Witzleben's report, were a case in point.[22] In preparation for the training course, the BDI had consulted with the other two top business associations, the employer association *Bundesverband der deutschen Arbeitgeberverbände* (BDA) and the *Deutscher Industrie- und Handelstag* (DIHT), and together they had rejected the idea of university-style '*Schulung*' or seminars. Other than the already-mentioned self-perception of German businessmen as the true facilitators of Germany's economic recovery and the economic miracle, there were two groups in particular which rejected US-style schooling for managers. The first was the

DIHT, in combination with the trades associations. They feared for the quality of German craftsmanship if US mass production methods were to be introduced.[23] The second group were the conservative industrialists in heavy industry, whose influence was undergoing something of a revival. They had their own elitist system, the *Bergassessor* training: a traditional Prussian state-examined programme, it took applicants seven to eight years to complete. It consisted of at least three years of university study in mining technologies, maths, geology, mining law and engineering, followed by at least four years' practical experience in the mining industry, either in ore, salt or coal mines, or a combination of those.[24] How much these men valued their special status and education is well demonstrated by two of their leading exponents, Hans-Günther Sohl and Hermann Reusch. Not only did they insist that all their incoming correspondence addressed them with their title *Bergassessor*, they also signed all their outgoing correspondence with the traditional miners' greeting '*Glück auf*. Sohl remarked in his memoirs how proud he was to have become a '*Bergmann*'; by this he meant not just a simple miner but rather a *Bergassessor*. Sohl emphasized how this group traditionally had held leading positions in industry and state administration. It went without saying that he also got married in his traditional *Bergassessor*'s uniform.[25] Hermann Reusch, for his part, stated as late as the mid-1960s that the training required to become a *Bergassessor* was the best available education for any manager to run a big *Konzern*.[26] Those attitudes left little room for innovation.

Following the two successful trial seminars, the BDI put the BBUG on a permanent footing when it founded the *Gesellschaft zur Förderung des Unternehmernachwuchses* (GFU, Association for the Enhancement of Entrepreneurial Young Blood) as the body that would organize the BBUG. Thirty companies were invited to participate in its establishment, paying some DM 20,000 each for an eighteen-month period to get the association off the ground.[27] The two trial seminars had set the format of the talks. The first two of the three weeks' seminar time were dedicated to business and managerial topics, including marketing, controlling and investment. Human relations had been introduced as well, most likely as a response to co-determination, which German businessmen saw as a threat to their leadership. Once this political hot topic had failed to materialize, industrialists lost interest in the subject in the late 1950s.[28] The third week was reserved for the wide topic of the entrepreneur's role and responsibility in state and society. In this section the discussion was based around day-to-day topics such as *Konjunkturpolitik*, the current economic cycle and the policy response to it; the growing antagonism between industry and agriculture; or changing labour relations. Standard topics were the role of the entrepreneur in politics and his contribution to arts and culture, which had to be seen as an attempt to get the future top managers engaged with the world outside their companies. The BBUG hosted guest speakers which included moral theologians, and bishops, academics from various fields as well as politicians, but also, perhaps surprisingly, high-ranking trade union officials. The inclusion of those wider aspects has to be understood as a revival of the efforts of Wilhelm Merton, the owner of the metal trading company Metallgesellschaft, who even before the First World War had tried to promote the education of socially responsible managers.[29]

There was one aspect in particular in which the BBUG really distinguished themselves from any American post-experience management training course.

Harvard's Advanced Management Program was – and still is – taught almost exclusively by academics who used the case-study method, with occasional guest speakers invited for a particular topic. At Baden-Baden, the teaching was done almost completely by 'men of practice', in particular when it came to discussions and talks on managerial and economic matters. Hans Hellwig, editor-in-chief of the economic paper *Deutsche Zeitung*, emphasized in the late 1960s that there was actually no teaching staff (*Lehrpersonal*) at Baden-Baden, only 'speakers'.[30] The ratio of speakers to participants is astonishing: while there were 134 seminar attendees for the first five talks, they were outnumbered by 153 listed speakers or seminar participants. Since several speakers attended more than one seminar, the actual student–speaker ratio was more likely 1:1.7 or even 1:2. Of the 153 speakers (including the guest speakers), only twenty-seven were not in one way or another engaged in commercial activities, either in a company, a bank or a business association. Of these twenty-seven speakers, thirteen were German or Swiss university professors from different subjects, including economists. There is hardly better proof that German businessmen believed first and foremost in their own skills and experience of the 'real' business world. The speakers who attended were the cream of the crop of the German economy. Hermann Josef Abs of Deutsche Bank attended, as did board members and chief executives of world-renowned firms such as Bosch, Daimler-Benz, Hoechst, Klöckner, Krupp, Siemens and Volkswagen, to name but a few. There were also representatives of leading medium-sized enterprises with famous names such as Alfred Flender (in his capacity as ASU chairman addressing concerns of medium-sized owner-entrepreneurial companies), Dyckerhoff & Widmann (the leading construction company), china manufacturer Philip Rosenthal and tableware manufacturer Württembergische Metallwarenfabrik (WMF). Speakers usually had a genuine interest in the careers and personalities of the participants and whenever possible made time in their diaries to participate in the seminars.[31]

The GFU's guidelines stipulated that 'only those gentlemen' could participate who were aged between thirty-five and forty-five, who had shown exceptional leadership potential and were expected to be appointed to the company leadership or company board within the next five years. Being a personal assistant and even having power of attorney (*Prokura*), which was otherwise a very high distinction within a German company, was insufficient to qualify. From this, two things become obvious: first, female participants were the absolute exception. Of the 134 participants of the first five talks, only two were women. Gender roles in the 1950s and 1960s simply did not allow for female executives. Second, the *Baden-Badener Unternehmergespräche* were a 'big boys' club'.[32] Table 4.1 shows the distribution by company size of the participants of the first twenty-five talks, which took place between 1954 and 1963.

Fifty-five per cent of all participants came from companies with more than 5,000 employees; a mere 17 per cent came from companies with a workforce of fewer than 1,000, companies that were usually run by the owner-entrepreneur. In other words, while the 'independent entrepreneur' was postulated as a role model, in reality it was salaried managers who took the vast majority of Baden-Baden places. Considering the time and effort industry invested in the Baden-Baden talks one wonders about the impact the seminars had on the professional careers of the participants, and the answer is that they were very significant. One-third of all participants became board members

Table 4.1 Participants of the first twenty-five *Baden-Badener Unternehmergespräche* 1954–63, by size of company workforce and the share of independent entrepreneurs among them

Company size by workforce	<500	500–1,000	1,000–3,000	3,000–5,000	5,000–10,000	>10,000	Total	Of which independent entrepreneurs
Total	**78**	**45**	**110**	**77**	**101**	**290**	**701***	**42**
Per cent	11.1	6.4	15.7	11	14.4	41.3		9.7

*Including one member of an association
Source: Grünbacher, 'The Americanisation that never was?', 255.

of leading companies eventually, while up to 15 per cent became chairman of their managerial board.[33] Unsurprisingly, amongst the early attendees at Baden-Baden, the list of famous names is considerable, including, to name the most prominent: Friedrich Wilhelm Christians, the successor to H.J. Abs at Deutsche Bank; Hans-Martin Schleyer of Daimler-Benz, later joint president of the BDI and BDA; Egon Overbeck, future chairman of Mannesmann; Klaus Haniel, heir to the Haniel family holdings, which included, amongst others, Hermann Reusch's Gutehoffnungshütte conglomerate; and Helmut Maucher, later chief executive of Nestlé.[34]

While the participation of independent entrepreneurs (or their sons) remained below 10 per cent, the largest single group of attendees came from a sector which had initially not been considered by the BDI to participate at all in the training. No fewer than 110 banking managers attended the first twenty-five talks, the next largest sectors being the iron industry with 78 and the electrical and machine tool manufacturing industries with 76 and 62 respectively.[35] Also, in line with Matthias Kipping's argument, the share of managers without a university degree decreased considerably, but there was a significant difference to the US: in contrast to American management cohorts, where the entry qualification for the top echelons was increasingly the business school degree MBA (Master of Business Administration), in Germany it remained a degree in engineering or law, with the latter taking a very prominent place in the training of bankers, as Table 4.2 shows.[36] The relative small number of '*Wiwi*' graduates, in particular amongst the bankers, who had the highest level of graduates throughout, is striking.[37] '*Wiwi*', short for *Wirtschaftswissenschaft*, is the German umbrella term for degrees in business studies (*Betriebswirtschaft*, the degree most similar to the MBA), economics (*Volkswirtschaft*) and the more old-fashioned *Staatswirtschaft*, a combination of political science, economics and legal studies. The available mini CVs of the eighty-two participants of the third, fourth and fifth seminars list only seven men who studied *Betriebswirtschaft*. Three of these came from SMEs, four – two of whom did not complete their degree – worked for big companies, one of whom had a PhD. This contrasts with two dozen or so participants who had completed a commercial apprenticeship (*kaufmännische Lehre*), ten with *Volkswirtschaft* degrees and another twelve who had studied *Staatswissenschaft*, which suggests that during the 1950s and 1960s, German industry and banks were not particularly interested in *Betriebswirtschaft*, which was still regarded as an 'American' degree. Instead nearly half of all participants

Table 4.2 Educational background of seminar participants from industry and banks

Seminars/Education	1–10	11–13	14–16	17–19	20–22	23–25	Total
Participants from Industry/Banks	226/44	76/14	76/12	73/13	72/13	67/14	590/110
Total	271*	90	88	86	85	81	701*
Wiwi (of which in banks)	44	19	13	15	15	23	129
	(4)	(3)	(1)	(1)	(1)	(4)	(14)
Law	35	17	14	13	22	19	120
	(16)	(7)	(7)	(6)	(8)	(6)	(50)
Engineering	57	24	23	22	23	21	170
	–	–	–	–	–	–	–
Other academic degrees	2	2	1	6	1	3	15
	–	(2)	–	(2)	–	(1)	(5)
Non-academic	132	28	37	30	24	15	266
	(25)	(2)	(4)	(3)	(4)	(3)	(41)

*Plus 1 member from a business association
Source: Grünbacher, 'The Americanisation that never was?', p. 255.

had a background in 'practical' subjects, e.g. in science, engineering or law, the latter especially prevalent within the banking sector. All this shows that the traditional recruitment base for Germany's top management did not change much during this period. To put it in a different way, while the percentage of university graduates on company boards increased in 1950s and 1960s Germany, and a *Betriebswirtschaft* degree may have been a good starting point for a career in SMEs, it was more of a handicap than a precondition for progression to a top company leadership. In the US, however, the MBA degree became increasingly important. In Germany, economists (and even more so entrepreneurs) saw the micro-economic approach taken by *Betriebswirtschaft* as nothing more than the 'assembly of common sense rules'.[38]

German universities have always been criticized for their *praxisferne* (lacking practical relevance) in their curriculum. Christian Kleinschmidt has argued that the purpose of the *Baden-Badener Unternehmergespräche* was to compensate for the lack of training and teaching at German universities that was relevant in real life. For this reason the invited speakers were almost exclusively successful businessmen.[39] This position is, however, flawed, as the participants were men who on average had been in their jobs for fifteen to twenty years, and thus they certainly *would* have known what daily business practice meant. Dedicating almost one-third of a training course to wider political, social and cultural affairs indicates that the seminars were intended to broaden the participants' horizon to those issues and to the entrepreneurs' responsibility to society as a whole.[40] The evidence shows that this intended widening of perspectives was only one aspect of the talks, though: there were other, more important, motives. First, the BBUG have to be understood as a networking circle where up and coming managers could meet their peers and establish contacts and personal friendships, and potentially also find a mentor among the great and the good of German industry. Second, the significant role German big banks played on the supervisory boards of almost all large companies (except for family companies whose shares were not traded), especially when new investments were coming up, has to be considered. The large number of bankers attending the talks indicates that for the bankers BBUG offered the extra benefit of allowing them to connect with the future leadership of their client companies.[41] Third, the BBUG also had a social educational function. In a contemporary study of German management and management traditions first published in the US in 1959, Heinz Hartmann, a German industrial sociologist who attended several sessions of the first seminar as an observer, described the purpose of the Baden-Baden seminars as being the production of 'a social type, an *Unternehmer*, rather than a manager'.[42] Hartmann saw German managers' personnel policy as being based on a typical German entrepreneurial self-conception, which made it not an expression of economic rationale but rather an instrument of entrepreneurial authority.[43] For this reason, Hartmann's book was not well received amongst the German industrial elite and they put in considerable effort to discredit his work. They called him ideologically biased and accused him of lacking in practical experience; his fieldwork was criticized as being outdated since he had carried out his research during 1953 and 1955, implying that there had been a radical shift in managers' mentality between the end of the fieldwork and the book's publication four or five years later.[44] It is both the manner and the tone of managements' attacks against Hartmann which confirm Paul Erker's statement about industrialists as '[an] exciting ... continuity in mentality and attitudes'.[45]

Outside the top level *Unternehmergespräche*, German company leaders and high-ranking business associations' representatives remained critical, if not scathing, of German academic training. In particular the training available for commerce (*Kaufleute*) was lambasted. A working paper on industry's views on commercial training at universities is representative of this view. Although the paper acknowledged that universities gave a good grounding in specialized technical aspects, training was seen as too theoretical overall with little or no relevance for real-life business situations. In particular the lack of '*Weltorientierung*', an understanding of social and political events and cultural issues at home and abroad, was criticized. This lack of insight was seen as leading to an absence of empathy for human concerns, which then turned into inconsideration and ruthlessness both within the company and in its overall conduct.[46] This is an important statement as it confirms entrepreneurs' self-perception as being socially responsible.

The criticism about the theoretical nature of German universities' business education, in particular in contrast to US institutions of higher learning, has been commented on and explained repeatedly.[47] However, entrepreneurs' negative critique of their junior staff's theoretical training also reflected an important aspect of self-perception that showed itself in so many other situations: they saw themselves as the men of practice who knew how the world worked and how business was done. While their criticism of a overly theoretical university curriculum was by and large justified, they were also implying that graduates did not have their level of practical knowledge and experience. At the same time, and even if this was a naive and uncritical thought process, this lack of practical graduate knowledge would have confirmed to entrepreneurs their own elite status, in particular if they themselves had not attended university: they had the knowledge, the graduates had not.

From the mid-1950s onward, management training below the elite Baden-Baden level became an ever more important topic. Obviously, the demographic shortfall which von Witzleben had predicted in his 1953 report affected not only top management and company leadership but also to an even larger extent the workforce, particularly the skilled workers, and there were predictions of severe labour shortages at the end of the decade. In 1950, following the outbreak of the Korean War, the German economy had gained first-hand experience of the negative impact engendered by a lack of skilled workers. The totally insufficient coal supply in the second half of 1950 and first half of 1951 had been caused to a considerable extent by the lack of skilled miners at a time when the mechanization of coal mining was only in its infancy. This experience would have been a stark reminder of what other sectors could face in the foreseeable future.[48] Although there had been considerable internal training and promotions within companies (*innerbetrieblicher Aufstieg*) during the Third Reich because of the industrial expansion and a shortage of skilled workers due to military service, the scale of this training was insufficient.[49] War losses, an aging workforce and in particular the looming demographic shortfall demanded urgent action. In contrast to the Baden-Baden entrepreneurs' talks, which had quickly developed into the *Kaderschmiede*[50] of German management training, this development received less prominence and attention than warranted by its urgency and much more extensive social impact.

At the BDI's annual members' meeting from 17–19 May 1953, Wilhelm Beutler, the association's senior chief clerk, highlighted the necessity to implement *Weiterbildung* (further training) of skilled workers and master craftsmen, as well as of middle management,[51] in order to sustain or improve productivity and allow those workers upward social mobility. By this time, some companies had already taken action and developed their own internal further education programmes. Unsurprisingly, due to the influence of Ludwig Vauble, one of the trailblazer firms was once again Vereinigte Glanzstoff Fabriken. Between 1951 and the end of 1953, VGF had organized eleven courses for master craftsmen (*Meisterschulungen*) – class sizes were typically twenty to twenty-five men – as well as two courses for *Abteilungsleiter* (department heads). Topics in both had been economic and social policy issues as well as the theory and practice of rationalization. Members of the VGF board and factory directors as well as some outside experts acted as instructors. The company's board minutes expressed surprise about the positive response the courses had received from participants. This astonishment on management boards about the lower and middle managements' willingness to learn came up time and again in companies which introduced *Weiterbildung* and is an indication of the paternalist and patronizing attitude of company leaders towards their workforce at this time. Of course, VGF management did not offer the training courses simply out of the goodness of their hearts or for the benefit of their workers. They had realized, even before the war had ended, that the company could survive on the international market only if it modernized, rationalized and improved its product quality, for which extra staff training and expanded activities in these areas was needed.[52]

Ludwig Vauble, who stated repeatedly that his whole post-war career had been shaped by attending Harvard's Advanced Management Program, became the driving force for the training programmes.[53] In 1955 Vaubel initiated the establishment of the

Wuppertaler Kreis (Wuppertal Circle), a co-ordinating body for the various training courses available at the time in Germany. Other than publishing course timetables three times a year, the Circle helped and advised in the development of training curriculum, but did not provide training itself, as it is sometimes claimed in the literature.[54] In 1957, the *Wuppertaler Kreis* published a 'leadership pyramid' in which four leadership groups were identified, and these became standard in German management at the time. Lower management at the bottom comprised mainly the *Meister* or similar occupations on the shop floor; middle management formed the second group; upper management, which meant a company's leadership personnel, i.e. those people with the authority to 'hire and fire', were the third tier. The top of the pyramid was reserved for 'entrepreneurs', that is company owners or board members.[55] It was estimated at the time that in Germany 5,000–7,000 positions in the two top categories had to be filled annually.[56] By the mid-1960s, there were only two other institutions besides the BBUG which offered entrepreneurs' training, namely the C. Rudolf Poensgen Stiftung (C. Rudolf Poensgen Foundation) and the Bad Harzburger Akademie für Führungskräfte der Wirtschaft (Academy for Business Leadership); all other institutions offered lower and middle management training only.[57]

The Poensgen Foundation had been set up on 15 June 1956 by IHK Düsseldorf with a donation of DM 100,000 in order to celebrate the Chamber's 125th anniversary. The target group were in the first instance managers from North-Rhine Westphalia, regardless of company size, who were aged between about thirty and forty. Ideally they needed to have some experience either in staff positions, as an assistant to the management (*Assistent der Geschäftsführung*) or as department head. It was up to the companies to nominate candidates, who then had to apply for a place with the Foundation. As part of the application, candidates had to include a case study they had either completed or were working on. Companies' selection criteria for candidates followed an international example, based on the French *Centre de Percectionnement de l'Administration des Affaires* model, where not the completion of a higher degree but effective performance in a leadership position was relevant. Seminars were limited to thirty participants and ran only in the afternoons for a total of eight weeks: this was split into a two-week introduction, a main block of four weeks in which the principles of company leadership were addressed, and a final two-week summary in which case studies were discussed. The costs of the courses were to be carried by the firms, but the participants were expected to give up their free time for the seminars.[58] Although other Chambers were offering training courses as well, usually for lower level management, the Poensgen Foundation seminars were unique for an IHK. Initially it was hoped that they would even draw clients away from the BBUG, although this idea was strongly opposed by the BDI, who did not like its own creation challenged.[59] Eventually, the Poensgen Foundation established itself as a (mainly) regional training institute for the leadership of small and medium-sized enterprises. In this way it could indeed be called a 'mini Baden-Baden', one which the participants from SME companies preferred to attend instead of the 'real' BBUG, where they often felt uncomfortable, inferior and out of place.[60]

In terms of participants' numbers, West Germany's most successful management training institution in the 1950s and 1960s, and since the mid-1970s also the most controversial one, was the Bad Harzburger Akademie für Führungskräfte der Wirtschaft. Perhaps more than any other institution the Bad Harzburger Akademie has to be seen and understood as a product of its time. The 'Bad Harzburger Akademie für Führungskräfte der Wirtschaft. Middle Management', as its full name ran, was founded in 1956 by Reinhard Höhn. As of 1953 he had been president of the *Deutsche Volkswirtschaftliche Gesellschaft* (German Economic Society), a society that had been established in the late 1940s to help reduce the division between capital and labour.[61] At the Society Höhn used the ongoing debate amongst German business leaders about the lack of skills and training as a catalyst to offer *Mitarbeiterkurse* (co-worker courses), which brought together middle and upper management and works' councillors for discussions on human relations, before he set up the Academy.[62] In its early days, the Academy offered two types of courses: first, training for '*Meister, Vorarbeiter und Gruppenführer*' (master craftsmen, foremen and group leaders); and second a course for '*technische und kaufmännische Führungskräfte*' (technical and commercial management). Five topics were on the curriculum in both programmes: human resource management; social policy in the industrial society; economic theory; modern management theory; and labour and social law.[63] In particular for the *Meister*, this curriculum would have provided a real learning curve, since although their social prestige was much higher than that of American foremen, their general education was far inferior to that of their US counterparts.[64] It can be assumed that even for many middle managers attending these early seminars meant a significant learning opportunity. By the late 1950s, Höhn had developed what became known as the 'Bad Harzburger Model', a system based on what he called '*Führen im Mitarbeiterverhältnis*' and '*Delegation von Verantwortung*', respectively leadership in a co-worker relationship and delegation of responsibility. At the centre of Höhn's model was his realization that even though industrial society in Germany after the Second World War had changed considerably, management methods and human relations had not: the leadership style was still authoritarian-patriarchal, just as it had been during the Industrial Revolution and even before.[65] As a result many master craftsmen, while defending their work authority against subordinates, still 'stood to attention when receiving their work directives' from their line managers, as a progressive personnel manager observed at the time.[66]

For Höhn, the co-worker relationship meant that *betriebliche* (operational) decisions would be taken by employees at the relevant level of operation and no longer by a few men at the top; therefore responsibility had to be delegated to the appropriate lower stratum. As a consequence, old structures, i.e. the traditional 'top–down' approach, would be reversed into a 'bottom–up' policy, in which a senior staff member would deal with a decision delegated to a more junior colleague only if that colleague was unable to handle it. The company would lay down the basic principles of company leadership for all employees in an '*Allgemeine Führungsanweisung*' (general leadership directive) and draw up a detailed job specification for each post.[67]

For the co-worker, the model meant significantly enhanced responsibilities and duties: he would decide and act independently within his area of responsibility, so that ultimately he would 'become an entrepreneur in his own sphere' (Höhn); he also had to advise and, if necessary, criticize his superior and provide horizontal information to other departments at the same level. Only in exceptional cases could he ask for a decision that fell into his remit to be taken by his superiors. The two levels of what Höhn called hierarchy of responsibility (*Verantwortungshierarchie*) had to communicate with each other through discussions (*Gespräche*).[68] He went so far as to say that because workers could now take responsibility at their workplace, they would do so in wider society as 'responsible citizens', thus contributing to a consolidation of democracy in the Federal Republic.[69]

During the 1960s and up to the mid-1970s, German managers and entrepreneurs sent their workers to Bad Harzburg in their tens of thousands every year. In one of the rare studies of the establishment, Daniel Schmid has identified two periods of particular growth for the Academy: during 1963–68, when participant numbers doubled from about 9,000 to 18,000, and in 1968–71, when they rose to over 35,000 a year.[70] The second growth spurt was certainly influenced by the mini recession which had hit West Germany in 1966–67 and demonstrated to managers that the post-war boom was finally over and that they now had to compete much more vigorously on the international markets. This recession almost coincided with the publication of Jean-Jacques Servan-Schreiber's 1968 book *Die Amerikanische Herausforderung*, in which severe consequences for European economies were predicted due to supposedly superior American management methods.[71] In any case, even by the end of the first growth period, the Bad Harzburger Akademie had overtaken the hitherto largest provider of management training, the Heidelberg Arbeitsgemeinschaft für soziale Betriebsgestaltung.[72]

This raises the question of why the Academy was so successful before its spectacular decline from the mid-1970s onward, even despite Reinhard Höhn's past as an SS *Oberführer* (Brigadier General) and co-organizer of the infamous *Reichssicherheitshauptamt* (Reich Security Main Office)? These facts about Höhn's past had been known since the late 1950s and became even more prominent with the serialization of Heinz Höhne's seminal book *Der Orden unter dem Totenkopf. Die Geschichte der SS* in twenty-two issues of *Der Spiegel* in 1966–67.[73] The answer to this question is multi-faceted. During the 1950s and 1960s, the Harzburg model was very popular with heavy industry's trade-union-affiliated labour directors.[74] This is surprising at first sight since the Academy was not in favour of economic democracy and the co-determination model the trade unions were striving for. However, workers' further training in general, and the principle of delegation of responsibility in particular, made the Harzburg programme an attractive proposition for labour directors at a time when such delegation was still a novelty. Once the Academy was properly established (initially with donations from industry), Höhn offered a plethora of different courses for different levels of management (lower and middle, and from 1962 top management), distinct job categories (accountants, mining supervisors or training instructors (*Ausbilder*) etc.) and, as a particular innovation, for secretaries. Courses were also tailored for individual companies who wanted to introduce his system.[75] At a time when many workers, particularly those in big companies, were dissatisfied with their jobs due to strict hierarchies and unfulfilled expectations, the Harzburg model ostensibly offered something different. Adelheid von Saldern with good reason calls the model a 'denazified *Volksgemeinschaft*', which had a strong appeal to both workers and employers as it called for *soziale Betriebsharmonie* (social harmony at the workplace).[76] This social harmony was advocated especially in small and medium-sized companies and had been expressed in various forms by ASU chairman Alfred Flender in a number of speeches. He was one of the driving forces for the humanization of work to achieve social harmony and encouraged his fellow SME entrepreneurs to transform their traditional paternalism into real social responsibility.[77] Despite delegation of responsibility, the Harzburg leadership model did not want to remove company hierarchies wholesale: in fact it relied heavily on them and only changed the form from patriarchal authoritarian to bureaucratic authoritarian hierarchy. Richard Guserl identified not fewer than 315 different organizational principles in the model, unsurprisingly making it a bureaucratic juggernaut.[78]

At a time when ever more German managers realized that they needed better trained and led personnel, the academy caused a schism amongst entrepreneurs and managers about how to bring about this improvement. For the more conservative entrepreneurs who resisted the introduction of 'American' leadership models, the Harzburg Academy offered a solution.[79] Reinhard Höhn's 'German' model demanded more worker initiative, which would be beneficial for the company; at the same time it left management's authority untouched. However, the mere availability of a 'German' model of management training and leadership encouraged a wider debate over 'scientific' management in Germany and as a result, there were two dozen management training institutes in the country and in Switzerland operating by the early 1970s, compared to only six in the mid-1950s.[80] What brought the Harzburger Academy down was therefore not so much the Nazi past of its founder but rather Höhn's inability to adapt his system, which in the face of new competitors began to appear overly bureaucratic and unwieldy. By 1989, after having lingered on through the decade, the Academy was declared bankrupt.[81] Yet Harzburg's failure does not mean that management training models based on the Harvard Business School prevailed in Germany, as has been claimed.[82] On the contrary, the *Universitätsseminar der Wirtschaft*, founded in 1968 and often hailed as 'the German Harvard' due to its teaching methods, had to shorten its ten-week flagship programme to four weeks to adapt to German requirements; and even at the start of the twenty-first century there was no US-style MBA training course available at a German university.[83] Post-war German management persisted in going its own way when it came to training staff; at best companies may have *adapted* American methods but they never simply copied them. Höhn's supposed 'German' model relied in many details on US ideas and philosophies but because it was similar to (or even based on) the German army's *Auftragstaktik* (missions tactics),[84] a concept which many entrepreneurs knew from their own military experience, he could successfully market it to conservative German entrepreneurs. In this way he opened the door for more progressive and innovative leadership styles. However, it says a lot about the industrialists' attitudes towards Nazism that the Academy's decline did not come about because of Höhn's past. Regardless of the Academy's fate, one figure sums up how important and successful lower- and middle-management training and *Weiterbildung* were in Germany: between 1950 and 1970, some 400,000 skilled workers, that is 50 per cent of the total number of *Facharbeiter*, experienced social advancement and 'exchanged the blue for the white collar'.[85]

It is important not to underestimate the impact of industrialists' unchanged mentality when they chose future leadership personnel or even their successors, a mentality they had often adopted from, or which was influenced by, their predecessors. '*Reist bei Tage!*' (travels by day) – hardly ever had a career been halted by fewer words than these comments by Paul Reusch when asked by fellow industrialist Peter Klöckner about the character and suitability of an applicant for a leadership position.[86] Mannesmann chairman Wilhelm Zangen said in his speech for the launch of the Poensgen Foundation that there were three things he looked for in an applicant: '1) character; 2) character and 3) character' and 'daß die Auswahl des Führungsstabes eines Unternehmens vornehmste und höchstpersönliche Pflicht des Leiters ist' ('that the selection of the senior management was the most noble and most personal duty of the director').[87] Zangen's statement emphasizes the importance managers and entrepreneurs placed on the selection of the right man, in particular for board membership and the succession to company leadership. At the same time the statement also implies that what he had been looking for in a candidate was someone with character traits similar to his own. As succession decisions were ultimately strategic choices, these could also deliberately be delayed for the benefit of the company. At IG Farben Ulrich Haberland was intentionally not promoted to full board membership during the last two years of the war. This then allowed him to take a leading role after 1945 in one if IG Farben's successor companies, Bayer, where he became chairman because he was classed by the Allies as 'untainted'.[88]

There was (and still is) an obvious difference between choosing a successor for a family-run company and one for a joint stock company run by appointed managers. In the former case, the successor was normally a family member, usually a son, which automatically limited the pool of candidates. If no suitable family member was available, either because heirs had no interest in the family business or because a potential successor seem to lack 'entrepreneurial spirit', the company's existence was under threat. Josef Winschuh therefore stressed time and again the need for owner-run companies to train their next generation, especially if they lacked their father's entrepreneurial skills, to compensate as far as possible for the shortfall.[89] Some findings from Rainer Koehne's study, especially the low job-satisfaction rate amongst younger entrepreneurs, suggest that many of them took over the family business more out of a sense of duty and tradition rather than because of the famous 'calling'.[90]

The situation in large joint stock companies with their salaried managers was obviously different. Although Dieter Ziegler has pointed out that as late as 1967, 100 of Germany's largest 300 companies were still family owned,[91] this does not mean that the day-to-day business operations were conducted by the family. For example, Alfried Krupp left the running of his company to his general plenipotentiary Berthold Beitz; the Haniel family entrusted the running of Gutehoffnungshütte after the Second World War to Hermann Reusch.[92] What is clear, however, is that the members of the managing boards, and in particular their chairmen, had a similar social background and newcomers or outsiders were not accepted lightly (see Chapter 5). Hans Günther Sohl describes in his memoirs how, during his academic internship, he lodged with a widow of a pit director and later spent his free time in the household of a Gutehoffnungshütte board member.[93] Arrangements of this type not only offered early networking opportunities but also introduced upcoming managers promptly to the social habits of their strata. Perhaps of even greater importance were student fraternities, where former members, the so-called *Alte Herren*, traditionally provided career advice and acted as mentors to younger students.[94]

Some top managers' careers may have been temporarily interrupted between 1945 and 1948 but the traditional and established networks of West Germany's economic elites never disappeared because overall there was considerable continuity of leadership personnel after 1949.[95] This continuity meant that the leadership of big industrial companies or banks were recruited mainly from the same social circles, as they had what was seen as the right *Stallgeruch* or social pedigree.[96] At a time when a university degree became increasingly important for a leadership role, but when less than 5 per cent of a year group went to university – at that time German universities had fewer than 150,000 students enrolled – this growing educational pre-selection reinforced the limited access to top jobs in the big companies for those outsiders and managers who were not from the elite upper bourgeois circles.[97] While the educational reform of the 1960s opened up tertiary education for a much wider social group and allowed the new graduates from a wider section of society to take up management and leadership positions in small and medium-sized companies, Michael Hartmann's research has shown the opposite trend for big businesses, where the social pool for top management positions became even more exclusive.[98]

One particular feature of leadership selection in German big companies was the *Hauskarriere*, the in-house career.[99] Only in very rare and exceptional cases was a board member or chairman brought in from another company, although promotion from the leadership of a subsidiary company to run the 'mother' company or holding company was not uncommon, as Dietrich Wilhelm von Menges's career shows. But he too had been chosen and prepared for the job, as was the common practice at the time, by his predecessor Hermann Reusch and in turn von Menges would pick his own successor.[100] An in-house career did not necessarily mean that the career had to be begun in the firm but the transfer had to be done soon after a manager reached a certain leadership position, usually departmental level. This meant that the incumbent chief executive had time to select the right man from a small cadre of candidates and prepare him for the role, often by making him his personal assistant, before promoting him to deputy board member where he gained further insight into their future position. This gradual approach left time not only to prepare the candidate for the role (or reverse a decision in case the chosen one did not fulfil expectations,) but also allowed time to influence the candidate and make sure that he had the right 'character', as Wilhelm Zangen would have said.

The unwritten rule in the large joint stock companies that a chairman of the management board was to retire around the age of sixty-five was usually adhered to. In many cases, the chief executive who had run the company for many years would then became the chairman of the supervisory board. While this title did officially not allow them to interfere directly in the day-to-day running of the company, it did permit them to hang on to power through the role of 'backseat driver', since it was the supervisory board's task to appoint the management board and its chairman. Both Hans Günther Sohl at Thyssen and Berthold Beitz at Krupp wore out several chief executives they had previously appointed because they eventually did not agree with the way the successors were running the companies.[101] Some egos were simply too big to allow a new man to take over 'their' position and to adapt to new economic circumstances and changed market situations.

This chapter has shown that after the Second World War, almost in contrast to their traditional conservatism, German top managers and entrepreneurs did relatively quickly accept that their management selection and leadership structures had to be broadened and their management training expanded. In the case of big company leadership, this need for training arose in the first instance out of the demographic situation that had been caused by the two world wars and the loss of life or career interruption they had caused. German company leaders did not, however, change their minds that 'entrepreneurs are born, not made', so no schooling could make up for those perceived as lacking the entrepreneurial spirit or appropriate character traits regarded as essential for senior positions. The *Baden-Badener Unternehmergespräche* have to be seen less as a training institution and more as a 'finishing school' for the next generation of top managers in the large firms where extra mentoring and networking opportunities were provided. The seminars, although they allowed a small number of participants from small and medium-sized companies, were run by the big companies for the big companies and Germany's three leading banks. Seminar participation, either as a trainee participant or as an expert discussant, would have confirmed to attendees an elite status and special calling in the economic sphere (and possibly beyond). However, training the next generation of entrepreneurs began as early as their selection. Family background and habitus, the right pedigree and ability to fit social norms were of paramount importance. Gatekeepers and mentors made sure that only the most exceptional candidates from outside the prescribed social setting could progress. Most of those few social climbers who had begun their career under the Nazis, and had been able to maintain a leading position after 1945, would lose that during the 1950s. The old industrial elites, led during the 1950s once more by the *Bergassessoren*, remained by and large socially closed off.

The situation in lower- and middle-management positions was quite different. Although the need for better training of the master craftsmen had been recognized and stated since the early 1950s, there were initially very few training institutions available and the whole concept of *Weiterbildung* had to develop during the 1950s before it could really take off in the 1960s. As the story of, and developments around, the Harzburger Akademie have shown, significant changes did happen in this training, which in part facilitated a massive wave of social mobility in 1950s and 1960s Germany. While initially driven by the need to improve productivity and competitiveness, the tentative development of a human resource management movement in Germany did not just help to modernize personnel management; in fact in its modern sense it was actually created in this process.[102] In the course of this development, old authoritarian methods of leadership were replaced by more flexible approaches which allowed a significantly larger worker participation in a company's operations. It was this feature which made the Harzburg Academy popular with the trade unions' labour directors in companies under co-determination, and from here it spread to other firms and sectors, including SME companies and the consumer goods and retail sector. Despite its underlying conservative philosophy, the Harzburg Academy's principle of delegation of responsibility contributed to the modernization of German management. But as the examples of both the Baden Badener Unternehmergespräche and Reinhard Höhn's academy have shown, German entrepreneurs preferred to do things their own 'German' way and did not copy American methods. From this perspective it is therefore wrong to speak of 'Americanization' of German management; it was instead, as Harm Schröter phrased it, rather a process of 'modernization' that occurred.[103]

5

Bürgerlichkeit: Culture and Honour, Upstarts and Old Elites

For German entrepreneurs, social status and their place in society was of very high importance. *Bürgerlichkeit*, being part of bourgeois society, conducting their lives in a certain way, following a set of particular norms and values which had been acquired through a strictly controlled process of socialization, guaranteed them a privileged lifestyle and high social prestige. However, for a number of reasons, it is not easy to properly place the post-Second World War German *Bürger* in society. In contrast to France and Britain, the German language has only the word *Bürger* for both its political meaning of 'citizen' and its class-based social meaning of bourgeois and/or middle class.[1] Acting within the framework of those bourgeois rules and cultural conventions reached its zenith in the period between the founding of the Wilhelmine Empire and the First World War.[2] Manfred Hettling and Stefan-Ludwig Hoffmann refer to the total of these conventions as the so-called *bürgerliche Wertehimmel* (bourgeois heaven of values), an imagined and idealized collection of norms and interpretation (*Sinngebung*) of how a good *Bürger* should conduct his life; the bourgeois heaven of values could go so far as to challenge the Christian heaven.[3] The development of these social norms had begun well before the industrialization but found its high point in the antagonism between the educated and property-owning middle classes and the aristocracy on the one hand, and the resentment between the middle classes and the proletariat on the other.[4] Although there are similarities and continuation lines, a direct transfer of ninenteenth-century bourgeois values and experiences to the post-1945 situation is fraught with problems but entrepreneurs' bourgeois values as they existed after the Second World War undoubtedly had their origins in the 1800s. This is true particularly among the German *Wirtschaftsbürgertum*, the economic bourgeoisie, which was able to preserve the strongest bourgeois continuity lines because of its relatively strong social cohesion and homogeneity compared to other European countries.[5]

One of these continuity lines is addressed by Manfred Hettling, who sees the development of *Bürgerlichkeit* as a process that cannot be described only by the social status of a person or the esteem in which they were held in society, but also by their own honour.[6] This chapter will show how the concept of honour did indeed survive in the social habits of entrepreneurs into the second half of the twentieth century. *Bürgertum* regarded temperance in all walks of life as a virtue, a trait which also continued well beyond the Wilhelmine epoch.[7] This bourgeois attitude is one reason why German capitalism developed differently from the Anglo-Saxon model. Robert Locke has pointed out that German business owners did not usually regard their companies as simple 'cash cows' but instead as living entities, which needed to be nurtured. Profit was therefore to be made for the benefit of the company, but not the sake of the owner (although if successful, he was certainly entitled to his share).[8] Similarly, although a higher social status had often found its outward expression in the villas of the post-1871 unification economic boom period, the *Gründerzeit*, excessive display of wealth was usually rejected by the *Bürgertum*, as was the accumulation of wealth for its own sake, which was seen and spurned as an 'aristocratic' vice.

Initially, research into the German bourgeoisie focussed on the nineteenth century when most of the bourgeois habitus developed; only in the new millennium was it expanded into the second half of the twentieth century.[9] This was due to the widespread belief that following the First World War and the 1923 hyperinflation, which reduced the *Bürgertum*'s material assets, its values as a social group had been hollowed out and the bourgeoisie themselves had become irrelevant. This is the argument made especially by Hans Mommsen, who as the grandson of the famous Theodor Mommsen was himself the product of a significant bourgeois family. The bourgeoisie's involvement with, and support for, the Nazis finally discredited them morally and socially.[10] However, this perception of the *Bürgertum* as an extinct social group had been challenged by post-war contemporaries long before Mommsen's remarks. In a speech at a CDU party meeting in Cologne on 6 September 1946, Robert Pferdmenges, deeply rooted in bourgeois traditions, rejected the claim that the bourgeoisie in Germany was dead. While he conceded that it may be battered, impoverished and shaken to its foundations, he emphasized that it was still, and would remain, alive:

> For the *Bürgertum* is not a matter of money or income. It is an attitude. The *Bürger* was, and wishes to remain, the guardian of tradition, the champion of a lifestyle which has . . . provided the soil on which our Western culture . . . was able to grow and has grown. . . . Without him [the *Bürger*] reconstruction in our country is unthinkable.[11]

Another insight into contemporary bourgeois attitudes is given by Ludwig Vaubel, who described in his diary a visit to Hermann Josef Abs' estate Bentgerhof in February 1949. The estate's exterior 'peasant scruffiness' is contrasted with the refined upper bourgeois lifestyle which had found its expression in the farmhouse's interior decoration described in detail and with admiration by Vaubel.[12] As will be shown in this chapter, the German economic bourgeoisie was indeed not dead, even though it had suffered the vicissitudes of war and was to experience a transformation due to the emergence of what has been termed *Staatsbürgergsellschaft* (civic society). As Dieter Gosewinkel explained, the economic bourgeoisie remained alive between the poles of four pairs of characteristics: property and education, personal interest and the common good (*Gemeinwohlorientierung*), creativity and rationality, as well as sense and sensibility which together remained determining parameters for their habitus.[13] These will be investigated by looking at industrialists' involvement in the fields of scientific and cultural patronage and their attitude towards honour. That there were different rules of how to apply honour, however, will be shown by the different treatment newcomers experienced in contrast to established entrepreneurs.

During the Wilhelmine and Weimar eras, student duels were a symbol of membership of a superior social class and a way of distinguishing themselves from lower strata of society.[14] Another way through which the economic bourgeoisie tried to maintain the demarcation between themselves and other social groups and retain its social exclusivity was through the limitation of marriage circles.[15] Cornelia Rauh's study on the family life of the economic bourgeoisie gives a very good example of these attitudes. Hermann Reusch went ahead with his engagement to his future wife, the daughter of a Hamburg banking family, only after his father had agreed that the marriage befitted his status.[16] In the *Wirtschaftsbürgertum*, spouses were also seen as 'a gift from heaven . . . a comrade in life . . . who has understanding for the constant overstraining [of the manager husband] . . . and provide the inner balance through the creation of domestic bliss' in the rare moments of family life enjoyed by the overworked businessman.[17] Most couples of the economic bourgeoisie and the managerial elites remained married to their partners until one of the spouses died. Divorce among entrepreneurs or top managers was very unusual: Otto A. Friedrich, who was divorced twice and married three times, is a rare exception to this social rule.[18] Where the attitude of top industrialists differed to those of small and medium-sized owner-entrepreneurs was in the social role of the wives: the owners of SMEs often relied on their wives as business partners and advisors in commercial affairs and thus expected them to have some knowledge of economic matters. In contrast, wives of the top managers primarily had to look after the house and children and sometimes had to fulfil representative functions, but the general attitude was, as Hermann Reusch expressed it, that 'womenfolk should stay away from business matters'.[19]

A centrepiece of German *Bürgerlichkeit* was patronage of arts and science, usually in the form of donations to cultural institutions like museums and learned establishments such as universities or research institutes. In the post-war period, the most important body in this field was the *Stifterverband der deutschen Wissenschaft* (Association for the Promotion of Science and Humanities). It was set up in 1949 by seventy business associations with the aim of promoting Germany's large research institutes. Financed through voluntary contributions of at least 1 per cent of the member companies' annual profits or dividends, it became one of the most important donors for institutions such as the Max Planck Society, the *Deutsche Forschungsgesellschaft* (DFG, German Research Society), the Alexander von Humboldt Foundation as well as the German Academic Exchange Service, the DAAD.[20] According to Gerard Braunthal, businesses raised and distributed DM 50 million in this way annually.[21] At a time when West Germany's economic success was far from certain, the scale of this commitment was striking. Other forms of donations on a more local level went to charitable bodies which looked after those fellow businessmen who had fallen on hard times.[22]

Cultural patronage was of similar significance and was taken up again soon after the war. One of the first industrial cultural organizations that was established after the war was the *Vereinigung der Freunde von Kunst und Kultur im Bergbau* (VFKK, Association of the Friends of Art and Culture in the Mining Industry), which was founded in November 1947.[23] Its aim was to promote popular art forms in the mining industry and while membership had nominally been open to all levels of mining employees, the actual target membership was upper management. In its cultural intentions the Association was conservative, even *völkisch*, in character and full of patronizing arrogance towards the ordinary miners working, quite literally, at the coal face. The association has to be seen as an expression of industrialists' feeling of social and cultural superiority and an attempt to preserve the traditional social order.

A very different organization to the VFKK was the Federation of German Industry's *Kulturkreis* (Cultural Circle). Founded on 17 August 1951 by thirty-five high-ranking BDI figures in the presence of the Federal President, Theodor Heuss, the *Kulturkreis* became one of the biggest patrons and supporter of the young Federal Republic's art and cultural scene, but also one with an underlying purpose.[24] In an exchange of letters, Hermann Reusch had asked his father about the scale of industrial cultural patronage prior to the Second World War. Reusch Senior explained that back then industrialists were usually not interested in art or art patronage at all; or if they had interests, then these were limited to the collection of Old Masters.[25] The underlying motive which drove both men was a realization that arts, and the patronage in particular of *modern* art, would become a means for industrialists' societal rehabilitation in the aftermath of their involvement with the Nazis. However, the role of the *Kulturkreis* and its chairman Hermann Reusch is not as clear-cut as it appears from this point. In a speech before the Circle's launch, Reusch emphasized that the *Kulturkreis* was explicitly not the industrialists' response to the current wave of cultural promotion by the trade unions, but rather that both sides were 'workers and craftsmen at the great cathedral of humanity'.[26] When he compared the promotion of art to the great constructions of medieval Christendom, Reusch implied that arts would benefit and improve all classes equally but he also evoked the myth of European Christianity and culture, which had led to the modern capitalist society. In his official opening address, he then referred to the internal debate about the circle's purpose. The initial idea to put the Circle onto the 'broadest possible base, which meant an emphasis of western anti-collective ideas (*Gedankengut*) and onto the notion of free entrepreneurship' was deferred in favour of more practical support for the arts.[27] In other words, the initially suggested level of entrepreneurial propaganda was seen as too crude and too blunt and instead it was decided that the Circle should concentrate on more practical art support. Its first activities, then, were of a traditional, conservational nature. The Circle gave DM 40,000 for the rebuilding of the famous Essen Volkwang Museum for modern art, while a staggering DM 300,000 was raised for the rebuilding of the baroque church organ at Ottobeuren Abby after the Bavarian government withdrew its promised support for the project.[28] While the Circle donated annually between DM 30,000 and DM 50,000 for museums, its perhaps most important task came in the form of bursaries for painters, musicians, composers, architects and writers. Between 1953 and 1964, nearly 400 stipends were given, mainly to artists who were to make up West Germany's avant-garde art scene. Amongst the recipients were Heinrich Böll, Walter Jens, Ilse Aichinger, Ingeborg Bachmann and Wolfgang Köppen. Controversial conservative writers like the brothers Ernst and Friedrich Georg Jünger remained exceptions amongst the recipients. Only the young Hans Magnus Enzensberger refused his award on the grounds that accepting it would 'compromise the credibility of his social criticism'.[29] How artistically open-minded the *Kulturkreis* actually was is best demonstrated by the fact that Peter Weiss was published in the anthology of *Jahresring*, the Circle's official publication.[30] Two years later, in 1965 the *Deutsches Industrie Institut* felt compelled to warn businessmen and to provide them with a documentation about 'the Weiss case'. This related to Weiss's new play, *Die Untersuchug* (*The Investigation*) which dealt with businesses' links to Auschwitz and which, in the DII's opinion, 'defamed free entrepreneurship and private property'.[31]

All this did not mean that the Circle was not used for social propaganda as well. In January 1952, five months after its launch, Reusch wrote to Circle members and informed them about the first thoughts on the content of a book about *Arbeitereigenheime* (working-class owner-occupied houses). In six chapters or 'scenes', the industrialists' very patronising view of the worker and the traditional and ideal family displayed itself. The first scene described the factory as at the heart of the worker's life, the second explained that since 'the workers' taste in general is 50 years behind the times', it was necessary to educate them and if required disregard their tastes. The following two chapters were dedicated to financing and planning, both architecturally and in terms of landscapes, with a view on workers' health, as well as the subsidies provided by the state and the company. 'Moving in' and the need for ongoing savings and economical housekeeping to service the mortgage was the topic of the penultimate scene. According to the draft, 50 per cent of all workers were '*siedlungsunfähig*' (unsuitable for owner-occupation) because they had married the wrong wife, one who had too much interest in cinema and not enough in prudent housekeeping. The last chapter described the model family who, after years of saving and doing without trips to the pub or cinema, had paid off their first mortgage and were now living happily off home-grown fruits and vegetables.[32] Although the letter said explicitly that the crude message of 'one's own home as a protective wall against proletarianisation' should not be used and the book should 'tactfully stay out of the political debate' and let the facts speak for themselves, its conservative political and educational message was very clear.[33] At the same time it was a thinly veiled attempt to impose middle-class values of domesticity, thriftiness and 'prudence', but also middle-class style and taste, onto the workers.[34] In late November 1952, the *Kulturkreis* was able to send the first copies of the book, now called *Das goldene Dach* (*The Golden Roof*) to its members, but it proved to be a sales flop. When the Circle's *Verwaltungsrat* met in April 1953, they reported that so far only 2,500 copies had been sold. This was explained by another telling statement, namely that many companies had not bought the book because they feared that it would raise overly high aspirations and expectations amongst their workforce. It was therefore suggested that the book's cover price be reduced to DM 6.80 (for a bulk purchase of 200 copies), with the *Kulturkreis* covering the estimated shortfall of DM 25,000.[35]

The *Kulturkreis* would have been well able to bear the costs. By pointing out that the Circle's activities not only had cultural value but also benefitted industry's reputation, Reusch had expected not only to raise the provisional membership fees for companies from 20 Pfennig per employee to 50 Pfennig (with a reduction for the wage-intensive coal industry), but also to increase the number of companies which were members.[36] In all this, public perception and reputation remained very much on the industrialists' agenda. When in 1955 the *Kulturkreis* was criticized for its self-imposed budget limit of DM 300,000, the *Verwaltungsrat* decided to counter this by spending DM 10,000 on documentation to show how much money industry had actually donated for arts and culture since 1945 in an attempt to correct the 'public's misunderstanding' on the matter.[37]

The *Kulturkreis* was important enough for the BDI to be given its own standing rubric (one of six) in the BDI's newsletter, the *BDI Rundschreiben*.[38] In the 1952 stipend awards ceremony, *Kulturkreis* chairman Reusch spoke of cultural patronage as a *Herzensangelegenheit* (an affair of the heart) with which industrialists were trying to look after Germany's cultural well-being. This was not just a way to show off industry's new wealth, to 'hand out alms' or 'affix a cultural tie pin'. He explained that *Leistungswille* (motivation to perform), by which he meant entrepreneurial performance, and artistic creation were both non-materialist and therefore similar.[39] Two years later, Reusch addressed another underlying reason for industry's support for the arts. He explained that the German 'economic miracle' had been achieved not by the masses mobilized by Communism or National Socialism but by human beings who had remained individuals. For this reason he appealed to his audience to help support young German artists of all fields since they were the ones who were working against *Vermassung* (massification).[40] Several times Reusch addressed participants of the *Baden-Badener Unternehmergespräche* about 'the Entrepreneur's role in contemporary culture', in an attempt to pass this message on to the next generation of business leaders.[41]

Considering Reusch's usual arch-conservative attitudes, it is surprising that he was the champion of modern art, especially within the *Kulturkreis*. Other than Reusch it was Gustav Stein, senior chief clerk at the BDI as well as chief clerk to the *Kulturkreis*, who was the main advocate for modern art. This 'progressive' wing faced considerable resistance from the 'traditionalists' in the Circle whose key protagonist was the Augsburg IHK president Otto Vogel. As early as 1953, Vogel had complained about the overrepresentation of modern art in the Circle. Tensions between the two cultural poles simmered until 1961 when there was finally a debate about the issue among the *Kulturkreis* board, which the progressives won easily. Wener. Bührer claims that in particular Stein was a modernizer by convention, and that for him the support for modern art was merely an expression of 'being modern'.[42] Whether or not this judgement is applicable to Hermann Reusch as well can be debated. He defended the heavily criticized portrait of Federal President Theodor Heuss, painted by Oskar Kokoschka and funded at least in part with donations from industry, against attacks from fellow industrialists; he also had his own official portrait painted in modernist style by Alfred Eckhard, indicating a sincere interest in modern art.[43]

Industrialists' cultural interests were to a very large degree dependent on an individual's upbringing. Other than the classical education which many future business leaders received at the humanist high schools, it was the domestic influences in the households of the *Bildungs- und Wirtschaftsbürgertum* (educated and economic bourgeoisie, the other two pillars of the German bourgeoisie) which were important to instil an interest in high culture. This interest in theatre plays, classical music or art exhibitions shows itself in many autobiographical accounts of managers. Günter Henle dedicated more than fifty pages of his autobiography to his work and hobby as a musical publisher; Otto A. Friedrich wrote his own theatre plays, and these were produced.[44] Ludwig Vaubel's diary is full of comments on arts and culture, books he had just read or plays he had attended. Quite interestingly and in contrast to others, Vauble questioned 'the failure of [Germany's] spiritual elite' (*geistige Elite*) of which he saw himself and other managers to be part, because of the role they played during the Nazi regime. At the same time he explicitly criticized the American cultural re-education programme which was attempted in the immediate post war years as superficial. Implicitly, and in line with German bourgeois thinking, he saw German culture as superior to its American counterpart.[45] Hans-Günther Sohl, another eager promoter of the *Kulturkreis* and its chairman after Reusch had stepped down, spent ten pages in his autobiography elaborating on his love for music and opera from an early age, and another ten pages on his patronage in later years of the Bayreuth festival and other opera and theatre projects.[46]

How deep the cultural habit had been ingrained in the attitude of German upper bourgeoisie, not just industrialists, is visible through their public appearances and speeches. In particular during the first half of the 1950s, hardly any public speech was delivered without the inclusion of a classical quote, usually from the German classics Schiller or Goethe, sometimes from the Greco-Roman classics, and industrialists followed this example.[47] When Gerhard Schroeder of Kloeckner stepped down as chairman of the *Wirtschaftsvereinigung Eisen und Stahl* in May 1956 he delivered a humorous speech full of literary and theatre allusions in which he pictured himself as the artistic director/actor of a theatre. He explained his different leadership styles as the association's chairman as *The Taming of the Shrew* followed by *The Magic Flute* followed by *Trouble Backstairs* (*Krach im Hinterhaus*). Many of the association's issues were like Shakespeare's *Much Ado About Nothing* but that ultimately *All's Well That Ends Well* and that he would now retire as an actor to read *Götz von Berlichingen*.[48] Citing this famous play by Goethe – which contains the infamous sentence 'He can lick me in the arse' – was Schroeder's very cultured but well understood rebuke of some association members and their behaviour.

While in the early 1950s cultural patronage, particularly in the form of the 'collective patronage' (Bührer) adopted by the *Kulturkreis*, may have been used to improve industrialists' public image, its significance went much further than that. Having an interest in, and understanding of, high culture helped to foster and further the feeling of being part of Germany's cultural elite. Cultural activities and interests, in other words, helped to shape a group identity. This can be seen in Herdenröder's hagiography, *Neue Männer an der Ruhr*. Industrialists' love for music or arts is constantly highlighted and stood in contrast to newcomers who had few cultural interests and 'found recreation rather at a football match or boxing fight than in a theatre or concert hall.'[49] Established entrepreneurs, on the other hand, saw their economic activities as being similar to that of a creative artist, something they emphasized repeatedly throughout the 1950s, 60s and 70s. In their speeches, entrepreneurs saw themselves together with artists as one of the last bulwark of the West against the '*Vermassung*' of society, which they saw as being contrary to the *abendländische* (occidental) conception of man.[50] Only artists and entrepreneurs, they claimed, had the *Persönlichkeit* (character) to withstand this 'massification', because both had a passion for '*schöpferische Intuition*' (creative intuition). Thus, Hans-Günther Sohl explained on the occasion of the BDI's twenty-fifth anniversary that '*steckt in jedem echten Unternehmer auch ein künstlerisches Element*' ('there is in each true entrepreneur also an artistic element').[51]

Another important attribute which defined West Germany's economic bourgeoisie was their honour, more specifically their *Kaufmannsehre* (merchants' honour). At least up to the middle of the twentieth century, the term *Kaufmann* (merchant) was used much more frequently amongst the German economic class than 'entrepreneur' or 'industrialist'. The most striking example of this was Hugo Stinnes, who referred to himself as *Kaufmann aus Mühlheim* (merchant from Mühlheim).[52] As with so many aspects of bourgeois honour, this attitude had developed in the nineteenth century, when the 'merchant' became a symbol of hard work, honesty and fidelity. In particular the ability (and willingness) to pay obligations and commitments in full and on time became a status symbol and a demarcation against other parts of society, and also helped to develop entrepreneurial *Standesehre* (professional honour). The term '*ehrbare Kaufmann*' (honourable merchant) itself dated back to the seventeenth century, when Hansa merchants from Hamburg set up a traders' deputation to the city's administration to make their claims heard but also to separate themselves from 'less honourable' elements of the business community.[53] With the rise in company sizes at the end of the 1800s came the advent of the salaried managers, and company honour became independent from that of the owner and his personal conduct.[54] However, this trend did not apply to the owners of small or medium-sized companies. For them, both their personal and their business conduct continued to inform their status as honourable merchants. If they went bankrupt, they would lose both their personal *and* business reputations, as the two were closely linked. The worst that could befall an independent entrepreneur was the loss of good reputation and personal credit.[55]

In the following section, Winfried Speitkamp's definition of honour as a code of conduct and an instrument for social, or here more precisely, *group* control, will be applied.[56] This definition will facilitate an effective analysis of entrepreneurs' actions and their attempts to maintain a certain group habitus which had a significant impact on social prestige and positioning. As Speitkamp has observed, 'Honour creates status'.[57] And yet although the significance of social status was retained, social practices related to honour did change noticeably during the reconstruction period.

When Max Weber, himself an ardent advocate of the 'highest' form of preserving honour, the duel, predicted that honour would lose its meaning in a modernizing society because of its feudal origins, he was wrong on several levels.[58] During the Weimar period, German students continued to fight duels with rapiers, and sometimes even sabres, despite considerable (if futile) attempts by the authorities to prevent these 'class-based' blood sports. Indeed, it was the duelling student fraternities which recruited up to 60 per cent of all student society members between the wars.[59] The facial scars obtained during those encounters became the students' badge of honour and their image is eternalized in the portraits they commissioned once they had developed into West Germany's post-war industrial leaders.[60] None other than BDI president Fritz Berg became the poster boy for this attitude: when he visited the US for the first time after the Second World War, a New York newspaper called him 'a typical German beer student' because of his duelling scars.[61] When students left university, they dropped their duelling habits but this did not mean that the middle classes were no longer prepared to defend their honour. They simply did it differently, mainly through the courts in tens of thousands of litigation cases every year, even though numbers of honour litigation cases dropped from over 80,000 before the First World War to fewer than 30,000 in 1936.[62]

After the Allies occupied Germany, business leaders were in for a big shock. Most of them had expected that they could continue their work in the belief that they would be needed for Germany's economic reconstruction.[63] None of them had foreseen that the Allies would automatically arrest almost all top managers of big industry and ban many entrepreneurs in small and medium-sized companies who had been Nazi party members from running their companies, sometimes for years. Owners of medium-sized companies were frequently affected for longer by this policy, because their firms were usually not seen as vital to the reconstruction. They could only express their indignation about this treatment. Heinrich Krumm, owner of the world-renowned Goldpfeil leather manufacturing company, spoke for many when he expressed his exasperation and bitterness about this treatment in the afterword to his published diary, stating more than ten years after the event: 'American Morgenthau justice was applied. . . . Looking back, even today I feel the greatest humiliation to appear in front of such a [denazification] court.'[64] Krumm had been banned from entering or running his company for four years. In contrast, top managers like Günter Henle, a man known for his resentment of the Nazis, were released from their automatic arrest after nine months as the leading men of the Ruhr were needed urgently for the reconstruction. Henle's autobiography provides a similar account to that of other men arrested. It describes the good camaraderie amongst the interned industrialists and states that he held no grudge against the British who had incarcerated him. However, he calls Bad Nenndorf detention camp where he was held 'the British secret service's infamous concentration camp' where they were kept in 'most primitive accommodations', badly fed and treated rudely by the guards.[65] Hans-Günther Sohl dedicates no less than twelve pages of his autobiography to his almost eighteen months of internment experiences. He emphasizes the 'many people he met' during this time and the 'interesting conversations' he had with them and finishes the account with a description of which industrialists took up which leadership positions after their release.[66]

These three examples demonstrate several things: first, it shows the humiliation the men suffered from the experience of the arrest and incarceration and later on from the denazification process, even though Henle and Sohl in their autobiographies emphasized (almost too much) that they bore no grudges. Second, Sohl's 'interesting conversations' describes the establishment of new networks amongst the internees from the business community (in contrast to those who were interned for political reasons), contacts which were maintained after their release. Third, this, together with the emphasis of harbouring no ill-will towards their captors, has to be understood as a retrospective feeling of vindication and moral righteousness, which could have only been reinforced by their economic success. At the time of writing their memoirs, the men could look back on their achievements in the reconstruction process and the economic miracle, and in their eyes these must have redeemed any misdeeds alleged by the Allies. The perception of unjustified internment and denazification turned those industrialists caught up in it almost into a 'band of brothers' who had suffered Allied retributory policy against 'unpolitical and innocent' businessmen. In their eyes, their true honour could not be touched by these measures; on the contrary, it was increased.

How significant honour remained for post-war Germany's business elite is best shown in the Reusch-Kirchfeld case, which, after dragging on for almost two years, was ultimately settled in an honour court. The case was so unusual that Dietrich Wilhelm von Menges, chaiman of Gutehoffnungshütte from 1966 to 1975, spent two pages in his autobiography describing it.[67] In 1942, the Nazis had pushed Paul Reusch, who since 1909 had held the chairmanship of the Gutehofffnungshütte managing board, out of the company because of his ongoing opposition to their armaments policies. Reusch's son Hermann, also a member of the managing board and his designated successor, resigned out of solidarity with his father. Because of his actions, Hermann Reusch would be regarded by the British as politically 'clean' and thus he was allowed to the company in 1945 to become acting chairman before he was given the role permanently in 1947. Early that year, Reusch had accused Franz Kirchfeld, another board member, who had also been tipped to succeed Paul Reusch as chairman, of having conspired against Reusch Senior. As an active Nazi party member, Kirchfeld had reached the position of state secretary in the economics ministry during the war. In 1946, he resigned from the Gutehoffnungshütte managing board, but stayed on as a board member of the subsidiary company Ferrostaal.[68] During 1947, Reusch intensified his campaign against Kirchfeld. One of his tactics was to ignore Kirchfeld in meetings or refuse to take his phone calls but without giving him any explanation for this isolation. It was only in November 1947 that he made his accusations known to Kirchfeld and subsequently asked von Menges to act as mediator and go-between. Reusch's allegation centred around the claim of 'disloyalty' against Paul Reusch and conspiring with Werner Carp and Wolfgang Curtius, who represented a branch of the Gutehoffnungshütte owning family which was opposed to Reusch's running of the company.[69] Other than outright fraudulent behaviour, 'disloyalty' was perhaps the strongest accusation that could have been levelled against a leading manager at the time. Kirchfeld's vehement denial of the accusations and his insistence that he had always been loyal to his mentor, Paul Reusch, fell on deaf ears. Eventually, in April 1948, he took the only route left open to him, declaring that his honour had been insulted and that the case had to be immediately resolved and his reputation restored. As both Kirchfeld and Reusch Junior had been members of student duelling societies during their time at university, they finally managed to agree to the establishment of an honour court which was to resolve the case once and for all.[70] In the process it came to light that there were no rules for such a course of action. However, the fact that Reusch sent his second the *Ehren- und Waffenordnung des Verbandes Alter Corpsstudenten* (Honour and Weapons Code of the Association of Former Corps Students), which outlined the rules for pistol and sabre duels, demonstrates the serious nature of the affair. Eventually both men desisted from pursuing this option.[71] Instead they agreed to the establishment of an honour court which consisted of one second from each side to which the opponents would send written statements in response to their adversary's case.[72]

As it turned out, Reusch was not able to substantiate any claim against Kirchfeld with anything other than hearsay and instead increasingly had to focus his allegations more on Kirchfeld's party membership and activities. Exacerbating the situation, even his confidants were making statements in support of Kirchfeld, but none against him. This included Reusch's second, Otto Meyer, chairman of the Gutehoffnungshütte's subsidiary MAN, an outspoken opponent of the Nazis. Meyer had been persecuted by the Nazis because of his Jewish wife and was almost sent to a labour camp in 1945. Subsequently, while the honour court declared that both men had acted out of 'honourable motives', Reusch's case was dismissed. The court declared the accusations unproven and Kirchfeld's honour restored. Despite this clear outcome he had to give up his board memberships in all Gutehoffnungshütte companies and subsidiaries, and, with only a pittance as compensation, had to leave the company altogether. However, with his reputation rehabilitated, after a short business interlude with Willy Schlieker, Kirchfeld was able to establish his own successful industrial trading and service company.[73]

The case shows several important things. In the first instance, it demonstrates how important personal honour was to the two protagonists. Once Kirchfeld claimed that he felt insulted in his honour by Hermann Reusch's accusation, Reusch could not ignore him any longer and had to talk to him. Second, the seconds who made up the honour court took their task very seriously and carried it out without any bias. As noted above, even Reusch's friend Otto Meyer, who had been persecuted by the Nazis, reported his findings objectively in favour of the former state secretary. Third, although Reusch had to shift his accusations ever more in that direction, Kirchfeld's Nazi party membership was never a real issue in the process. Even in the 'under-Nazified' Gutehoffnungshütte, there were several other party members on the managing boards who went on to continue their careers.[74] When Curt Haniel, chairman of the Gutehoffnungshütte supervisory board, expressed his displeasure about Kirchfeld's party membership during the ongoing dispute, this was therefore only a smokescreen.[75] The real reason for Haniel's bias was a long-running imbroglio within the owner family of Haniel/Carp. Both Reusch Senior and Junior had supported the Haniel family, for which they acted as major-domus in the running of the company. In some instances they even put the Haniel family interest ahead of the company, although officially Hermann Reusch tried to stay out of the family dispute.[76] Because of this, he had tense relations with the Carp branch of the family. It therefore made sense for Curt Haniel to support Reusch in this conflict. By so doing he strengthened his own position in the family quarrel as he knew that Reusch's loyalty would only increase.[77] Finally, it is worth noting that both men did accept the ruling of the honour court, althought naturally this was easier for Reusch, since he had ultimately achieved his goal of removing Kirchfeld from the company and in doing so had eliminated a potential leadership rival. For Franz Kirchfeld, even though he had to leave the company with only a few thousand Marks as compensation (unthinkable in today's 'golden parachute' management culture), the verdict meant that with his reputation restored and his honour intact he could eventually start his own successful business. Had he challenged his dismissal and the measly settlement he had received in a court of law, he only would have tarnished his reputation. The Reusch-Kirchfeld case seems to have been the only post-war honour court case which involved top industrialists: any other disputes would have been settled in courts of law or through the mediation of friends. In one such case in December 1949 and January 1950, Hermann Reusch was called in to act as mediator in a dispute over dismantling adjustments between Mannesmann and Krupp. That he had been chosen demonstrates the high esteem in which he was held among his peers in matters of reputation and objectivity, irrespective of his otherwise often extreme views.[78]

While high-profile honour cases such as the Reusch-Kirchfeld dispute provide a very helpful insight into the mentality of leading industrialists, the question of honourable conduct and how to enforce it if necessary were not limited to Germany's top businessmen. The question had been taken up in various forms by the Chambers of Industry and Commerce soon after the war had ended, but its roots lay in the interwar years. Compared to other professional sectors such as lawyers, medical doctors or journalists, who had introduced honour courts in the nineteenth century, businessmen were late to establish them.[79] It was only after the First World War that Berlin merchants called for the introduction of merchants' honour courts. This was in response to a number of high-profile business scandals in the aftermath of the 1923 hyperinflation and subsequently the 1929 Wall Street Crash, which threatened to tarnish the reputation of the Berlin business community altogether.[80] Their endeavours have to be understood to a significant extent as attempts by the established merchants to demarcate themselves from the nouveaux riches and their greed, real or perceived. Setting up the courts had the added benefit for established businesses that it allowed to keep the newcomers in a position of lower status within the group they had just acceded to.[81] However, it took until 1935, and presumably resulting from some pressure from National Socialist authorities, before a definition of honour was found that was widely acceptable and applicable to all sectors of the economy. According to this definition, an honourable merchant was someone 'who subordinates himself under, and supports the idea of, work in and for the common weal through his comments, actions and omissions'.[82] This definition was wide open to interpretation. For the Nazis it allowed the exclusion of Jews, who, by their definition, never worked for the common good. On the other hand, it permitted some protection for Jewish businessmen, at least until about 1938. Petra Bräutigam's study of south-west German medium-sized companies has shown that there was considerable loyalty towards Jewish employees and colleagues amongst the region's leather industry; those who broke this loyalty were shunned.[83] At the time, opinions about the usefulness of the honour courts were divided amongst the Chambers of Industry and Commerce. At IHK Wuppertal, a majority of members seemed to have regarded it as very effective in individual cases but it took more than two years to appoint the court's members.[84]

After the war, it had been the IHK which took the initiative to re-establish honourable business conduct. By 15 February 1946, the Bonn Chamber had established a procedure for an arbitration court (*Schiedsgerichtsordnung*); by late 1948 at least seven other Chambers in the British zone had followed the Bonn example and set up arbitration courts based on the model of the American Arbitration Association for any trading on product bourses.[85] This initial step was meant to guarantee a smooth running of business and fulfilments of contracts by binding both sides to the arbitration outcome. In case of non-observance of the court decision, a participant could be excluded from the specified product bourse. By mid-1948, in the wake of an improving economic situation, the Chambers started looking towards the establishment of honour courts as a way of preventing irregular business practices. That they took this action is a strong indication that there was a level of business misconduct in the post-war years. On the other hand, an initial query at the Cologne Chamber found that its previous honour court had never been used, and it was speculated that 'the sheer existence of the honour court had contributed to a better conduct of the mercantile community'.[86]

The draft proposals for the honour court at IHK Essen shows how much importance was given to proper business conduct. Entrepreneurs and their legal representatives were obliged to keep *Sitte und Anstand* (customs and manners) befitting those of an honourable entrepreneur. Gross violations would be pursued by the honour court, which could impose reprimands, fines or deprive the right to hold a Chamber office. The verdict could also be publicized in Chamber publications or released to the press for wider publication. The court regulations specified that the chairman had to hold the legal qualification of a judge and possess appropriate commercial knowledge.[87] They set a very high standard. The sanctions, in particular the option to release the verdict to the press for wider publication, could easily spell the end of a business since they signified the loss of trust in the indicted entrepreneur. However, it is open for debate why there were only a relatively small number of honour court cases: IHK Essen recorded only about half a dozen instances throughout the 1950s, for example.[88] Based on the significance of honourable conduct, this indicates that the overwhelming number of businessmen running small and medium-sized companies adhered to their own code of conduct and honour, and did so presumably out of conviction and due to their prevailing social mores. A letter by Kurt Birrenbach, chairman of the Thyssen supervisory board to a Herr G.V. Winterhalter, a representative of Birrenbach's former company in Buenos Aires, exemplifies what a bad reputation meant. Birrenbach states that 'Ka', the man Winterhalter had enquired about, had such a bad reputation that Winterhalter's company could not have business contacts with 'Ka', and that even just being associated with him could damage the company's reputation. Birrenbach warned emphatically that 'out of deep and amicable concern that your name should never be associated with this kind of people'.[89]

It may have been those isolated cases which created the belief amongst leading businessmen that there should be a more general and all-encompassing honour code guiding commercial activities, similar to those in the legal and medical professions.[90] Thus in February 1957, the Federation of German Industry announced in one if its circulars that in co-operation with the Federal Employers' Association, they had drafted guidelines for the establishment of industrial honour courts, which would be circulated in due course.[91] Although the existence of the guidelines could not be verified, the BDI announcement had longer-term impacts on some industrial sectors.

The experiences of the *Wirtschaftsvereinigung Eisen und Stahl* (WVES, Iron and Steel Association) during the late 1950s and early 1960s, i.e. before the full onset of the late 1960s steel crisis, will demonstrate how far reputation and honour lost their value amongst top businessmen when big financial stakes were involved. However, in contrast to the functional decline of honour, there remained a strong attachment to the concept of honour itself amongst the leading men of the steel industry. The German steel industry had always been a very close-knit community. This tradition arose not least out of its history, since the industry perceived itself to be surrounded by outside enemies and threats.[92] During the imperial era, there was the fear of ruinous competition, both from abroad and amongst the steel plants themselves, which prompted them to organize in trade associations to which they thought they had to adhere if they wanted to survive. Through the First World War, the steel industrialists had to deal with state intervention aiming to maximize war production.[93] In the Weimar period, they were confronted by more powerful trade unions, a perceived left-wing government and a system of forced arbitration in industrial conflicts, which, time and again, seem to favour labour over industry. In 1928, the steel industrialists even broke the law by ignoring one of those rulings in the infamous *Ruhreisenstreit* (Ruhr iron struggle) when they locked out almost a quarter of a million workers after another arbitration judgement had gone against them.[94] Challenging state authority in such a way was possible only through very disciplined compliance with association policies. The brief honeymoon the steel barons experienced at the beginning of the Nazi rule turned quickly into massive state interference after the introduction of the Four Year Plan in 1936, and culminated in the construction of the Hermann Göring steel plant at Salzgitter.[95] Finally, from 1945 to 1951, the western Allies tried to implement policies of breaking up of the vertically integrated steel companies, dismantling and decartelization which were described by heavy industrialists as a direct threat to their economic survival. All this changed in the 1950s. Under the European Coal and Steel Community (ECSC), many of the companies that had been split up reformed and once the Federal Republic had passed a much watered-down decartelization bill in 1957, political threats of this kind seemed to recede. The disappearance of political threats against heavy industry in the new environment of Ludwig Erhard's market economy meant that the traditional group coherence was no longer necessary. Accordingly, honour as an instrument of group control, as Speitkamp has defined it, did indeed lose its significance within the Iron and Steel Association.

The first significant case of dishonourable conduct within the Association was a serious indiscretion which happened after the 1957 general election. The Association had planned to raise prices after the elections but had to forgo some of the price hikes because they were leaked in advance and Hans-Günther Sohl, as the WVES's chairman, found himself in the awkward position of having to explain the increases to the Federal government. Wilhelm Ahrens, WVES's senior chief clerk, could only complain about this apparent 'lack of common spirit'.[96] Only two months later, in February 1958, Ahrens was in for an even bigger shock. He had sent confidential material to ten leading men of the German steel industry – and one of them passed the material on to the press. Ahrens was so 'seriously appalled' about this lack of integrity that he considered not circulating sensitive material before a meeting and instead distributing information in the meetings themselves.[97]

By 1960, German steel output had reached record levels and the pressure and competition to sell the steel became fierce, which led to constant price concessions and reductions in the agreed price lists by almost all steel producers. In a meeting of the *Diskussionsabend* (DA, Discussion Evening) in November 1961 a new low point was reached. The DAs were highly confidential meetings in private settings, where the top company representatives of the WVES discussed and agreed strategies, including product pricing. The DAs had been introduced by the steel industrialists to avoid accusations of cartel agreements, as they were nominally classed as private, rather than business, meetings. Otto Wolff von Amerongen, owner of the steel trading house Otto Wolff, took personal records of the meeting.[98] Wolff von Amerongen gave one particular agenda point of that November meeting the symptomatic name '*Dreckwerfen*' (mudslinging). It appeared as if Sohl, as chairman of the DA, had deliberately provoked his fellow steel bosses into accusing each other of breaking the agreements to which they had previously all given their word, in order to force an open debate about the behaviour. Wolff von Amerongen recorded thirty minutes of dishonourable accusation and insults. Managers were accused of lying to the chief clerks of an iron and steel sub-association, and calling the chief clerks '*Würstchen*' (literally, this means 'little sausage' but as a diminutive could mean 'poor soul' or 'nobody') and '*Hanswürstchen*' ('clowns'). All of these terms, including 'liar', could have led to a civil court action for the sullying of honour, and show how much nerves were on edge.[99] This lack of civility amongst a group of people that placed such a premium on their reputation is astonishing. Just three years earlier the DA had felt it necessary to discuss the mere rumour that the metal workers' trade union had provided DM 30,000 for the making of the film *Das Mädchen Rosemarie*, about the life and death of West Germany's most famous prostitute, Rosemarie Nitribitt. Her murder in 1957 had never been solved but there had been strong rumours and allegations that leading businessmen had availed themselves of her services. Such disreputable conduct, or worse, the very fact that one of them might be linked to such a high-profile murder case, was not welcome news and had to be prevented at all costs.[100]

After the 'mudslinging' meeting, group coherence seemed to have been restored for a short time but in the spring of 1963, the WVES had to announce the establishment of an honour council for the *Walzstahlvereinigung* (Rolled Steel Association), its most important sub-association. The reason for the establishment was a 'market disturbance' as a result of increasing imports, which led to companies to constantly undercut each other's prices. Herbert Köhler, the association's new senior chief clerk, expressed his confidence to Sohl that 'the mere constitution of an honour council will be sufficient to restore and renew the trust amongst the plants'.[101] The honour council was vested with significant powers. It could appoint independent auditors and 'all parties involved' – the term 'accused' was avoided – had to co-operate fully with the inquiry. If a company was found in breach of agreements, it could be fined DM 10,000 in minor cases. If violations were deemed to be more severe, fines could be imposed which asked for the complete repayment of any illicit rebate granted, plus the same amount of money again to be given as 'a voluntary donation' to the industry's scientific foundation, the *Stifterverband der deutschen Wissenschaft*.[102]

Only two months later, in September 1963, Sohl had to announce that monetary fines were not enough and that the penalties should try to 'grab the person concerned by his honour'.[103] If there were repeated offences, 'personnel consequences' should be applied. This meant that the company had to dismiss the *Verkaufsleiter* (sales manager); if even the board manager responsible for sales was involved in the repeated breach, his contract was to be terminated immediately by the supervisory board. To increase the

Figure 5.1 Hans-Günther Sohl (1906–1989), until 1945 deputy chairman of the Vereinigte Stahlwerke conglomerate, and after the break-up of Vereinigte Stahlwerke chairman of the Thyssen Steel company. He replaced Reusch as the leading man of the German steel industry during its boom years of the 1950s and crisis years of the 1960s. He was the longest-serving chairman of the Iron and Steel Association (1956–69) and BDI president in 1972–76. The photo shows him as BDI president. © Bundesverband der deutschen Industrie, BDI Archiv SF 00 340 009.

pressure on companies to comply with these regulations, Sohl now openly threatened what he had only hinted at during an earlier meeting in May, *Gruppenkampf* (group fight). *Gruppenkampf* had been the last resort of the pre-1933 steel cartels to enforce compliance. If a company refused to follow the agreed rules, the others would terminate any form of co-operation with the offender; in the tightly knit community of the Ruhr's iron and steel industry, this was a heavy penalty. But with the traditional role of honour as a group regulative no longer working, this time it did not bring about more orderly market conduct, as Sohl had hoped. New agreements were broken almost as soon as the Association had worked them out. Worse, in January 1964, the honour council had to write to Sohl to inform him that not only were they unable to detect serious misconduct because the companies involved had closed ranks, but they also had to report that managers were refusing to give their word of honour to confirm their statements. They argued that they regarded their *Ehrenwort* so highly that they would not use it lightly in what they regarded as minor matters.[104] Although this could have been a very simple excuse not to incriminate themselves further, it also shows the great significance businessmen still attached to their word of honour. However, by refusing to give it on matters of such importance to the association, they demonstrated that the traditional group honour was, if not disappearing, then at least changing.[105]

Before the WVES was eventually able to restore price stability in 1966 through the establishment of four *Verkaufskontore* (sales offices), Sohl had to report to the DA about the 'most shocking meeting of his professional life', which had taken place at the Rolled Steel Association's advisory council. Otto Siering of Hüttenwerk Oberhausen refused to participate in any other meeting, because 'at the table sat men who only lied'.[106] There was now clear evidence that some companies had gone so far as to forge their output statistics, a decision that could have come only from the very top of a company, the management board. At this stage, mutual suspicion had replaced any trust and honourable conduct amongst Germany's steel managers.[107] While this development may have been shocking for some of the participants, as the statements of Ahrens or Siering demonstrate, paradoxically it was by no means a sign that the concept of honour had lost its significance for the business community. Seen in the context of the time, it was rather an indication that traditional forms of loyalty were being replaced by new ones. In the wake of the re-ordering of the steel industry by the Allies (and despite considerable re-concentration efforts by the German steel industry), and with the disappearance of outside threats for the Iron and Steel Association, allegiances shifted.[108] Now even more than before, managers' loyalties were with their companies – and their own reputations. Although the steel boom of the 1950s was petering out in the early 1960s, there were still new and bigger production lines coming on stream. In anticipation of further expanding steel markets, chief executives had convinced their supervisory boards to enhance production capacity by building new steel plants. Now, in the face of market saturation and falling prices, it was necessary to undercut agreed prices and shift production in order to use the new capacity. In other words, managers' egos had become more important than association agreements, a turn of events which at least some of the steel managers recognized as having significant negative consequences for the industry.[109] Seen in this way, the 'crisis of honour' within the Iron and Steel Association serves as a good example of Konrad Jarausch's theory of socio-cultural changes as a gradual process caused by small, day-to-day experiences.[110]

Honourable, that is conduct which conforms to group behaviour, was important to German entrepreneurs but in the first instance this honour was owed only to insiders or those who acted in line with the group. In contrast, first-generation newcomers, unless they had special patronage and protection, could not expect any favourable treatment – on the contrary, in fact. The case in point here are the experiences of Berthold Beitz, Walther Rohland, Willy Schlieker and Ernst Hellmut Vits. Beitz had been chairman of the Hamburg insurance company Iduna since 1948 and thus he had had no links to heavy industry. So when Alfried Krupp von Bohlen und Hallbach appointed Bertold Beitz to be his general-plenipotentiary effective from 1 November 1953, this surprise move caused incredible resentment amongst the traditional Krupp directorate. That ill-feeling against the outsider is best illustrated by an event in 1959. Krupp had been commissioned to build the deep-sea diving capsule for the ocean explorer Jacques Picard. At a press event to demonstrate the capsule to the public, Beitz climbed into the submersible only for a member of the Krupp directorate to mumble audibly: 'And now the lid on, this is the opportunity.'[111] This public comment clearly illustrated the 'old guard's' displeasure with, and disrespect for, the newcomer. As an outsider to heavy industry, Beitz could survive as managing director only because he had the complete trust and confidence of Alfried Krupp, who saw Beitz as an opportunity to break with the firm's past. Sustained by Krupp's trust, Beitz was able to 'sit out' the old management until they retired, or he was able to hasten that move for them.[112]

The fate of Walther Rohland, who during the war had risen to become chairman of Vereinigte Stahlwerke, and that of Willy Schlieker, a man who had built one of Germany's most modern post-war shipyards from nothing, are much more typical of the treatment doled out to newcomers. Rohland had begun his career during the 1920s when he joined Deutsche Edelstahlwerke (DEW), a company which was part of the Vereinigte Stahlwerke conglomerate. In 1932, aged only thirty-four, he was made a member of DEW's board. Six years later, in 1938, he had become deputy chairman. From 1940 to 1943, he was chairman of the *Ausschuß Panzerwagen* (committee for tank production) within the armaments ministry, which led to his nickname of 'Panzer Rohland'.[113] Appointed chairman of Vereinigte Stahlwerke in 1943, he ran the company until his arrest by the British in November 1945. Although his denazification in January 1948 classed him, like so many others, as a 'fellow traveller', he was not able to return to his position within Vereinigte Stahlwerke or one of its successor companies. He himself explained in his autobiography that this was because of Russian propaganda, which referred to him still as 'Panzer Rohland', but also because of his outsider-status. He claimed that since he was neither a *Bergassessor*, and nor had he been a member of a duelling student fraternity, nor did he like hunting, one of the Ruhr industrialists' favourite pastimes, he was treated as an outsider.[114] In the light of Rohland's undisputed managerial abilities, this is only half the truth. In fact Rohland had high expectations of running the biggest successor company of Vereinigte Stahlwerke, August Thyssen Hütte, but he was beaten to it by his former deputy. Sohl's later claim that in 1948 no other Vereinigte Stahlwerke board member was interested in the chairmanship of that company because of its alleged uncertain future, is wrong.[115] Rohland was not only beaten to the Thyssen chairmanship, he failed to get appointed to any company chairmanship either: even the supervisory board memberships that were offered to him were no longer those of top companies, but only second-tier ones. Bypassed in this way he set up his own consultancy company, Wedexro, for which Sohl provided some consultancy contracts in Germany and abroad.[116] Sohl's action here are interesting: although Rohland was no longer an 'insider' he nevertheless showed some solidarity to his former boss and arranged some contracts for him, although whether this was due to a guilty conscience or out of genuine loyalty is impossible to say. In any case, Sohl's actions showed far more solidarity than that of many other industrialists, who criticized Rohland's *Umtriebigkeit* (being always on the go) when he explored new business opportunities in India and Pakistan.[117] The general explanation for Rohland failing to regain any significant position in the post-war steel industry is that he lacked full social integration in the industrial circles, as his own statements about not having been a duelling student, a hunter or a *Bergassessor* demonstrate. Rohland also lacked proper pedigree, with his father having been only a small textile manufacturer.[118] However, for a man who was seen as so talented that he would have made his career without Nazi party membership, this explanation is insufficient.[119] There were two more reasons why he did not make the way back to the top, as so many other managers had been able to. First, it was the way he rose to become Vereinigte Stahlwerke chairman, which marked him out as too ambitious, even amongst his fellow industrialists.[120] In his diary, Ludwig Vaubel indicates that over-ambition could actually damage a manager's career when he wrote that he had to take seriously a colleague's warning on the matter.[121] Second, and this is what really damaged Rohland's post-war prospects, as 'steel dictator' during the last phase of the war he had ruthlessly demanded ever higher production targets, irrespective of the military situation and the damage the revised limits did to the steel plants' equipment. Not even his activities to prevent Hitler's 'Nero Order' were enough to make his fellow industrialists forget the brutality with which he had operated before and by so doing, had threatened the interests of the industry.[122]

Willy Schlieker's case is even more illuminating of how outsiders were treated. Like no other Schlieker has to be seen as the example of 'Speer's Kindergarten', ambitious young men who organized Speer's armaments industry.[123] In 1942, aged only twenty-eight, Schlieker had been put in charge of the Ruhr's iron ore allocation system. In this role he became very unpopular with the great and the good of the iron industry because he attempted to apportion the resources in a fairer and more efficient way than hitherto, and in one that was not based on reputation and influence. After the German defeat, Schlieker worked for a brief period for another outsider, Friedrich Flick, where his knowledge of the steel industry made him into the '*Hauptaktivum*' (main assets) of the firm.[124] Because of his extraordinary knowledge of the Ruhr industry, the British Military Government made him an advisor on industrial policy. In this position he annoyed the steel barons twice more when in 1946 he openly advocated the nationalization of the iron and steel industry, and then he complained to the British about the close co-operation between the newly established Iron and Steel Association and the *Verwaltungsamt für Stahl* (Steel Administration Office), a body set up by the British for the running of the steel industry.[125] Following an anonymous and false accusation, he lost this post. In 1948 he bought the name of a defunct steel mill with the intention, as he put it, 'to encroach into the *Naturschutzpark* (nature reserve) that is the iron industry'. With the new company he was able to establish a virtual monopoly on the production of electric sheet plates because at the time the previous suppliers were subject to Allied dismantling.[126] The son of a shipyard worker, Schlieker expanded his endeavours into shipping construction where he bought and modernized a number of shipyards. During the Korean War, he increased his fortune by engaging in a barter trade with American coal for German steel.[127] Although economically very successful, Schlieker was even more of an outsider then Rohland. Both at the Ruhr, and even more so in Hamburg's traditional business circles, he was seen as a nouveau riche and uncultured upstart. This impression is confirmed in his mini-biography featured in *Neue Männer an der Ruhr*. With an annual turnover of more than DM 450 million across his companies, his biography speaks of Schlieker now being recognized, albeit grudgingly, by the Ruhr elites. Quite striking, though, is the fact that only in his case does the book mention the denazification he had to undergo; in the cases of the other industrialists this blot on their CVs had been omitted. Schlieker's wish to be 'first and foremost a *Fabrikant*' (manufacturer)[128] contributed to his downfall. Without any business network and having concentrated all his wealth in his firms instead of holding a wider share portfolio, his structural economic weakness became obvious in 1962 when he faced a cash-flow problem. It was then that his main creditors, the Salzgitter and Phoenix Rheinrohr steelworks, refused to extend his payment deadlines and, together with Dresdner Bank, prevented Schlieker's rescue attempts. At the time, Phoenix Rheinrohr held 50 per cent of the shares of Blohm und Voss shipyard, while Salzgitter had significant interests in Howaldswerft shipyard, Schlieker's two main competitors. Thus it made more commercial sense for them to let Schlieker go under than to rescue him, as they could take over his workforce and his very modern production facilities.[129] However, commercial reasons were not the only factor here. Schlieker's former close associates from the time in the armaments ministry, Ernst Wolf Mommsen and Hans-Günther Sohl, now in charge at Phoenix and the Thyssen group respectively (to which Phoenix belonged), refused to come to his aid.[130] While Sohl in his memoirs expressed regret about Schlieker's downfall, this should be rather seen as crocodile tears, as August Thyssen Hütte was able to absorb Schlieker's highly profitable thin sheet works. The case also questions Sohl's claim that he had adopted a business principle from his former mentor Albert Vögler, 'who had said that if he had to choose between friendship and business, he would always choose friendship'.[131] In contrast to Rohland's case, Sohl was not willing to give breathing space to the newcomer. Schlieker's cash-flow problem was rather an opportunity to pay him back for his previous lack of respect for the Ruhr's great and good.

Finally, the importance of group solidarity becomes most obvious when we compare the experiences of Heinrich Dinkelbach and Ernst Hellmut Vits. Dinkelbach, from a humble background, had risen to become one of the managing directors of Vereinigte Stahlwerke, where he had managed to introduce a standardized accounting system for all its 177 subsidiary companies. Although nominally a Nazi party member he was one of the very few steel managers not summarily arrested by the British, but instead appointed trustee for the expropriated steel companies. Grunenberg speculates that this had to do with him being a Roman Catholic and steeped in that religion's social teaching, with connections to Karl Arnold, the left-of-centre CDU Minister President of North-Rhine Westphalia since 1947.[132] However, it is more likely that his appointment was because of the so-called 'Dinkelbach memorandum' of October 1945. In the memorandum he suggested hiving off those steel plants which had already received Allied permission to operate from their mother companies in order to get the reconstruction going, something the other steel managers saw as an unacceptable, deliberate break-up of their companies. When Dinkelbach as steel trustee also favoured co-determination, he had finally gone too far and suffered the wrath of his peers. From 1946–47 until well after the *Stahltreuhand* had been dissolved in 1953, Dinkelbach was continuously and heavily criticized for his activities.[133] For his work as steel trustee and the attempts to break with the Ruhr's traditional cartel policy, he had to pay the price of ostracism, receiving only offers for supervisory board membership of second-tier companies.[134] This contrasts very much with the career of Vits, the managing director of Vereinigte Glanzstoff Fabriken. During the war, he had also been chairman of the Reich association for chemical fibres but unlike Rohland, had never pushed too hard for total war mobilization. Although also a party member, the British military government appointed him a trustee of VGF in 1945 and then, in 1947, financial advisor to the Combined Coal Group, another Allied control body loathed by German industry.[135] What is different in Vits's case is that in none of his roles did he step out of line, but rather skilfully advocated the interests of German industry.[136] What is more, Vits acted as witness for the defence during the Nuremberg industrialists' trials, which Ludwig Vaubel commented on in his diary as 'a thankless task' of having to step 'into the spotlight . . . displaying a strong *esprit de corps* while others chickened out'.[137] It was not least the display of this *esprit de corps* which allowed Vits to continue his successful career unimpeded during the 1950s and 1960s.

How important this feeling of *Zusammengehörigkeit*, or belonging, has been in the post-war years becomes obvious when heavy industry's behaviour in the case of Krupp is considered. As part of his sentence at the Nuremberg War Crimes Trial, Alfried Krupp was required to sell off significant sections of his company, a move which also formed part of the American decartelization programme. However, the company was supposedly unable to find a buyer for these prized assets, as the other Ruhr industrialists, in a show of solidarity, refused to make any offers. This charade continued until Alfried Krupp's death in 1967, when the sales obligation ceased.[138] Although in many cases it would have made economic sense for companies to acquire parts of Krupp, either to consolidate their product range or as an extension to company re-integration subsequent to Allied decartelization, their group loyalty to an 'insider' and a perceived victim of Allied persecution did not allow this to happen. Breaking this code of behaviour would have led to social and economic ostracism. Not even Friedrich Flick, big industry's *enfant terrible* was prepared to take this risk.[139] In any case, the different treatment the 'insider' Krupp received to the 'outsider' Schlieker is striking.

This 'one of us' feeling and the resulting group loyalty and group honour was extremely prevalent amongst entrepreneurs in the post-war period, as two more examples will demonstrate. When Jakob Reichert, the senior chief clerk of the Iron and Steel Association's predecessor organization, the Wirtschaftsgruppe Eisenschaffende Industrie, committed suicide in early 1948 and his widow faced economic difficulties, the WVES stepped in without hesitation and provided an exceptional pension for her although there had been no requirement to do so.[140] Similarly, when a former Gutehoffnungshütte manager, who had moved to the European Coal and Steel Community's High Authority on behalf of the WVES, died in a car crash while on a work trip, the Association's board minutes stated that the association '*darf jetzt nicht kleinlich sein*' ('must now not be petty').[141] Although the widow was entitled to three months' of her late husband's ECSC salary, and again had no legal claim against the Association, the steel managers found it necessary and appropriate to pay the funeral costs and also award her a pension from the WVES coffers.[142] This feeling of '*Ehrenschuld*' (a debt of honour) was widespread amongst German entrepreneurs outside heavy industry, too. During the 1930s, Berlin merchants felt 'honour-bound' to support and raise funds for an old age pension home for merchants who had fallen on hard times because of the 1923 hyperinflation. Once again, by the early 1950s, they had recapitalized their *Notkasse für notleidende Kaufleute* (emergency fund for merchants in economic distress) with DM 600,000. As this happened in the face of an overall very poor economic situation in early 1950s Berlin, it has to be assumed that much of the funds raised were provided from the personal wealth of the members.[143]

A strong honour code, based on traditional nineteenth-century bourgeois perceptions, and which clearly distinguished between 'insiders' and 'outsiders' and was combined with a very strong demand for, and willingness to give, group loyalty determined entrepreneurs' social interactions well into the post-war years. Exceptions were possible only to maverick entrepreneurs who had a strong enough power base of their own, best symbolized perhaps by Friedrich Flick;[144] but he, too, had to make sure that he did not go too far. Only in the 1960s did some of these aspects of group cohesion begin to disappear, as has been demonstrated with the example of the unruly and not very honourable discussions at the *Diskussionsabende*. But these quarrels, too, did not mean an end to 'honourable' conduct overall; they merely signify a change in what was seen as permissible within the new framework of the more competitive social market economy. This change allowed a wider scope of business conduct for the individual companies over the rule of the associations. However, as will be shown in the next chapter, the associations remained at the heart of the German business community.

6

Politics: Business, Associations and the State

In the post-war years, there were two very striking features about German industrialists' interactions with the 'polis'. First, they claimed in their overwhelming majority to have never been politically active, that they in fact were apolitical because they were focussed so much on running their businesses. While it is true that very few German industrialists in the interwar years got actively involved in high politics – the most famous exceptions being Walther Rathenau, Gustav Stresemann and, until his unexpected death in 1924, Hugo Stinnes – this does not mean that industrialists were not entangled in politics in the wider sense. To assume so would reduce politics merely to discussions in, and acts of, Parliament. Such a gross reduction would completely disregard any lobbying by businessmen and other players with economic interests, such as the farmers' lobby, for or against any legislation which had the slightest economic implications.[1] Businessmen did influence Weimar politics and perhaps the most political act by heavy industrialists in the interwar years was the lock-out of almost 250,000 workers during the so-called *Ruhreisenstreit* of 1928, in response to an industrial arbitration tribunal decision which had ruled against them. Weimar industrialists, furthermore, tried to influence politics through the press empires which had been set up by former Krupp director Alfred Hugenberg, who was also chairman of the conservative Deutsch-Nationale Volkspartei (DNVP, German National People's Party) and Gutehoffnungshütte chairman Paul Reusch, although the actual political influence of these newspapers is disputed.[2] The second important feature was the re-establishment of industrial associations and the prominent place those took for some time in German public life. Associations had traditionally been at the centre of industrialists' political lobbying and it is therefore not surprising that so much energy was used to re-establish them after the war.

This chapter will show that the claim of being non-political was very much a myth, based on an 'unpolitical German bourgeoisie' which had developed in the late nineteenth century, as discussed in Chapter 5.[3] After 1945 they deliberately used a very narrow definition of '(un)political', but this time it was merely an excuse in the face of Allied denazification policies and the post-war accusations of collaborating with the Nazis. In reality, even though many leading men did not (re-)join a political party in the Federal Republic, entrepreneurs and managers were nonetheless heavily involved in West German politics. Closely intertwined with the question of industrialists' political involvement were business and industrial associations and the matter of their political power, which came to a head in the second part of the 1950s as a public debate about, and warning against, the *Herrschaft der Verbände*,[4] the rule of the associations, over the state.

During the time of the Weimar Republic, many owners of small and medium-sized companies had been politically active at a local level in the liberal Deutsche Demokratische Partei (DDP) or the national-liberal Deutsche Volkspartei (DVP). When they had to explain their political activities of the pre-Nazi period and then their subsequent Nazi party membership to denazification panels, they described themselves as '*gänzlich unpolitisch*' (utterly unpolitical).[5] This self-proclaimed lack of political involvement – political illiteracy, if you will – was an attempt to explain away the fact that they *had* been involved with the Nazi reign on a very large scale. Reutlingen, a town in Wuerttemberg dominated by small and medium-sized businesses, can be seen as representative of many other German business communities. At the end of the war, 62 per cent of all Reutlingen business owners had been members of the Nazi party. During their denazification process they excused their membership as 'having been for economic reasons only', in order to avoid negative actions by party officials against their companies.[6] After the war, many German entrepreneurs renewed and upheld the claim of being apolitical. Partly as a response to the humiliation of the denazification process, where they had to explain and defend their Nazi party membership, participation in a political party became anathema for many of them. In the climate of the Cold War some feared that if Western Europe was attacked by the Soviet Union, they would be even more victimized by the Soviets, for being 'capitalists' and for being members of democratic parties.[7] Hans-Günther Sohl gives a similar excuse in his autobiography, where he stated that he refused Adenauer's invitation to join the CDU because his experience of his Nazi party membership 'still stuck in his marrow'.[8]

Gabriel A. Almond's contemporary study criticizes industrialists for their 'political irresponsibility', for not playing a more dynamic role in the development of post-war German democracy. However, this argument of the non-political entrepreneur in general and of the Ruhr's heavy industrialists in particular follows the industrialists' own narrow definition of 'political'.[9] On a closer look, he provides plenty of examples of entrepreneurial involvement in politics in some form or another. Most significantly, 15 per cent of the first Bundestag's MPs came, broadly speaking, from the business community, a figure which rose to 25 per cent of deputies after the 1953 elections, although many of these were association functionaries, not entrepreneurs.[10] This rise had been due to a decisive campaign during 1951 and 1952, led by BDI chief clerk Gustav Stein, to find more willing and suitable parliamentary candidates. During a speech to BDI *Geschäftsführer* and BDI regional associations (*Landesverbände*) in early summer 1952, he explained that industrialists' influence of the elections with legal means was 'economic policy of the highest level and fundamental (*ureigenst*) form' and that industrialists had to provide ideational (*ideelle*) support. He demanded the creation of entrepreneurial class consciousness (*Standesbewußtsein*) and to quietly act in a political way and called for more entrepreneurs as parliamentary candidates. He concluded the speech by declaring that: 'The 1953 election campaign will be the battle of Lechfeld of modern entrepreneurial history. Either we will be submerged by collectivism, or we prevail, despite heavy losses, for which we are prepared.'[11] The speech's content and language reveal several interesting points; first and foremost it obviously once again debunks the myth of the 'unpolitical entrepreneur'. That Stein had to emphasize the legality of any support for political parties demonstrates that there was still a lingering fear of being accused of extra-legal machinations, which could have led to further attacks against the entrepreneurial class. Similarly, talking about ideational support only and not financial donations (the size of which will be discussed below) is another sign that entrepreneurs were concerned about their reputation, that they did not want to have been seen as 'buying' the election or influencing its outcome by throwing their money around. Declaring the 1953 elections to be businesses' modern equivalent of the Lechfeld battle in 955, which traditionally has been seen as the birth of the German nation, was strong language even for the time, and was reminiscent of the tone of Nazi newsreels. It shows that, despite all the progress the German economy had made since 1948/9, and for which entrepreneurs liked to take the credit, there was still a high level of insecurity, even fear, about the Federal Republic's political future, and with it that of the country's economic order.

Stein's campaign certainly paid off. During the BDI's members' meeting in May 1953, he could report significant progress. Once again deliberately bypassing the '*materielle Unterstützung*', i.e. the financial contributions, he was very pleased with the record numbers of parliamentary candidates from business backgrounds.[12] The 1953 general elections resulted in 336 government coalition MPs (out of a total of 487); fifty-five of them were from agriculture and its affiliated associations and 111 came from industry, trade and commerce.[13] To put these figures into perspective: in 1959, there were a total of three million self-employed in West Germany, about 210,000 of whom had businesses with more than ten employees. The total population numbered some 55 million in 1960, and thus the 'unpolitical' business community was rather over-represented in parliament.[14] While a good number of these deputies came from small and medium-sized companies, dispelling the myth of the unpolitical SME entrepreneur even further, about twenty MPs came from large companies and influential industrial associations; however, the largest number of MPs linked to business worked in the lower tiers of industry's self-administering bodies, including the Chambers of Industry and Commerce. Arguably the most important new entrant into Parliament from the perspective of big business was the DII's central figure, Fritz Hellwig.[15] He quickly rose to become chairman of Parliament's Economic Policy Committee and was eventually named by industry as a contender to succeed Ludwig Erhard as economics minister when the latter was rumoured to be a potential Federal President in 1959. Hellwig stepped down as MP shortly after the presidential affair to become a member of the Coal and Steel Community's High Authority, a loss bitterly bemoaned by Stein.[16] In any case, Stein's pleasure in 1953 about the large number of MPs linked to business did not last long. When he addressed the Institut für die Niedersächsische Wirtschaft (Institute for the Economy of Lower Saxony) in June 1956, he complained that only two men of stature were representing business interests, namely Robert Pferdmenges and Hans Wellhausen.[17] In 1961, the year Stein himself was elected as an MP, he extended his criticism. He complained about the lack of political activity amongst businessmen at local level and pointed to the fact that only 5 to 7 per cent of councillors in town and city councils were business tax payers; and amongst those were a large proportion of small traders, which meant that the

Figure 6.1 Gustav Stein (1903–1979), BDI *Hauptgeschäftsführer* (senior chief clerk) and together with Fritz Berg one of the association's conservative hardliners. Stein was one of the BDI's most politically active functionaries and himself a Member of Parliament from 1961 to 1972. © Bundesverband der deutschen Industrie, BDI Archiv SF 00 358 001.

'prestigious entrepreneurs' (*repräsentative Unternehmer*) had an even smaller representation. Overall he criticized what he regarded as mediocre candidates that represented the bourgeois parties in local government.[18] One has to remember that Stein himself was not an entrepreneur, but that he held a post which, in another context, he himself would have called that of a bureaucrat or a functionary. Nevertheless, he not only criticized entrepreneurs for prioritizing their businesses over engagement in local government, but also devalued the efforts of small traders altogether by implying that they were not actually businessmen. Put differently, in his view only a businessman whose company was of a certain size could be a 'real' entrepreneur. A similar level of snobbery was directed against the bourgeois parties in general. By saying that their representatives in local government were mediocre, he implied that 'real' businessmen would and could do a better job.

Stein had made similar comments before. For example, at the sixth *Baden-Badener Unternehmergespräch* in May 1957, he had given a talk on 'the political responsibility of the entrepreneur'. His central argument was that a state needed an elite and that entrepreneurs were this elite. 'Where once the best men of a city parliament [the merchants] determined the fate of a city, there sit now completely inadequate people. . . .

Do not leave the field to those kind of people who, for the sheer lack of expertise, are unable to take the right decisions.'[19] Stein did not have to spell out to his audience that he thought only entrepreneurs were able to take these decisions. He had acted as editor of the 1954 book *Unternehmer in der Politik* (*Entrepreneurs in Politics*), which he most likely had initiated in the first place. In the book's foreword he explained that it had been written as an attempt to strengthen democracy in West Germany and to spare it the fate of the Weimar Republic. He then spelled out what many entrepreneurs at the time believed about political and social leadership and their role in it: because the previous leading class of society, e.g. the landed aristocracy, no longer existed or was no longer able to lead politically, it was now up to them to lead the country. Stein argued that due to his personality, the entrepreneur was at the core of a new aristocracy of merit, an aristocracy which guaranteed order and material wealth.[20]

While industrialists saw themselves as the country's new elite, called upon to lead in both economy and in politics,[21] 'the firm' remained at the centre of most businessmen's thinking. Although there was general satisfaction amongst industrialists about their extended representation and influence in Parliament after the 1953 elections, business remained at the centre of their actions. This is demonstrated by Günter Henle's decision before the 1953 election not to stand again. When he announced this to Adenauer, very much to the Chancellor's displeasure, Henle explained that his decision was driven by the need to take more care of the family business.[22] As a former diplomat, Henle's withdrawal from active politics was a blow to Adenauer, who valued Henle's foreign policy advice, in particular on France, as well as his support for the European Coal and Steel Community. He saw Henle as one of the few entrepreneurs who 'thought in political concepts'.[23] Prioritizing business over politics applied not only to owner-entrepreneurs such as Henle, though, but also to salaried managers. Hermann Reusch, as chairman of the board of managers of Gutehoffnungshütte one of those '*beauftragte Unternehmer*', tried unsuccessfully to convince his fellow board member Martin Blank not to stand again for the Bundestag in 1953, citing the reason that he was needed in the company.[24]

Not all industrialists enjoyed their time in parliament. MAN board member and FDP MP Hans Wellhausen, chairman of the Bundestag Finance Committee, expressed his deep disappointment about the 'spreading of parliamentarianism' in a letter to Reusch when he stepped down as an MP in 1957. By this he meant the 'escalating egotism and lobbyism in Parliament' which he saw in particular in his party colleague, Thomas Dehler, but also in the CDU's pension reform. He accused the party of 'making political conquests through social policy' and giving in time and again to demands of the *Mittelstand* lobby; he then extended criticism to the orthodox policy of Finance Minister Fritz Schäffer. Despite his overall disappointment, he reserved the option of another candidacy in four years' time if the situation were to improve.[25] While some parts of Wellhausen's criticism would not be out of place today, it also demonstrates his understanding of politics. For him, this was not so much about what the majority wanted (or what would please the majority), but what he thought was right. His frustration shows that he approached parliamentary proceedings from the point of view of a manager and the belief that he knew better how government business should really be conducted.

Only a small number of deputies with a real industrial background chose the parliamentary benches over their executive offices and became full-time politicians, or at best, part-time managers. Amongst them were Kurt Birrenbach, supervisory board chairman of Thyssen, who became the CDU's foreign affairs spokesman, and Gutehoffnungshütte's Martin Blank, who had co-drafted the FDP's economic policy manifesto.[26] The majority of MPs with a business connection, in particular those whose who had come from jobs with business associations, stayed on in both roles. The best examples here were Robert Pferdmenges, who, next to the bank's owner, Baron Oppenheim, not only remained the leading man at Bankhaus Sal. Oppenheim but also supervisory board member of more than twenty companies; similarly Gustav Stein, the BDI's senior chief clerk, also continued his work at the industrial federation. In particular the parliamentary seats held by association officials were increasingly seen as almost an association entitlement. The seat which had been held by Günter Henle became known as the 'Henle mandate' and it was up to the Iron and Steel Association to nominate a candidate for it.[27] The strength of this entitlement is expressed in Sohl's autobiography. When the Iron and Steel Association's long-serving chief clerk Hans Dichgans stepped down as an MP (he held the seat from 1961 to 1972), he was succeeded by Herbert Köhler, the association's new chief clerk. The handover prompted Sohl to write, unhesitatatingly, about the entitlement of 'the continuation of the association's Bundestag tradition'.[28]

Business's influence in Parliament extended further than the sheer number of MPs. Because of their particular knowledge (and, of course, particular interests), many of them served on important committees, for example, the finance and tax committees, often as chairman or at least as deputy chairman, so that they could influence debates about draft legislation at a very early stage.[29] There was, of course, also considerable behind-the-scene political lobbying, either directly by industrialists or by Robert Pferdmenges, who, as Adenauer's economic confident and advisor, was 'the crucial contact point between government and industry'.[30] The 'Pferdmenges connection' worked the other way round as well: when Adenauer was in political trouble, for example, he could use his banker friend to influence individual deputies and through them the liberal party, the FDP. Such action was suggested to him by his *Fraktionsführer* (chief whip), Heinrich von Brentano, during the coalition negotiation following the 1961 general election, when the FDP came up with considerable political demands and Adenauer was threatened by the real possibility of not being re-elected as Chancellor with an absolute majority in the first or second ballot.[31] In 1953, Pferdmenges initiated the establishment of Chancellor Adenauer's *Küchenkabinett* (kitchen cabinet), made up of businessman and bankers; since 1949 he had also been a member of Adenauer's own 'Federal Chancellor's Working Party for Economic Policy Questions' (*Kleiner Arbeitskreis des Bundeskanzlers für wirtschaftspolitische Fragen*). Another member of this committee was the newly elected president of the Federation of German Industry, Fritz Berg.[32] Berg was the man who would take political lobbying in Germany to new heights. As a member of the *Küchenkabinett*, which had been established as an economic counterweight to Erhard, Berg had almost unlimited access to the Chancellor.[33] An arch conservative, choleric, rash in his outbursts and categorical in his statements, Berg symbolized the stereotype of the uncompromising master-in-the house industrialist. In addition to the confidential talks he had with Adenauer at least once or twice a month, they had also extensive mail correspondence and telephone conversations. This elevated status may have contributed to some of his imprudent press statements. In July 1962, he spoke out in favour of financing political parties out of the public purse, because 'this would save industry money ... since we could then follow the route taken in other countries and simply buy the necessary numbers of MPs'.[34] The BDI press office was forced to publish a strong denial of the quote and demanded a correction and apology from the journalist.[35] At the height of the debate about the revaluation of the Deutschmark, Berg explained that he 'only had to go to Adenauer to get Erhard's plans for economic damping off the table'.[36] On this occasion, however, he got it wrong. Hardly a week after Adenauer had given Berg his word that there would be no revaluation of the German currency, on 6 March 1961 the Deutschmark was indeed revalued from DM 4.20 to DM 4 to the dollar. A furious Berg offered his resignation to the BDI board – and withdrew the BDI's monthly donation of DM 100,000 to the CDU.[37] Two years earlier, during the early stages of the 'presidential crisis' Berg also played a dubious role. Federal President Theodor Heuss's second term in office was ending in autumn 1959, which meant a successor had to be found as the Constitution did not allow a third term. When suddenly Ludwig Erhard's name was mentioned for

Figure 6.2 Fritz Berg (1901–1979). The longest-serving BDI president, Berg was very much the man of conservative heavy industry despite the fact that he himself was classed (and saw himself) as a *selbstständiger Unternehmer*. Berg's politically incorrect comments throughout his career were infamous. © Bundesverband der deutschen Industrie, BDI Archiv SF 00 347 001.

the post, Berg had to deny that it was he who had made the suggestion.[38] Although it would have suited Berg to get rid of the economics minister, with whom he had an increasingly tense relationship, by directing him into a merely ceremonial role (and thus also prevent him from becoming Chancellor), it is more likely that Adenauer himself had started the rumour.[39]

Business tried other forms of political influence and opinion-making, which was intended to reach a far wider audience. This came in form of advertisement through *Die Waage* (The Scales), an incorporated society which had been founded in 1952 with the aim of supporting the social market economy and backing the re-election of the bourgeois parties. Equipped with an annual budget of about DM 2 million, in 1954 it placed advertisements in 70 per cent of all West German newspapers, reaching an estimated 90 per cent of the total readership.[40] The *Waage's* perhaps best-known advertisement was published on the eve of the 1953 general elections. In two columns, West Germany's dire economic circumstances prior to the currency reform were compared with, and contrasted to, the improved situation in the summer of 1953. The ad ended with an appeal to continue the economic improvements by voting 'for a party that declares themselves for Erhard's Social Market Economy'.[41] Although the economics minister was explicitly named in the advert, it was not an outright electoral appeal for the CDU. For one, Erhard at the time was not a CDU party member; he officially joined the party only in 1963 just before he succeeded Adenauer as Chancellor. Until then he was in some respect politically closer to the FDP.[42] Second, in 1953, the smaller parties in Adenauer's coalition government, the FDP and the DP, were in some ways even more business friendly than the CDU, which still contained a strong socially oriented labour wing. Influential MPs from FDP and DP had strong links to the business community, such as the leading DP parliamentarian Hans-Christoph Seebohm, who was president of the IHK Braunschweig, or FDP man and MAN board member Hans Wellhausen, the co-writer of the FDP's economic policy programme.[43]

A noteworthy detail about *Die Waage* is the fact that it was initiated and supported not by heavy industry, which was otherwise often at the forefront of involvement into political schemes, but by the consumer goods industries, in particular from the retail sector, and the chemical industry.[44] The reason for this is simple: the consumer goods industry had profited from Erhard's economic reforms in the wake of the currency reform more than any other industry. Heavy industry, in contrast, had been rather neglected by Erhard, at least until the Korean crisis and the launch of the *Investitionshilfe Gesetz*. Furthermore, there was also considerable resistance amongst the coal and steel industrialists to Erhard's anti-cartel policy, which they perceived as going against their traditions and interests.

The sheer scale of direct or indirect monetary contributions to bourgeois political parties not only challenges the claim of the 'unpolitical' entrepreneur, they directly refute it. The suspension of BDI donations to the CDU mentioned above was only temporary and was lifted prior to the upcoming elections. As early as 14 April 1961 the CDU treasurer was able to announce that despite the so far only hesitant individual donations, the 1961 election campaign could be regarded as financially secured. Industry had confirmed that it would make two donations of DM 10 million each.[45] Links between entrepreneurs and the bourgeois parties went back to the occupation period and the early years of the FRG. They usually ran under the label of 'defence against the socialist threat' and encouraged the CDU to nominate candidates for the elections to Chamber of Industry and Commerce bodies.[46] In 1952, Lower Saxony's Chambers of Industry and Commerce, together with industrial and employer organizations, established the *Institut für die Niedersächsische Wirtschaft* (Institute for Lower Saxony's Economy). The Institute's purpose was to act as a 'cloak' for clandestine political financing, so that none of the IHK or other associations appeared publically as party donors; in North Rhine-Westphalia, the *Verein zur Förderung der Sozialen Markwirtschaft in Nordrhein-Westfalen* (Association for the Advancement of the Social Market Economy in North-Rhine Westphalia) had the same function.[47] The significant donations, however, were collected by and channelled through the industrial associations or given by individual firms. A good example of the latter happened in the run-up to the 1957 general election. Fritz Berg, this time in his capacity as member of the *Staatsbürgerliche Vereinigung*, another body established to launder political donations, in a letter to Thyssen's supervisory board chairman Birrenbach asked for campaign donations. Berg explained the *Vereinigung's* need for funding for the forthcoming elections, and, in contrast to the real political situation, painted an almost apocalyptic electoral scenario with the socialists rampant, and asked for the sum of DM 200,000. In his reply, Birrenbach agreed with Berg's political analysis and volunteered to donate DM 250,000.[48] As it happened, Birrenbach himself was a CDU parliamentary candidate and was elected to the Bundestag, as the CDU achieved the first and so far only absolute majority in post-war German federal elections. There is the slight irony that the victory was in large part due to the CDU's pension reform, which had been heavily opposed by businesses.

Overall, BDI donations to the conservative political parties prior to general elections were considerable. For the 1949 elections, which were seen by many entrepreneurs as a 'fight for survival' in case of a Social Democratic victory, between DM 2 and 3 million were provided for the CDU, FDP and DP or their precursor organizations. In an interview with *Der Spiegel* in November 1959, Gustav Stein confirmed annual average donations to the conservative parties outside the election years 'of not more than' DM 7 million, with another DM 5.7 million channelled through the *Staatsbürgerliche Vereinigung*. During election years, donations were significantly higher; for example, DM 19.4 million was provided for the 1957 federal elections alone.[49]

Compared to other European countries, where political donations were not uncommon, it was in the first instance the scale of the donations and their denial which made West German industrialists stand out. Their hypocrisy becomes even more obvious when they accused the trade unions of political meddling through their donations for the Social Democrats. Ultimately, the involvement of industrialists and industrial associations in politics shows two things: first, although there was only a relatively small number of men in Parliament who were related to business and industry, these numbers were still considerably higher than businesses' share in the total population. Their actual political influence was enhanced by their work in important committees, in which they often enough held the chair, and in which they could influence legislation in their favour. Furthermore, even if industrialists outside

Parliament did not belong to a political party, unpolitical they were certainly not. Second, much of the political influence held by business in West Germany's state or federal parliaments was wielded through industrial associations, mainly in two ways. Associations were able to get a number of highly qualified staff as candidates, either into safe constituencies or onto secure party list positions and from there elected into Parliament, where they took up key positions in influential committees. The parties conceded these positions in the first instance because of the significant amounts of money the associations had provided for them, either due to 'special funds' or, more commonly, through fundraising campaigns, in particular before elections. Here, too, the reality of political involvements belied the public statements as pure hypocrisy. The influence of associations in German political and economic life cannot be underestimated. By 1953, there were again 550 *Fachverbände* (industrial branch associations) in the Federal Republic, and an estimated total of 1,800 economic and socio-political associations representing some 100,000 employers.[50] Association membership was not a token gesture either. Braunthal estimated that German companies were paying as much as 2 per cent of their total sales turnover to the Federation of German Industries and other associations, either as membership dues or special donations.[51]

This very strong bond to associations had been in the making for almost 80 years. Ranging back to the 1870s, Germany's industrial associations had developed into very powerful, but sometimes competing, organizations. Following the creation in 1876 of the *Centralverband der deutschen Industriellen* (CDI, Central Association of German industrialists), which had been initiated by south German textile industrialists and heavy industrialists, a large number of *Zweck-* (for a particular purpose), *Fach-* (for sections or branches of an industry), regional and *Spitzenverbände* (top or umbrella associations) emerged during the *Kaiserreich.* A significant part in the CDI's creation had also the *Verein zur Wahrung der gemeinsamen wirtschaftlichen Interessen in Rheinland und Westfalen* (Association for the Protection of the Economic Interests in the Rhineland and in Westphalia), which had been established in 1871 by heavy industry and textile industrialists in present day North-Rhine Westphalia.[52] The association became simply known as the *Langnam Verein* (Long Name Association) as even for German tastes the name was too cumbersome in everyday use. Both within the *Langnam* association and the CDI, heavy industry quickly became the dominant, but not hegemonic, influence. It was because of their preference for cartels and the pursuit of protectionist tariff policies, which they had in common with the agrarian lobby, that in 1895 the rival *Bund der Industriellen* (Federation of Industrialists) was established by sections of the export-oriented manufacturing industry as a second top association.[53] Of the two, the CDI remained far more influential, better organized and financially prosperous, since two important manufacturing sectors, chemicals and machine tool manufacturing, did not join the *Bund der Industriellen.* Only during the First World War did the two associations begin to work together and set up the *Kriegsausschuß der deutschen Industrie* (KADI, War Committee of the German Industry), to strengthen their position in negotiations with the government. Subsequently, in April 1919 they merged into the *Reichsverband der deutschen Industrie* (RDI, Reich's Association of German Industry).[54] The RDI had significant political influences, with contacts to the ministerial bureaucracy in both the Economics and Finance Ministry, but also because they were able to win high-ranking civil servants as association chief clerks. Although heavy industry was again dominant in the RDI, providing the association chairmen from 1919–25 (Krupp director Kurt Sorge) and 1931–33 (Gustav Krupp von Bohlen und Halbach), compromises with other industrial branches had to be found. This is particularly true on the trade union issue and whether or not they should tolerate Social Democratic participation in government. On both accounts heavy industry, together with small and medium-sized companies, found themselves at odds with the electrical, chemical and parts of the manufacturing industry which were far more flexible and willing to compromise in both fields.[55] This split in entrepreneurs' opinion on how to deal with the trade unions would re-emerge again during the late 1940s and 1950s. The infamous activities of at least large sections of the RDI in the last phase of the Weimar Republic were not aimed at bringing Hitler to power but rather at replacing the democratic system with an authoritarian one that was more favourable to their wishes. It was therefore not industrialists' support for the Nazis, but rather their unwillingness to defend the Republic, which contributed to Hitler's accession to power.[56]

Following Hitler's 'seizure of power', the industrial associations were brought (or fell) into line as well, signified by the dissolution of the RDI in 1933 and the creation, in January 1935, of the *Reichsgruppe Industrie*, which also contained the Reich's employer associations. There was little resistance to this process because it had considerable benefits for industry. Trade unions had been dissolved and the *Führer* principle introduced in companies and associations, allowing a much more authoritarian leadership. More importantly from the associations' point was that association membership was now compulsory but as long as they were not challenged in their decisions, the Nazis continued to allow industrial self-organization and administration. Matt Bera's recent study has shown that active collaboration of an association chief clerk could massively increase his power (as in the case of Karl Lange, of the Machine Tool Manufacturing Association) to unprecedented levels, or led to him and the association being side-lined (as in the case of Jakob Reichert of the Iron and Steel Association).[57] It was Reichert's inability to retain the association's influence which in turn led to him not being re-appointed to his old post after 1945 even though he had not been a party member. His place was taken by men who *had* joined the party and had learned how to operate their new powers effectively under the Nazi system. From an association's perspective, the most important point was that these men would be able eventually to carry some of the new association powers into the post-war era.

After Germany's defeat, the initial price for the associations' compliance came in the form of Allied dissolution or suspension of all industrial associations, except the Chambers of Industry and Commerce. Despite this ban, and in the absence of any functioning state administration, industrialists came together as early as May or June 1945 to discuss their situation, take stock of supplies, equipment and workforce and consider how to best restart production. The experiences in the iron and steel industry were typical of this development.[58] The invitation to one such meeting happened '*auf Anordnung Herrn Sohls*' ('as ordered by Herr Sohl'), which demonstrates the continued self-confidence German steel industrialists, based on their almost 100-year-long tradition, still had despite the lost war and occupation.[59] The meetings took place in so-called *Kreisen* (circles), such as the *Sohl-Kreis* (Sohl circle), the *Notkreis* (emergency circle), or the *Eisenkreis* (iron circle). A clear distinction between the different circles and their function is difficult, almost impossible;[60] it is not clear if the sometimes interchanging terminology was due to the chaotic post-war situation or a deliberate attempt to make it more difficult for the military government to scrutinize their work.

It was the British military government's need to increase economic production that led to the passing of 'Technical Instruction no. 49' in July 1945, which allowed the formal rebuilding of the Chambers of Industry and Commerce and of industrial associations, but the latter were initially allowed to operate at provincial level only and thus took longer to re-establish themselves properly. The creation of the *Wirtschaftsvereinigung Eisen und Stahl* was in many ways typical of developments. When it was set up in March 1946, it was already allowed to operate on a regional or *Land* level, before in April the following year its operation could span the whole of the British occupation zone.[61] By early 1946, the French and Americans had created standardized rules for the establishment of associations in their zones, where they remained restricted to *Land* level. For the Americans, this was part of their decartelization policy, while for the French it was an attempt to prevent a German resurgence. The military governments in all zones insisted on a number of basic rules for the creation of new associations. These included, in particular: voluntary membership only; a leadership that had been vetted and declared 'denazified'; the prohibition of sliding voting rights, which in the past had always favoured the big companies. Finally, while by 1949 the Allies had allowed industrial branch associations to operate within all three of the occupation zones, they were not permitted to establish a national peak association, or *Dachverband*, prior to the creation of the Federal Republic and the transfer of some rights to the new state. Even the British, who felt they needed some associations' assistance, reacted decisively when any of these rules were violated. When in the summer of 1946, the chairman of the *Vereinigung Eisen- Blech- und Metallwaren Industrie* (Iron, Sheet and Metal Goods Industry Association), Fritz Berg, tried to set up an amalgamation of twenty-three different industrial associations for all three zones, his attempts were quickly terminated by the British.[62]

The discussion about the future of industrial associations amongst managers had begun even before the British military government had given permission to re-establish them. The initial outlook was bleak, with Mannesmann director Zangen even claiming that they would now be superfluous. Others believed associations sanctioned by the occupation authorities were necessary to promote industrial interests but conceded that they would 'not have the ability to rule as they had before'.[63] There were also very different opinion on how the newly reformed association should be structured. Günter Henle strictly rejected Rohland's idea of compulsory membership and proposed to return to the pre-1933 voluntary participation. He accused both Walther Rohland and Hans-Günther Sohl of being unable to free themselves from the ideas of the authoritarian leadership structures to which they had become accustomed in previous years.[64]

Hermann Reusch was one of the hardliners and driving forces for the re-establishment of the associations. How important they were to him is highlighted by a memo from February 1946. It stated that 'following the (re)creation of the Iron and Steel Association, the next important problem was that of lack of labour'.[65] In other words, the GHH's leadership regarded the rebuilding of the associations as a more important issue than the question of labour supply and therefore of productivity. Unsurprising, by the end of the year, Gutehoffnungshütte and its subsidiaries held memberships in not fewer than fifty-six associations or chambers.[66] However, for Reusch the simple re-establishing of the organizations was not enough; he also wanted a return of the old power structures, which meant he refused to co-operate with companies that had been subject to *Entflechtung*. Reusch also caused significant upset by ignoring and passing over the Iron and Steel Association's elected chairman, Karl Barich, because he was merely chairman of a small steel plant and not one of the big players.[67] True to his line, it had been Reusch who in February 1948 pressed on with the creation of a top association by setting up the *Arbeitsgemeinschaft Eisen und Metall* (Working Group on Iron and Metals). The organization defined the term 'industrial branch' very liberally, as it included non-metals organizations such as precision mechanics and optics, machine-tool manufacturing and electrical engineering.[68] With the inclusion of these branches, Reusch was quite simply circumventing, or rather ignoring, Allied restrictions on the establishment and operation of industrial organizations. Over the next twenty months or so, the *Arbeitsgemeinschaft* morphed into the *Ausschuß für Wirtschaftsfragen* (Committee on Economic Affairs) which was set up in October 1949 as a provisional top association, before it was renamed Bundesverband der Deutschen Industrie in January 1950.[69]

The creation of the *Ausschuß für Wirtschaftsfragen* brought a novelty to the running of a German top association. In the past, the chair or presidential post had always been reserved for a member of big businesses, most the time for a representative of heavy industry. In 1949, Hermann Reusch could have been the front runner for the post. Already involved in the running of the Iron and Steel Association, and untainted by any Nazi party membership, he would have ticked all the right boxes were it not for his temperament and reputation and for heavy industry's overall negative reputation. As a firmly conservative manager, he had already alienated both the trade unions as well as the British military government, so both would have opposed his appointment. What was more important was that even sections of the manufacturing industry were suspicious of him as a representative of big businesses.[70] Reusch knew that as a man from heavy industry and big business, he was also not acceptable to the wider public: the Nuremberg industrialists' trials of Friedrich Flick and the Krupp directors were too fresh in people's minds. He himself stated that 'today the independent entrepreneurs has to have the leadership in those [association] affairs'.[71]

The perfect candidate for the post, then, was found in Fritz Berg, who was ideal for so many reasons. Berg was the owner of a medium-sized company which had specialized in the production of tubular furniture, in particular metal framed beds, where the company had a 38 percent market share in 1938, employing 1,500 workers. Born in 1901, he had begun to study *Betriebswirtschft* in 1921 with the renowned Professor Schmalenbach. In 1925, he had followed his professor to a study tour to the US, were he decided to abandon his studies and stay and work for three years, so that upon his return to Germany he spoke English fluently. He had married a Canadian, a fact which helped him to gain some favours with the British occupation authorities. Since his failed attempt to set up a top association in 1946, Berg had been mentored by Hermann Reusch. By 1948, he was both president of the Hagen Chamber of Industry and Commerce and chairman of the Iron, Sheet and Metal Goods Industry Association.[72] From Reusch's perspective, Berg had two more advantages: like Reusch, he was an arch-conservative, patriarchal entrepreneur; and he had no power base of his own. Neither Berg's IHK presidency nor the Metal Goods Association chairmanship had that much weight, so Berg was, at least in the early part of his presidency, dependent on Reusch.[73] Almond's description of Berg as almost an 'anti-Reusch' and a moderate leader is rather generous and based on the assumption that Reusch was still interested in, and a contender for, the BDI presidency, but this assumption is not convincing for at least two reasons.[74] First, there is no evidence in Reusch's papers that he was considering a run for the BDI top job. Furthermore, his statement about the necessity of having independent entrepreneur at the Association's helm shows that he knew very well that he had too many opponents to get the post.

As the owner of a regional SME, Berg had not been in the national limelight before 1949, a circumstance which helped him to cover up and get away with some dubious activities between 1945 and 1948. In April 1945 he had been appointed acting mayor of his hometown Altena by the Americans although he had been a Nazi party member since 1937 and had been appointed by the Nazis to several honorary posts within the city administration and IHK. His appointment was criticized by German authorities and businesses alike, because as it turned out, he misused this position for cronyism and favouritism.[75] Berg used his first stint as president of IHK Hagen to reorganize the Chambers in part – and, as it turned out, to his advantage. He seemed to have had no scruples about co-operating with the British, who had replaced the Americans as occupation force. In turn they began to rely ever more on his advice, even in matters concerning denazification. The British military government also supported Berg's association career, partly because their commanding officer was, like Berg's wife, Canadian, and partly because Berg simply bribed their officials. By August 1946, the British had completed his denazification and classed him in the lowest category, 'exonerated'. German authorities, on the other hand, had labelled him as a '*Nutznießer*' (beneficiary) of the Nazi regime and as politically unacceptable (*untragbar*). These accusations had some effect. Presumably as a result of an anonymous denunciation from within his own association about his manipulation of raw material allocation, he was arrested in January 1947. Charged with the illegal possession of a firearm and corruption, Berg was sentenced to eight months in prison and a fine of RM 200,000. On appeal the sentence was reduced to a nominal RM 100 fine, with the corruption charges being dropped altogether. By mid-1948 he had managed to regain his old positions both within the IHK and the metal industry association.[76] Berg's ability to bounce back in this way was a sign not only of his ambition but also of his knowledge of the system of industrial associations and self-administrative bodies, as well as of his ability to work within such a system. It was the basis of his future career as head of the BDI.

The inaugural meeting of the *Ausschuß für Wirtschaftsfragen* had been well-choreographed, with Berg's speech drafted for him, most likely by, or at least on behalf of, Reusch, who was the meeting's 'master of ceremonies'.[77] At the gathering, thirty-two industrial sector associations joined the new top association. The shoe industry had not yet established its branch association and the coalmining industry, as well as the Iron and Steel Association, did not join because of their ongoing *Entflechtung* under Allied decartelization policies and because of co-determination issues. Eventually thirty-five associations represented 335 industrial branch association and 154 *Landesverbände* (regional branch associations) and about 90 per cent of all industrial companies in those sectors.[78] Reusch's opening speech was almost predictable. He described the development of industrial associations to this point. Then he stressed that industry had to consider the common weal which depended on a thriving manufacturing industry, which, of course, was a call for industry's special place in society. When he called for more European co-operation 'as the only possibility to save the *abendländische* (occidental) culture', it was a warning against the Communist peril but also his demand for equal treatment of Germany's industry vis-à-vis that of other European countries.[79] For Reusch, who would turn into one of the strongest critics of the European Coal and Steel Community because he saw it as a sell-out of German industrial interests, equal treatment meant quite simply German industrial hegemony in Europe. On Reusch's suggestion the assembly then elected Berg as president, while the textile industrialist and president of IHK Augsburg Otto Vogel, and Wilhelm Menne, chairman of the Association of the Chemical Industry, became vice presidents. This composition of the BDI's *Präsidium* (executive committee) was not an accident. Vogel was to represent small and medium-sized consumer industries as well as southern German industrialists; Menne was the man of the 'new' industries; Berg was clearly seen as the man of heavy industry. This division of seats gave an indication of the BDI's future role which was as much to be one of an arbitrator between different industrial sectors' interests as it was to be a lobby group.

Although Fritz Berg became 'his own man' the longer he held office and no longer needed the patronage of Reusch, the BDI's various factions did not attempt to replace him. Many small and medium-sized entrepreneurs saw him as one of their own. Heavy industry, especially the steel industry (irrespective of the fact that it did not join the BDI before the mid-1950s), remained if not the dominant, than at least a highly influential, force within the BDI at least up to the mid-1960s, also saw no need to replace him because his conservative mentality was very close to their own.[80] Together with Reusch and the two chief clerks – Wilhelm Beutler, formerly a chief clerk of a steel association, and Gustav Stein – and also Otto Vogel, Berg stood for the conservative element amongst entrepreneurs who prevailed over the modernizers like Otto A. Friedrich or Heinrich Kost, who in this regard was an exception amongst the coal managers.[81] Both Werner Bührer and Hans-Peter Ullmann agree that a real change in mentality, which also meant a move away from the hard-line conservatives within the BDI leadership, occurred only in the aftermath of the 1972 general election and as part of a generational change.[82] This generalizing statement is not necessarily true for Berg's successors as BDI president, Hans-Günther Sohl (in office 1972–77) and Hans-Martin Schleyer (1977). Both were still confirmed conservatives – Schleyer was even called the 'spokesman of the right-wing extra-parliamentarian opposition' – but in their language they were much more flexible and less confrontational than Berg, the quintessential blustering conservative patriarch, had ever been.[83] Sohl's six-year presidency also marked the first time, and considering its decline, also the last time, that heavy industry held the BDI top post.

The activities the BDI have been, and still are, associated with political lobbying and rejection of, or agitation against, social policy change or other demands from the trade unions. During the 1950s and 60s, these particular activities were often discharged through the Deutsche Industrie Institut. Contemporary commentators' views of the BDI as an 'unpolitical interest group' (Almond) or merely as an interest group rather than a pressure or lobby group (Braunthal) are somewhat benign as they disregard the underlying political view of BDI protagonists.[84] That said, one of the BDI's most important tasks, and one that is often overlooked by historians, was the reconciliation of interests amongst its different constituent member associations. In the aftermath of Allied policies and confronted with an uncertain political situation in the Federal Republic, industrialists had realized that their best chance of survival lay in having a united front against their critics and when dealing with either the government or the trade unions. Different associations within one industrial sector or even competing top associations, as there had been before 1914, were seen as a dangerous fracturing of industrial power and influence. It was not least because of this background that the BDI was extremely successful in its attempts to unify, and only very few of these conflicts were leaked to the public. Two of these occurred in 1954. First, a minority group openly criticized the BDI's pro-cartel policy, which called for a return to Germany's traditional way of limiting competition. Second, the BDI had to contain a much more severe falling-out between the automobile industry and parts of the iron and steel industry in the so-called '*Straße–Schiene Konflikt*' (road–rail conflict).[85] In order to prevent a further deterioration of the Federal Rail's revenue due to a parlous drop in freight tonnage – road haulage was becoming increasingly popular – transport minister Hans-Christoph Seebohm had initiated a draft bill limiting the size and freight weight of lorries and trailers. This was vehemently opposed by the automobile industry, which saw a direct threat to a growth market and demanded intervention from the BDI. In this dispute the iron and steel industry seemed to have sided with Federal Rail not only because the latter was an extremely important customer but more importantly, because it determined freight prices and rebates. Nevertheless, the WVES followed the BDI's prescribed compromise terminology, which led to internal disputes during which no punches were pulled. When Victor Arntzen, a director of the Hoesch steel company, gave his personal opinion to a CDU committee, in which he criticized the automobile industry's 'undignified manipulation' of the debate, BDI senior clerk Stein wrote an angry letter to the WVES and demanded that Sohl put him straight. In his reply to Sohl, Arntzen expressed his understanding for the BDI's need to appear publicly unified but he rejected the BDI's assumed 'grand ducal authority', especially since the BDI did not believe in what they were saying on the matter. Arntzen's reply displays the underlying willingness to obey group loyalty, but also his expectation that the car lobby and the BDI should adhere to a certain code of conduct, which in his opinion neither was following. Although the WVES agreed with him in principle, Arntzen was told by his association that it had to agree to a compromise within the BDI because of the pressure from other members. He was also reminded that given the automobile industry was also a significant customer, he should refrain from criticizing it in public.[86]

Arguably the most prominent clash of industrial loyalties, and one with far-reaching consequences, emerged from late 1957 onwards when oil began to replace coal as an industrial and domestic fuel and as a chemical raw material. On the eve of the coal glut, the *Unternehmensverband Ruhrbergbau* (UVR, Federation of Ruhr mining companies) had stated that 'Ruhr coal is not sold but distributed to the consumer by the Ruhr mines' dispatch departments'.[87] As in other European countries, during the reconstruction period the price of Ruhr coal had been kept low by the government regulation for the benefit of other industrial sectors. This meant that the coal industry was unable to invest long-term, and thus coal output was well below demand. The UVR quote shows the hubris coal managers held at the time, and their inability to see that because of the short supply, customers were looking for alternatives and more modern forms of energy. The BDI itself had got things wrong, too. As late as June 1957, four months before the onset of the crisis, the *Landesverbands-Geschäftsführer* (chief clerks of the regional associations) meeting recorded that 'German coal mines do not have to fear any sales difficulties unless the High Authority [of the ECSC] would intervene in the import of US coal'.[88] Only the trade unions had warned about the changing market situation. Oil was replacing coal increasingly as a fuel and energy source and German coal stockpiles grew rapidly to previously unimaginable levels. By 1959, coal worth DM 1 billon had to be stockpiled, and pit managers were demanding from the government the introduction of import duties on light and heavy crude oil and a curbing of cheap US coal imports.[89] Eventually the BDI had to mediate between the coal mines on the one side and the petrol industry and other oil consumers on the other side. In a meeting in December 1958 the BDI executive committee discussed how to help the coal mines and opinions differed. Berg, who wanted to 'keep coal as the basis of a healthy German energy policy' called for a cartel, which was opposed by Otto A. Friedrich. While there was almost an agreement to redeem the existing long-term coal imports from the USA, at a cost of DM 30–40 per ton, to be paid in part with government aid, the chemical and the glass manufacturing industry were opposed to any price increases for either oil or coal.[90] Nine months later, in September 1959, the BDI held a further executive committee meeting dedicated exclusively to the oil–coal problem. The meeting concluded with a compromise statement and old-style rhetoric. Since the problem was not one of the coal industry's making, they should receive support, but not subsidies (as this was seen as the first step to the nationalization of the industry); neither, however, should there be a tax on fuel oil. Instead a joint coal–oil cartel should provide relief for the situation, which was blamed outright on failed government policy, especially Erhard's market liberalizations.[91]

During the 1950s and 1960s, the BDI was without a doubt an association for, and dominated by, big industries, despite its chairman himself being a SME entrepreneur. This dominance became increasingly criticized and challenged in the second part of the 1950s. German manufacturing industries have traditionally been classed as either '*produzierend*' (producing) or '*verarbeitend*' (processing), with the former usually being dominated by the big coal, iron and steel concerns, and the latter predominantly being SMEs. From the mid-1950s onward, the producing companies in the iron and steel sector began to encroach into the processing sector by acquiring more and more processing companies in an attempt to expand their business activities. Independent entrepreneurs began to feel threatened by this incursion and challenged both this expansion and the large companies' behaviour overall. In May 1957, ASU chairman Alfred Flender led the charge. He condemned a demand from the steel industry for a DM 750 million loan at 1 per cent interest as a compensation for the construction of the Mosel canal (which would have increased the French steel industry's competitiveness). He went on to criticize the encroachment of 'the big firms' into the processing sector and demanded a renewal of the 1928 AVI (*Arbeitsgemeinschaft Verarbeitende Industrie*, Working Committee on Processing Industries) agreement, which had limited such an expansion.[92] The following year he attacked the government as being dependent on big business and very sharply criticized the power of the joint stock companies and their '*Hausmeier*' (*major domus*), the men who ran the companies on behalf of the big shareholder. While he mentioned C. Rudolf Poensgen and Albert Vögler, he was polite (or politically astute) enough not to cite Hermann Reusch or Hans-Günther Sohl in this context. Flender welcomed the creation of a *Mittelstand* committee within the BDI but he remained sceptical about its success since 'any *Mittelstand* policy is non-credible as long as it brings tax advantages for the big companies'. Flender went on to use a new and hostile style of rhetoric amongst entrepreneurs when he used the term '*Großkapital*' to describe big businesses and accused some of their top executives as being 'Managers' (in the 1950s' German meaning of the word), which meant that he saw them as being 'functionaries' – perhaps the biggest insult for an entrepreneur at the time.[93]

Such outbursts from Flender and other SME entrepreneurs had an impact. The government set up a *Mittelstand* credit programme of DM 100–200 million to provide small businesses with loans between DM 100,000 and DM 3 million.[94] In late 1956, the BDI had not foreseen the storm that was brewing. It refuted the claim that the BDI was run by a 'big business clique', but that any problem simply arose because of insufficient credit lines for the SME sector.[95] Over the next year, however, pressure grew to such a level that the BDI was forced to act. In January 1958 it launched with some fanfare its *BDI Mittelstandsausschuß* (*Mittelstand* Committee). In the opening address, which was given by Berg himself, the BDI president tried to schmooze the SME representatives by highlighting that 88 per cent of all German industrial firms employed fewer than 100 workers and that the small and medium-sized businesses were crucial for the 'definition of property within the western culture' ('*Eigentumsbegriff ... unserer abendländischen Kultur*'), as well as being the bulwark against socialist levelling attempts.[96] Little action followed this rousing rhetoric and in October 1958 Berg had to report back on an unpleasant meeting he had with Adenauer. The Chancellor had threatened that unless the BDI took the initiative and addressed the crisis between big and small businesses, the Government would take legislative measures.[97] Adenauer's threat seemed to have had some effect. At a meeting of the *Geschäftsführer* of the BDI's member associations in April 1960, the senior chief clerk of the construction industry association came up with a positive assessment of the *Mittlestand* committee's activities. He stated that although many associations had SME membership of 80 per cent, they had previously not set up their own SME committees. It was the activities of the BDI committee that had shaken many associations and businesses out of their *Mittelstandsromantik* (the romanticization of small and medium-sized owner-run businesses) and shown them their actual power and influence within the BDI.[98] Despite this sappy statement, Hartmut Berghoff has shown that the reality of support for the *Mittelstand* was quite different and mainly lip-service.[99] *Der Spiegel* argued at the time that despite this gap between reality and rhetoric, it had been the BDI's member associations that were dominated by SMEs, and it was these that had time and again re-elected Berg, not the associations dominated by big industry.[100] It is therefore clear that for the SMEs, Berg had two distinct advantages: they still saw him as 'one of us' and he was, like most of them, a very strong opponent to Economics Minister Erhard's neo-liberal market economy.

After the Second World War, an aspect of German industrial associations' work was to prevent their individual members from making unsuitable remarks and avoid bad publicity. In times of increased media coverage, this task grew in importance and at times amounted almost to censorship.[101] There is some irony in the fact that it was the associations' ability to keep disputes, apart from a few exceptions, strictly as internal matters, that helped to create the public impression – and even the myth – of a super-strong, monolithic organization that could wield power over political matters. Berg's growing visibility during the 1950s and his almost unlimited access to the Chancellor only emphasized this point. By the middle of that decade, there was a growing public unease about the political influence of the associations. The spirit of the time was caught quite well by Theodor Eschenburg's booklet, *Herrschaft der Verbände* (*Rule of the Associations*). In reality the booklet was principally backward-looking to a 'better' past in which an 'ideal' state existed where 'unbiased' civil servants ran the country. It was therefore much more a criticism of a new understanding of democracy in West Germany in which the participating actors (political parties, religious denominational groups, farmers' lobbies etc.) were actively trying to push their interests vis-à-vis weak and incompetent politicians. In fact, industrial associations were mentioned only very briefly and towards the end of Eschenburg's pamphlet. The BDI had learned its lessons not least from the DII's early PR exercises and reacted swiftly and decisively in defence of industrial associations, despite the fact that they or their lobbying were hardly mentioned in the booklet.[102] One of their more prominent actions was to organize a widely publicized symposium titled '*Der Staat und die Verbände*' ('The State and the Associations'), the proceedings of which the BDI published under the editorship of its chief clerks.[103] The event had been opened with two speeches by eminent professors of constitutional law and civil law, who, of course, both confirmed the legitimacy of association in the democratic state. Then seventeen guests, among them the 'usual suspects' in defence of industry (e.g. Fritz Hellwig and Wolfgang Pohle), discussed the role of the associations. Also among the guests were ten more university professors, including Eschenburg, who this time acted as chief witness in defence of the associations, confirming their democratic right to exist and their role in the industrial society.

The BDI's swift action and widely disseminated public relations campaign did pay off: after all, it was difficult to argue against the associations' 'democratic rights', even though the case was presented in a very one-sided fashion. By the late 1950s and early

1960s, the debate about the influence of industrial groups had almost disappeared from public discussions, despite Berg's continuing (if not growing) presence in the public-political sphere, and despite the gaffes he made time and again in his speeches and statements.[104] The symposium and its organization, or at least the auspices of the event by the chief clerks, is a prime example of how much they were the public face of their associations, but their role went much further. In most cases, the *Geschäftsführer* and *Hauptgeschäftsführer* were much more than executive organs for their presidents; they were the actual power behind the throne. They provided, even guaranteed, the continuity of an association's policy in those cases where the association's chairman or president changed frequently or where they had to look after other affairs, including their companies. The Iron and Steel Association, for example, had four chief clerks or senior chief clerks between its foundation in 1946 and 1973 (Wilhelm Salewski 1946–52, Wilhelm Ahrens 1948–60, Hans Dichgans 1955–73, Herbert Köhler 1960–85). At the same time, the chairmanship changed eight times and there would have been even more changes had it not been for the exceptionally long chairmanship of Hans-Günther Sohl, who held the post for the unusually long period of thirteen years (1956–69).[105] Usually trained as attorneys-at-law and qualified to carry the title *Rechtsanwalt*, the *Geschäftsführer* were usually more hard-line than the chairmen or presidents of the associations. This was true not only for the industrial associations but had already been the case in the process of the re-establishment of the Chambers of Industry and Commerce, where the *Geschäfsführer* in many cases had been the real driving force behind attempts to prevent the trade unions from gaining parity or any influence in the Chambers at all. There is some irony in the fact that these men, who were themselves only hired hands, had in actual fact more interest in the body they were serving and were defending the status quo more vigorously than some of the entrepreneurial members. The *Geschäftsführer* had a symbiotic relationship with the associations. They kept the business going and in return for their loyalty, association or Chamber presidents allowed them free rein – and some of them took advantage of these arrangements. Hans Ballhausen, senior chief clerk at IHK Braunschweig and in the late 1940s one of the moderating voices in the dispute with the trade unions, was eventually caught up in financial irregularities and embezzlement for which his president, Transport Minister Seebohm, had to take some of the blame because of insufficient oversight.[106]

The reason why the 'hired hands' were often so much less compromising than the entrepreneurs and managers was simply that they wanted to retain their power and their jobs within the organizations. Heinz Hartmann was told in the late 1950s by an insider that the only reason preventing a merger between the BDI and the BDA (as had happened in Britain with the creation of the Confederation of British Industry, the CBI) were the vested interests of the associations' respective salaried officers.[107] Not least because of these vested interests were associations' chief clerks seen by some managers, in particular independent entrepreneurs, as 'functionaries' and they received considerable criticism from the ASU.[108]

There were a number of reasons why entrepreneurs or managers took on the extra burden of association work. Sometimes it was out of a sense of duty to stand for office in an association, but often it would have been the enticement of power and influence that was the driving force for taking on a position. In an analogy to O. A. Friedrich's famous definition of an entrepreneur ('someone with the passion to operate constructively and independently'), Hartmann defined entrepreneurs who took on positions in associations as those 'who have a passion for independent political action'.[109] This longing for power came at a cost, which was time. It was not surprising that in 1950, when the reconstruction of firms was just picking up pace, Josef Winschuh declared that the biggest sacrifice an entrepreneur could make was to spend his time in industrial organizations and associations, instead of his own company.[110] Compared to owner-entrepreneurs, managers of larger companies would have found it much easier to make the time to serve in an association as they had much more opportunity to spread the workload, or hire an extra assistant to ease the additional amount of work; this was much more difficult for small or medium-sized family or owner-run companies. How true this point was is shown by the fact that although by the late 1950s there were more than 90,000 small and medium-sized enterprises in the Federal Republic, the ASU itself had only about 500 active members.[111] The example of the Iron and Steel Association shows that once the economic recovery picked up pace, there was an increased interest by top managers in taking on the association's chairmanship. In 1954 two candidates, Gerhard Schroeder of Klöckner and Thyssen's Hans-Günther Sohl, put their names forward. Prior to that, the association's chairmen, apart from Hermann Reusch as foundation chairman in 1946–47, were either from smaller steel companies or were less prominent men from bigger companies. The appointment of men from smaller companies had been for good reasons at a time when the Allies were still in the process of breaking up and restructuring the Ruhr industries. They were less suspicious to the Allies and at the same time men like Sohl, Reusch or Winkhaus could concentrate on rebuilding their plants and keeping the trusts together. Once the industry's enforced '*Neuordnung*' (reordering) had come to an end and the re-concentration began, there was no longer any need to keep a low profile.[112]

For an organization which used to solve issues unanimously, the 1954 dual candidacy caused some unrest. The matter was eventually settled by Schroeder taking the post for two years but on the condition that the members had to agree to elect Sohl thereafter.[113] Sohl's subsequent long tenure at the head of the association shows several things: first, by the mid-1950s, he had become the leading man of the steel industry. Second, although the association hit very choppy waters in the 1960s, Sohl seemed to have retained the overall trust of his fellow managers, despite some glitches. The following will show that a manager's loyalty was primarily with his company and only after that with the association. So on at least one occasion Sohl (mis-)used his position as association chairman to access information that would give his firm an edge over competitors. His indignation when he was challenged about this behaviour was therefore rather misplaced.

The situation had arisen because of the intended expansion of a steel plant. In April 1960, *Der Spiegel* reported that the state-owned Salzgitter steel plant (built by the Nazis as the Reichswerke Hermann Göring) was planning to build a new six-metre-wide warm rolling mill and a secondary cold rolling mill to supply tin plates to the nearby VW plant at Wolfsburg.[114] As all large investment projects in the steel industry had to be reported to the association, Sohl knew about the project early on and lobbied with the Federal Government and eventually directly with Adenauer in an attempt to prevent the Salzgitter expansion, arguing that it would create significant overcapacity on the German steel market. By July 1960, the project had indeed been stopped, but now it had become known amongst association members that Sohl had planned the construction of a new rolling mill for his own company, Thyssen, and this caused consternation amongst his peers.[115] At the next *Diskussionsabend* meeting on 19 August, Sohl was accused, with good cause, by some of his peers of having abused his position as association chairman to prevent the Salzgitter expansion so that the new Thyssen rolling mill had less competition. That he had failed to inform the DA about his intentions made his action despicable in the eyes of the other DA members. Only Otto Wolff von Amerongen, with whom Thyssen jointly owned a sheet mill, argued that Sohl had acted in the greater interest of the industry.[116] The sharp reaction of the other managers would have prevented Sohl from committing a similar breach of trust within the association and the DA. Nevertheless, the advantage Sohl had gained for his company as a result of his privileged position would have lasted for years and therefore was well worth the trouble and extra workload he took on as association chairman.

The *Diskussionsabend*, established in October 1954, deserves special attention when discussing business associations. Although not a traditional association – it was referred to by its members as 'a non-binding meeting in a private setting'[117] – it had considerable influence over the steel industry and emphasized the special role the steel men expected for themselves. In a retrospective presentation to its members in 1976, Herbert Köhler described the DA as direct successor to the *Ruhrlade*, the influential body of the top twelve Ruhr industrialists which had been set up by Paul Reusch in 1927.[118] Because of the *Ruhrlade's* role in the 1928 *Ruhreisenstreit* in particular, and its role in the fall of the Weimar Republic in general, the reprinting of Köhler's remarks in his memoirs were sensitive and in the commissioned official history of the *Wirtschaftsvereinigung Stahl*, this interpretation is disputed.[119] While there were some differences between the DA and the *Ruhrlade* – the DA's membership was not limited to the Ruhr area alone; representatives of medium-sized steel companies were invited as well; its membership numbers was not fixed – the underlying purpose was the same. The DA was supposed to act as a co-ordination body for the industry in all matters relating to the economy (including pricing), society (wages and trade union matters) and politics (responses to political developments, including the ECSC) matters.[120] In reality, at least for some considerable time, the DA was much more than a co-ordinating body; it acted very much like a cartel, in which prices and quotas were not just discussed but agreed.[121] The DA's decisions were then formally adopted by the Iron and Steel Association's next meeting. Although the DA meetings were held at the private residences of its members (at least until the growing membership made this impractical and the meetings had to be relocated to hotels or the Düsseldorf Industrie Club), their decisions were anything but 'non-binding'. The fact that Köhler had suggested to the assembly's chairman (Sohl) the introduction of an honour code to curb dissenting actions and Sohl himself threatened '*Gruppenkampf*' against members who were non-compliant with the DA's decision, shows clearly otherwise. The DA was in all but name the re-run of the steel industry's cartels prior to the Second World War. It showed the continued mentality of the industry's managers as 'being special'.[122] The DA's expanding membership in the early 1960s, on the other hand, highlights the changes that were happening in the industry. It was no longer possible for decisions to be taken only by a handful of leading men from the big steel works; the managers of the smaller plants had to be included in the decision-making process as well. Matthias Kipping argues that it was the German iron and steel industry's much stronger inner cohesion which made it so much more competitive than its French counterpart.[123] Although he does not mention the DA by name, and despite the quarrels described above, it was one of the instruments which contributed to this cohesion.

This chapter has shown that while German industrialists' claims after 1945 of being unpolitical came as a direct response to Allied denazification panels, the reality, especially after the founding of the Federal Republic, was very different. Political activities outside party politics, including financial contribution to bourgeois parties, was rampant and almost inevitable for men who feared the rise of left of centre parties, which they equated with a socialist government and thus 'the end of capitalism'. What made German industrialists' donation to political parties distinct from those of industrialists in other European countries is not only the scale of the donation, but also the hypocritical claim of being unpolitical, which went hand in hand with criticism of trade union donations for the Social Democratic Party. The very peculiar understanding of democracy which businessmen often displayed when they went into high politics were exemplified by Hans Wellhausen's comments on parliamentary workings. For them, democracy was not the rule of majority and political compromise, but rather the rule of an elite who implemented measures they saw as right. However, although industrial interests were represented disproportionately to their share of population, in many cases industry's political interests in Parliament were taken care of by association managers, which gave those men further power well beyond their associations. Germany's traditionally strong trade organisations had received a further boost through the organization of the Nazi war economy, and it is not surprising that those powerful organizations re-appeared soon after the war had ended and that they kept some of their increased influence. Furthermore, German businessmen and association functionaries had learned that a united front gave them more power than the fragmented association landscape before 1914 and that when faced with dismantling and the threat of socialization of businesses, a united front made them stronger. It is for this reason that both intra- and inter-association conflicts were usually dealt with internally and not in public. This contrasts with and, according to Wyn Grant, explains the political weakness of British businesses, where even an association president spoke of the 'anarchy' in which UK business organizations found themselves.[124] This cohesive, top-down German structure and discipline allowed Heinz Hartmann to make the claim that the BDI was '10 times more influential than the NAM'.[125] Despite the sometimes fierce internal rows, few other institutions symbolize this associational influence to the same level as the non-association' *Diskussionsabende*.

The timing of the DA's creation in 1954 was not accidental. In the wake of the European Coal and Steel Community's establishment, Allies' deconcentration policy had come to an end in 1953 and with Gerhard Schroeder there was for the first time (except for the founding chairman, Hermann Reusch, 1946–47), again a top man at the helm of the Iron and Steel Association. Nevertheless, there were some innovations at the DA, most notably the inclusion of Karl Barich, chairman of Hüttenwerk Geisweid (and during 1948–49 and 1952–54 chairman of the Iron and Steel Association), together with Theodor Wuppermann, of Wuppermann steelworks, and Walter Pfeiffer of Ohlen ironworks, both of them owners of the respective plants.[126] The inclusion of these 'minor' players would have been unthinkable for the *Ruhrlade* and was a sign of gratitude for their loyalty during the 'difficult times' of Allied occupation and restructuring. Similarly, ever more representatives of non-Ruhr steel works were admitted. This was a sign of a less authoritarian leadership by a small group and the realization by Sohl and others that they could no longer expect not being challenged in the Iron and Steel Association about their DA decisions. Ultimately even this most conservative organization modernized and 'democratized' its operations. The special role steel managers believed they held in the industrial fabric of post-war Germany came eventually to an end with the steel crisis of the late 1960s. Despite the decline, the DA continued its work, but to Köhler's displeasure without the traditional confidentiality, high-level participants and wide remit of topics.[127] Although the German industrial associations can be called the strongest and most disciplined in the western world and held considerable political influence, ultimately this did not turn the Federal Republic into an 'association state'. Both the 1957 pension reforms,[128] which were heavily criticized and fought against by businessmen, and the 1961 revaluation of the Deutschmark are the key examples that association power had limits and that Adenauer carried out his policies even against the interests of his main backers.

Part III

Business

7

Living with the 'Enemy': Trade Unions, Workers and Communists

The claim that the German economy did so well in the post-war years because of good labour relations and worker participation within companies is now almost generally accepted.[1] This chapter will show that despite this claim, and although industrialists were happy to utilize trade unions against dismantling and deconcentration and to offer tactical concessions to the workers, they fiercely resisted trade union involvement in general and co-determination in particular. Indeed, although it was usually the industrialists who accused the unions of class warfare, it was in fact managements' attitudes which, for a number of reasons, were far more hostile towards the unions than vice versa.

German businessmen's relations with trade unions have not always been easy, to say the least. Although in November 1918 Hugo Stinnes had negotiated for the industrialists with trade union men under the leadership of Carl Legien, the famous 'Stinnes–Legien' accord, the employers had done so only out of fear of the immediate socialization of their firms, thus they had agreed merely out of opportunism.[2] In the agreement, industrialists made significant concessions, which many of them had previously refused even to contemplate: the trade unions were recognized as being legitimate representation of the workers and thus as partners in industrial bargaining; the eight-hour working day was accepted as industry standard; and employers had to accept the creation of *Arbeiterausschüsse* (workers' committees) to represent workers in companies with more than fifty employees. The 1920 Works Council law reduced workers' say (*Mitsprache*) to social affairs only, however.[3] Any disputed issues would be discussed in a joint body, the so-called *Zentralarbeitsgemeinschaft* (ZAG, Central Working Community). The acceptance of trade unions did not come about because the industrialists had seen reason but, as Carl Duisberg, one of the chemical industry's leaders explained: 'I am an opportunist and adapt to the circumstances' – at least as long as these circumstances did not touch the capitalist economic order as a whole.[4] Stephen Silvia argues that although it was heavy industry which in 1924 provoked the breakdown of the ZAG, German industrialists learned during the Weimar period to live with trade unions and, at least in the 'modern' industries, even co-operated with them.[5] Nevertheless, with the growing influence of the socially reactionary representatives of heavy industry on the RDI, management's attitude concerning the trade unions hardened towards the end of the 1920s. It deteriorated further with the onset of the Great Depression, even amongst the representatives of the 'technocratic organized capitalism' of the new industries. By 1931, big business, especially heavy industry, was opposed outright to the Weimar Republic but not necessarily in favour of the Nazis,[6] so when Hitler was appointed Chancellor, many industrialists were still not fully convinced about National Socialism. Nevertheless, they expected the Nazis to curb the trade unions, which they increasingly saw as detrimental to business. The Nazis' subsequent crushing of the unions on 2 May 1933 and their replacement with the German Labour Front (*Deutsche Arbeits Front*, DAF) was therefore welcomed by most industrialists. The DAF embodied the National Socialists' idea of the *Volksgemeinschaft* within the economy, the *Betriebsgemeinschaft* or factory community, in which the class divide had supposedly disappeared, as both employees and employers were forced to join. An even more welcome change was the implementation of the '*Führer* principle' in the economy, which meant that a company owner or company chairman became the *Betriebsführer* (factory leader) and the workforce became his *Gefolgschaft*, or retinue.[7] This setup, in particular the *Führer* principle, meant that the industrialists' traditional position of 'master-in-the-house' could no longer be challenged. The so-called 'trustees of labour', who were supposed to present workers' interests, had limited influence at best. It is therefore not surprising that most industrialists, although some would later criticize it heavily, favoured the Nazi model of company hierarchy and management–labour relations.[8] Karl-Friedrich Diedrich, head of the personnel department of a south German industrial plant, condemned not only this twisted self-perception, but also management's pre-war attitudes altogether. In his 1950 PhD on human relations in German companies, he stated that '*Die Betriebspolitik des* DINTA ... *bereitete den Übergang zur nationalsozialistischen Arbeitspolitik vor*'. ('Management policy by DINTA prepared the way for the switch to the National Socialist labour policy').[9]

More recent scholarship has suggested that during the latter part of the war and the early post-war years, when German industry was increasingly exposed to Allied air raids and then to dismantling, management and workforces did indeed merge into a form of genuine *Betriebsgemeinschaft*, because together they had endured initially Allied bombing raids and then had to fight the dismantling of their factories.[10] While the reconstituted trade unions did so for ultimately different goals – the disappearance or even only disabling of the plants meant first and foremost unemployment for the workforce – they also strongly opposed dismantling. Thus they joined the industrialists in their battle to save the plants.[11] Perhaps for the first time the fight against the threat to the factories gave the industrialists a common cause with their workers.[12] In many cases managers tried to utilize the unions to further their own agenda, or at least against the occupying powers, even as late as 1949. In August that year, the metal workers' union had called for protest rallies against the dismantling of the Salzgitter steel works when the industrialists demanded a full-blown protest strike against this policy, which the union refused.[13] Even Hermann Reusch, usually the trade union basher-in-chief, had tried to use the unions for his own ends. In October 1946, he wrote to a leading member of the *Freier Deutsche Gewerkschaftsbund* (FDGB)[14] to argue that under current food provisions, coal production could not be increased. To make his point, Reusch included several statistics in his letter and expressed his expectation that

'I assume that you can use these graphs occasionally for the right purpose'.[15] Reusch's intentions here are obvious: he hoped that the trade union, whose political standing with the occupying forces was higher than that of the industrialists, would use his statistical material to argue with the British military government either to increase miners' rations or to reduce production targets. As early as January 1946, in a meeting of the *Eisenkreis*, a predecessor to the Iron and Steel Association, Reusch asked for urgent talks with the trade unions about the works council law which had been passed by the British. The members of the *Eisenkreis* were prepared to accept workers' representation as inevitable, but they wanted it to be limited to the supervisory boards. Under no circumstances should worker representatives be allowed onto the managing boards, as they supposedly lacked the necessary qualifications and should not have any direct control of daily operations. Industrialists' beliefs were still unshakably along the lines that only management could manage. To prevent the union from coming up with further demands, Reusch wanted early talks with them so that they had no opportunity to make new claims.[16] Vociferous calls for meetings with the unions were heard again in January 1947, after the first details of the Allied Law 52 about the expropriation and possible socialization of heavy industry had become known.[17] Without a doubt, the steel industrialists were prepared, as they had been in 1918, to make drastic compromises with the trade unions in order to save as much as possible of their threatened position.

Talking with labour representatives did not mean that industrialists had changed their view on the trade unions and *Wirtschaftsdemokratie* as understood by the unions, however: far from it. At the time when the managers tried to use the unions as a tool to combat the military government, they were not prepared to make any real concessions to them. When the metal workers' union proposed to talk directly to the Iron and Steel Association and not to a separate employer organization about social policy and industrial bargaining matters, the *Eisenkreis* rejected this outright. The meeting's minutes did not mention any explicit reason for this decision, but on other occasions the trade unions had been fobbed off with platitudes such as 'this had never been done before by the Iron and Steel Association' and that 'there had always been a separate employers' association', so similar arguments would have been likely. The real reason to refuse the unions, however, *was* actually mentioned in the *Eisenkreis* meeting in passing: it was the fear that the unions could penetrate the associations through companies via the back door of those employer organizations responsible for both social and economic policy. Furthermore, it was of course 'unacceptable to have the structures of employers' or business associations' prescribed by trade unions'.[18] In parallel to this old-fashioned, anti-union attitude, heavy industry was prepared to defend its traditional paternalism. In early 1949, when the WVES was called upon by the retail association to reduce the activities of *Werkskonsumanstalten* (factory shops) for the benefit of the retail trade, this was rejected immediately. The shops had proven their worth in the recent past and the managers argued that 'the workers would not stand for their closure'.[19] Quite simply, the steel industrialists were not prepared to abandon one of their most cherished paternalistic institutions and they did so by pleading workers' resistance to such a plan.

Rainer Schulze's study on the role of the Chambers of Industry and Commerce in particular has shown that the industrialists' claim that the trade unions had been advantaged by the occupying powers in the immediate post-war years is a myth.[20] Due to their pre-existing and continuing networks, irrespective of the internment of some leading figures in late 1945, industrialists had advantages over the unions, particularly in terms of information flow. After years of persecution, exile and underground work, the unions found it much harder to re-establish themselves and articulate their policies. Businesses' underlying anti-union attitudes were not present only in big industry, however: they were even more widespread amongst small and medium-sized businesses, where 'attitudes and leadership style remained for much longer those of pre- and early industrialisation period'.[21] Nevertheless, management boards in large firms especially had hoped for the support of the trade unions in the rejection of Allied claims of complicity with the Nazi regime. But it was only *after* the British had expropriated the big Ruhr companies and *Entflechtung* began in August 1946 that the iron and steel industrialists were prepared to make concessions to the unions. They now offered labour some 'participation in planning and control' of the companies as well as in the supervisory bodies.[22] Some of these concessions, in particular the inclusion of trade unionists into the Iron and Steel Association, were not genuine but tactical in nature, as a comment by Reusch suggests. They nevertheless would come to haunt the managers during the German co-determination debate in 1950–51.[23]

British plans for the restructuring of the coal and iron and steel industries' organizational and operational structures posed two significant threats to management rule. These were the splitting up of companies and the '*Verbundwirtschaft*', the Ruhr's vertical integration of companies, and the imposition of co-determination in these sectors by the British military government. In an attempt to limit the power of management, which they still saw responsible for the rise of Hitler, the British co-determination plan was based around two key measures. First, all supervisory boards of heavy industry had to be made up of equal numbers of representatives from capital and labour, with an independent chairman. Second – and under normal circumstances, this would have been even less acceptable to management – a worker's representative, the so-called *Arbeitsdirektor* (labour director), was to take a seat on the management board with the same rights as all other members. In contrast to the industrialists' post-1949 agitation against co-determination, there was not much outward resistance to the British plan. This was simply because the Germans could not challenge the military authorities in a meaningful way. More significant was the fact that the managers could not speak out against co-determination because in so doing they would have lost trade union support in the fight against *Entflechtung*, which they dreaded even more.[24] Thus for the time being, the Ruhr managers were stuck with labour representatives on their supervisory and management boards, and in the case of iron and steel, also with trade unionists in their association.

After the creation of the Federal Republic of Germany, it was up to the German Parliament to pass its own legislation on co-determination, which the trade unions hoped to introduce to all industrial sectors. Business strove very hard to prevent this and if possible overturn the British legislation, or at least get it significantly weakened. Principally the whole of German industry, not just the coal and steel industries, agitated against co-determination, with the BDI at the fight's forefront. In a speech in November 1950, Fritz Berg went so far as to call the trade unions' demands for co-determination 'a threat to democracy'.[25] While from today's perspective, this was a totally overblown claim, it highlighted the fears of businessmen that such a development could be expanded from heavy industry to other industrial sectors and could also be introduced to small and medium-sized companies. From there, socialization was surely just a small step away. It also highlighted Berg's (and others') understanding of democracy, which was not identical with majority rule. Chancellor Adenauer, who at the time needed the political support from the trade unions to get the Schuman Plan approved in Parliament, was able to achieve a compromise which was then portrayed as a trade union victory by the industrialists. On 7 June 1951, the co-determination law was passed by the Bundestag, confirming both the *Arbeitsdirektoren* on the management boards and equal representation of capital and labour on the supervisory boards of iron and steel and coal companies with more than 1,000 employees – but at the same time, it prevented the spread of co-determination to other sectors. For companies outside the coal and steel sector and with more than 2,000 employees, the 1952 *Betriebsverfassungsgesetz* (Company Constitution Law) set the workers' representation on the supervisory boards at one-third of members, with no labour representative on the board of managers.[26] The dispute over workers' participation in companies was thus not concluded by the law; it continued to flare up time and again. Certainly Louis P. Lochner's 1954 claim that German heavy industry had accepted co-determination was plain wrong and nothing more than a part of his pro-business propaganda.[27]

While not at all uniform in their response to labour representatives, the relationship between many managers and trade union representatives did not necessarily improve throughout the 1950s, and not even during the 1960s. When the trade unions in the early 1960s called for an extension of co-determination into the chemical, electrical and automobile industries, there was an outcry from both the BDI and the BDA and co-determination in heavy industry was again called a *systemwidriger Fremdkörper* (detrimental contaminant). In 1967, when Karl Schiller, the Grand Coalition's economics minister, initiated the *Konzertierte Aktion* (concerted action) between the state, industrialists and trade unions in response to the 1966 mini-recession, most industrialists were incensed at the idea of direct talks with the unions on economic policy.[28] As late as 1974, Sohl spoke of the 'abolition of our economic and social order' when faced with the expansion of co-determination into other industrial sectors, despite his own good experiences with it.[29] Almost twenty years earlier he had made the first public statement in this regard. When asked in early 1955 by newspaper journalists about his co-operation experience with trade union supervisory board member Viktor Agartz, who had the reputation of being a radical hardliner, he replied that their working relationship relating to co-determination was very good and very professional. Sohl may have been wrong-footed by the question but this was an embarrassing setback in PR terms. This admission, and the journalists' interpretation that management in heavy industry was beginning to change their minds on co-determination, gave rise to an angry letter by MP Wolfgang Pohle to Sohl. The Thyssen boss's comments had come at a very inconvenient time. In January 1954, the county court in Düsseldorf had ruled that for holding companies such as the GHH, the *Betriebsverfassungsgesetz* and not the co-determination law was applicable. It had been this legal loophole, aside from the significant cost factor, that had kept Reusch from pursuing full *Rückverflechtung* of the Gutehoffungshütte trust, as it allowed him to keep the unions off the board.[30] At the time of Sohl's statement, Parliament was in the process of debating the inclusion of holding companies into co-determination as well, just as the BDI had feared after the original verdict. Pohle complained to Sohl that in the light of such statements, it was impossible for him to argue in Parliament against the expansion of co-determination to holding companies.[31] In his autobiography, Sohl confirmed that Agartz had worked loyally on the board and that he had not noticed any of Agartz's supposed 'radical leftist commitments'.[32] Sohl's retrospective glorifying description of the co-operation between employers and employees during the reconstruction period has been heavily criticized by Toni Pierenkemper. In contradiction to Sohl's autobiography, which denies the existence of any antagonism between management and labour, Pierenkemper points out that Sohl was seen by the DGB as one of the biggest anti-trade union rabble-rousers, right up to his time as BDI president in the 1970s, and this is certainly confirmed by his 1974 statement discussed above.[33] Similarly, Sohl's claim that he was able to get Thyssen's works council chairman, Johannes Meyer, with whom he had a very good working relationship, appointed as labour director against the wishes of the trade unions is misleading. The co-determination law explicitly stipulated that the labour director could not be appointed against the majority votes of the labour representatives on the supervisory board.[34]

How much the Thyssen chairman and other steel men were opposed to co-determination becomes obvious from an incident in 1958. The Saar industrialist Ernst Röchling was summoned to a *Diskussionsabend* where he faced heavy criticism for, and had to explain why, he had allowed that the neutral eleventh man on the supervisory board of three Saar steel plants to be nominated by the trade unions and not the management. Röchling explained that Hermann Josef Abs, whose advice was usually taken as gospel, had thought this step was unavoidable but this explanation was dismissed outright with the argument that Röchling's actions had caused a precedent in favour of the unions which was never to be repeated.[35] The main reason for managements' opposition to co-determination remained unspoken. It was simply the challenge to the 'elite' managers and their 'calling' which derived from 'unqualified' workers sitting on the supervisory board and even more worryingly, in their opinion, on the managing board. Having labour representatives on these bodies was a direct challenge to the notion that 'only management can manage' and one that simultaneously both undermined their status as company leaders and their claim of elite status.

Despite the anti-union rhetoric, in particular from heavy industry, there were some activities by the employers which did not fit the hostile tone and showed a more co-operative side. During the 1957 metal workers' strike in Schleswig Holstein, it turned out that many companies were collecting union membership fees from their workers' wages and forwarded them to the unions. During periods of industrial action, these monies went straight into the unions' strike funds. WVES chief clerk Ahrens suggested that if the strike arbitration were to fail, this support for the unions should be stopped.[36] By mid-1960, the *Diskussionsabend* had to report that the situation had become even more confused than ever; eleven companies on the Ruhr still collected the fees, while six, together with the companies at the Saar, did not. Most surprising is the fact that the

Klöckner works on the Ruhr did collect the contributions, but the Klöckner plant in Bremen did not.[37]

This confusion was shared by almost all industrialists, and not only those who were affected by co-determination. They were happy (or at least grudgingly willing) to deal with *their* workers and their workers' representative within the company, even collect their dues. The attitudes highlight the underlying mentality of the 'good' workers, who were part of the *Betriebsfamilie* (company family) and the 'bad' trade union representatives, who, as outsiders, tried to create unrest amongst the workforce. This explains why industrialists were vehemently opposed to trade union 'functionaries' and treated them with suspicion. The symptomatic depth of this mistrust is shown in the diary of Ludwig Vaubel. In December 1948, he had castigated the trade unions' attempts at social levelling, when they had demanded equal distribution of Vereingte Glanzstoff Fabriken foundation funds for both workers and management. In spring 1949, however, he expressed his utter surprise about the high quality of the political leadership in the Bremen and Hamburg regional governments, most of whom had been trade union officials before they moved into active politics. Vaubel simply had not believed it to be possible for them to perform their duties so well.[38] There were plenty of public comments by the ASU's Josef Winschuh in the same tone. For example, in a speech in January 1950, at a time when unemployment in the Federal Republic reached a record high, he accused union officials of not caring about the workers and only thinking of their careers. Workers, he explained, were interested in social benefits and not in politically motivated socialization. Indeed, workers welcomed a modern form of patriarchal attitudes, which were even indispensable in small and medium-sized enterprises.[39] Winschuh reinforced this traditional employer attitude in a speech in 1952, when he claimed that in 1951, employers' voluntary social benefits to workers had doubled since 1936 and were now 25 per cent higher than the compulsory contribution to the social insurance schemes. With his claim that 'Social policy is a matter for the entrepreneurs, not the trade unions', he practically denied the unions their right to exist.[40] It was not only conservative hardliners who held this view on company benefits. Heinrich Nordhoff, the influential chief executive of Volkswagen, also stated that it had not been the trade unions who had 'eked out company benefits, but those had been willingly conceded by the entrepreneurs'. Despite this attitude (or because of it), Nordhoff was one of the managers who blazed the trail for close co-operation between management and works council, as long as this did not involve co-determination, which he too opposed.[41]

Occasionally, there was some behaviour which was ostensibly inconsistent. In his own company, Fritz Berg had the motto '*Alle Mitarbeiter im Betrieb bestimmen mit, aber der Unternehmer entscheidet allein*' ('all employees in the firm have a say, but the [final] decision is the entrepreneur's alone'), but on the shopfloor he was addressed informally by his first name by long-serving *Meister*.[42] In the light of social convention in 1950s and 1960s Germany, this is remarkable: addressing someone by their first name was the preserve of close friends, not colleagues, and certainly not that of a worker to his line manager or company boss. Berghahn, in his biography of Otto A. Friedrich, highlights these strict social conventions when he thinks it is important to mention that Friedrich and Berg were, despite their very different political outlook, on first-name terms.[43] The fact that Berg, the quintessential patriarch, allowed such informal behaviour from his experienced *Meister* is more an expression of the idea of the *Betriebsgemeinschaft* or *Werksfamilie*. In the 1950s, some of these men would have worked (or more appropriately, 'served') in Berg's company as long as, or even longer than, he had done. This had created a special form of trust, not least because the company knew that they had to rely on – and indeed *could* rely on – the *Meisters*' skills and expertise. However, Berg's position as 'head of the family' would never have been challenged by them.

In general, the attitude of owner-entrepreneurs of small and medium-sized businesses was possibly more hostile to trade unions than that of their big company colleagues, but at the same time also more caring towards their workers, which at times led to conflicting statements. Josef Winschuh in a speech in April 1952 entitled '*Sinn und Unsinn der Wirtschaftsdemokratie*' ('The Sense and Absurdity of Economic Democracy') spoke out for *innerbetriebliche Zusammenarbeit* (intra-firm co-operation) between management and workers because employers had to learn to see the 'worker as a human being' and thus needed to contribute to the 'humanization of work'. At the same time he condemned co-determination as the road to socialization and *Vermassung* of businesses and society. Winschuh pleaded for workers '*Mitwissen, Mitdenken, Mitwirken*' ('sharing knowledge, thinking collectively, contributing') but rejected outright joint leadership or co-determination.[44] ASU chairman Flender went even further in November 1956, when he declared that not only did the *Faktor Mensch* (human factor) need to be replaced by *Mensch als Persönlichkeit* (man as a personality) but that the master-in-the-house-attitude had become outdated, even if many entrepreneurs were not yet ready to accept this fact.[45] Just one year previously, however, he had taken a rather narrow view of life and its meaning. When he declared that 'the times of bombing raids and dismantling have shown that jobs had been more important than housing and many other things',[46] he reduced human existence to the *Betrieb* and the *Betriebsgemeinschaft*. In the mid-1950s, most entrepreneurs would have agreed with his narrow view on the company as the purpose of life, but younger workers in particular had developed a very different outlook on life.

Anti-union sentiment arose not least out of, or combined with, entrepreneurs' paternalist attitudes, which were present in companies of all sizes. In April 1949, Hermann Reusch received a letter of complaint from IG Metall, the metal workers' union. They described how a GHH estate manager had repeatedly insulted and beaten workers. After an assault on a worker with learning difficulties, the chairman of the works council had requested a visit from union representatives at the estate. However, when they turned up, they were driven off the estate by the manager, apparently on the orders of GHH board member Ernst Hilbert. IG Metall had so far not publicized the incident because of 'the previously good relationship between them and GHH'. Reusch seems to have started an investigation immediately because four days later, Hilbert confirmed the event and elaborated on it. The estates manager had admitted his actions and conceded that they had been entirely inappropriate. As if the estate manager's admittance was enough to excuse his despicable behaviour, Hilbert went on to say that 'the union had to appeal to us and cannot just intervene directly in the company (*in den Betrieb*)'.[47] Other than giving an example of how rude the treatment of subordinates could be in the late 1940s, the incident shows to what length the chairman of GHH was prepared to go to maintain his patriarchal position in the company after the initial complaint by the union. Although the incident has to be seen as a serious one even for the late 1940s, it is surprising that the chairman of a 70,000-strong company that was still undergoing reconstruction, investigated the case himself. When Reusch replied to the union, his tone was polite (in contrast to many other of his dealings with the unions) but he pointed out in no uncertain terms that it had no right to get involved in the company's operations and to settle the matter directly with the estates manager. This was a matter for the company's administration, 'which will be available to you any time for a discussion'.[48] Reusch's attitude, while clearly also intended to keep the unions out of operational affairs, highlights the underlying paternalistic mentality of Germany's post-war company leaders, even when it concerned only a single unskilled worker.

The mentality of many entrepreneurs and managers who ran small and medium-sized companies had at its core a paternalism which had developed during and immediately after the First World War.[49] In contrast to both the 'older' (e.g. Paul Reusch) and 'younger' (e.g. Sohl, Winkhaus, H. Reusch) generation of managers who had been spared military service in either the First or Second World War because of their importance for the war economy, the wartime experiences of those who had served certainly shaped their outlook. Comradeship and duty of care for their men was therefore extended to their workforce. Heinrich Krumm, in his diary, reflected back to his time as leader of a 120-strong signals detachment in the First World War and the early revolutionary period, where, as he said, 'I could experience for the first time what it means to lead men' ('*was Menschenführung heißt*').[50] The best representative of this group was Hans-Constantin Paulssen, who from the 1930s had been director general of the aluminium producing company Aluminium Werke Singen near Lake Constance and the Swiss border. Never a party member, he had nevertheless been appointed *Wehrwirtschaftsführer* (armament economy leader) by the Nazis and had increased Germany's crucial aluminium output during the war. This led to him being barred from the company, similar to Krumm, until his denazification as 'fellow traveller' in 1948.[51] Paulssen's conclusions from his First World War experiences were the call for, and support of, the factory community within the companies, a theme that was also very strong in the philosophy of other firms.[52] In marked contrast to many other industrialists, Paulssen did not reject trade unions and their work outright, but he saw them as the underlying factor for inflation due to their wage demands. Because of his moderate stance in social policies, in 1954 Paulssen became president of the Federation of German Employers' Associations, where his explicit aim was to 'work for the public good'.[53] Paulssen's attempt to continue with the policy of social partnership of his BDA predecessor Walter Raymond, another south German industrialist, put the BDA in sharp contrast to, and conflict with, the hardliners in the BDI camp who stuck to the traditional 'master-in-the-house' approach, but also to the ASU, which criticized him on a regular basis.[54]

Hermann Reusch's incendiary remarks in 1955 that the co-determination in the iron and steel industry had come about only due to 'brutal blackmail' by the trade unions had led to some 800,000 coal and steel workers downing tools in protest at the statement.[55] Irrespective of this outcome, most industrialists agreed with what Reusch had said in the speech but were not necessarily in agreement about whether it had been wise to make such a politically incorrect statement. Although Paulssen would have never made comments of such a kind, the BDI was able to 'achieve agreement' with him on the matter; in other words, he did not speak out against Reusch overstepping the mark.[56] This is not the only reason why Paulssen was not, as Berghahn has claimed, an 'Americanizer', someone who wanted to reshape and modernize German industry and industrial relations along American lines.[57] Rau-Kühne's description of Paulssen as a 'south German patriarch with Swiss accent', the latter because he tried to adopt some aspects of the Swiss social model, is much more fitting.[58] Paulssen's adherence to a traditional *Betriebsgemeinschaft* with clear hierarchies, his social manners which were formed by his military service, but in particular his political ideas of the early post-war years, in which he favoured a political reconstruction carried by influential but unelected men, mark him out as a social conservative patriarch rather than a modernizer of industrial relations.[59] It is only the contrast to the even more hard-line managers, and his often disparaged willingness to talk to labour representatives, that make him appear as a modernizer. A much more progressive influence on labour relations was that of Friedrich, who in 1956 met with Hamburg DGB representatives for 'open exchanges of opinion' to discuss the end of 'class hostilities'. In his capacity as chairman of the Hamburg BDI branch, he then invited union representatives to speak to the local BDI section, which was the first occurrence of this kind and would remain a rare happening.[60] Friedrich could get away with it because of his strong position within Hamburg industrial circles and the more liberal Hamburg mentality. Fritz Berg, Hermann Reusch or Otto Vogel certainly would not have participated in such an event and as Michael Schneider has concluded managements' choice of words towards the trade unions and co-determination points to 'an ideological continuation from the 1920s to the 1970s'.[61] For the 'old guard' of industrialists, managerial leadership was a matter only for entrepreneurs, because ultimately this leadership claim was one of their legitimations.

Whereas the relationship German entrepreneurs had with trade union officials who were not members of their company was difficult, ranging from outright hostility to bare acceptance as negotiation partners, there was one point on which all businessmen did agree. This was their opposition and out-and-out antagonism to German communists and communism. The qualification 'German' is important: as will be shown in the next chapter, there were exceptions to this rule if it involved business deals with communist countries. German industrialists' fear of communists and communism always had something almost irrational about it, ever since the Bolsheviks had staged Russia's 1917 October Revolution. Attempted communist coups in Germany – notably the 1919 Spartacist Revolt and the 1923 uprisings in the Ruhr and Saxony – had a significant impact, and the attendant fear did not abate. Industrialists took little comfort from the fact that in all cases the uprisings had been swiftly and ruthlessly quashed through the actions of either the paramilitary Freikorps, as was the case in 1919, or by official military units. Even though the German Communist Party, the KPD, achieved a very respectable 16.9 per cent of the vote in the November 1932 Reichstag election, anti-communist forces in Germany, especially in the army and paramilitary units, would have prevented a KPD takeover.[62] Although the Communists were the political group that had been the most persecuted by the Nazis and which had suffered disproportionately heavy losses, they remained well organized even in hiding. Their involvement in anti-fascist committees in the immediate aftermath of Allied occupation would have served as a warning and reminder to industrialists (if they needed one) that their fear of communism was still justified. The conduct of Soviet occupation forces and events east of the Iron Curtain would have contributed to the continuing 'red scare' in industrial circles, as did the general political uncertainty of the time; in any case, by mid-1945 the fear of Communism was back on the Ruhr. In June 1945 Walter Rohland wrote a memorandum for the American occupation authorities on the future of the Ruhr industries which he pre-circulated amongst his colleagues. Conjuring up the fear of 'communism and chaos', he explained that so far the 'politically uneducated' German worker was 'currently not inclined towards Bolshevik ideas'. This statement was annotated with a question mark by one of the GHH directors, presumably board member Georg Lübsen.[63] It was a clear indication that the managers had only limited trust in their workers.

In the 1949 federal elections, the Communists achieved 5.7 per cent of the vote but in 1953, their share had dropped to 2.2 per cent and they failed to return to the Bundestag. Things were similar in North-Rhine Westphalia, which had become the KPD's stronghold in West Germany. In the regional elections in 1947, they had gained 14 per cent, with a particularly strong following amongst coal miners. Thereafter, however, their fortunes declined, polling 5.5 per cent in 1950 and only 3.8 per cent in 1954, which meant they were no longer in the Landtag.[64] In 1956, the party was banned by the Federal Constitutional Court because it was found to pursue undemocratic and unconstitutional objectives. Despite the very clear decline of the KPD, caused not only by West Germany's improving economic situation but also because of political disillusionment following Cold War events, German managers, and in particular those from heavy industry, remained wary of the 'red peril', almost at a paranoid level. In an early attempt to counter the communist threat, some Ruhr managers joined the Movement for Moral Rearmament, an organization created in 1938 by an American minister, Frank Buchman. The movement was interesting to the managers because of its Christian ideology and strong anti-materialist and anti-communist sentiments. Despite the movement's considerable successes at Gelsenkirchener Bergwerks AG – in particular in relation to the easing of tensions with trade unions and the curtailing of communist works councils – its success was short-lived; by 1952, German membership had halved to 660 compared to its peak year of 1949.[65]

The continuing fear and paranoia about the danger from communism, which indicates a persistent strong feeling of insecurity, showed itself again in 1955 when at Hoesch's Dortmund steel plant Westfalenhütte seventeen communists were elected to the works council, against six Social Democrats and two Christian union members. The result was a severe shock to the Ruhr managers and the DII tried to provide a detailed press analysis of the election outcome.[66] It is difficult to give a definitive reason for the communist success, but the KPD had traditionally a very strong grassroots organization and so it is perfectly possible that the victory was due to the candidates' personality and persuasive messaging. In any case, the result made co-determination at

Westfalenhütte more difficult, as the communist works council had little inclination to co-operate with the labour director, which this time irritated management.[67] The 1956 ban on the KPD did not ease industrialists' fears. In 1958, the DII reported extensively about '*kommunistische Betriebsagitation*' ('communist workplace agitation') that the party was thought to be conducting underground. In 1959, under the rubric of 'trade union issues', the DII highlighted the regional focal points of communist propaganda and listed no fewer than 287 communist newspapers in circulation; by 1961, the figure had risen to 301.[68] At the Saar, Ernst Röchling saw himself confronted with '10 per cent identifiable communists' in Völklingen's city council. In the previous local elections, he claimed, 10 per cent of the voters had voted for the communists who were now running under the label of 'Deutsche Demokratische Union' (DDU). They had achieved 5 per cent of the 1960 regional elections vote and had sent two deputies to the Saar Parliament.[69] Röchling's portrayal was rather one-dimensional. While the DDU did indeed take in former KPD members and was called 'left-wing', it was not the KPD in disguise. In any case, its 1960 electoral success was short-lived; it failed to regain parliamentary seats in 1965.[70]

At first glance, businesses' anti-communist paranoia is reminiscent of the 'Red Scare' and McCarthyism in 1950s America but there were important differences. Although strictly anti-communist, the Adenauer government never subscribed to the prevailing paranoia on this issue, despite the fact that they used fear of communism whenever it suited them in domestic politics. Also, industrialists' fear of communism did not abate as quickly as McCarthyism eventually did, as Röchling's statements show. This is also in contrast to the German public, who in general were more afraid of the Soviet Union than they were of communists at home, so that this anxiety can be seen as a particular trait of many German industrialists. Their fear can be explained in two ways. On the one hand, it could have been an expression of considerable mistrust in their own workforce and of West Germany's political – and even economic – system. After all, if the social market economy was as successful as the industrialists claimed, why had the number of communists increased? This explanation would to some extent challenge the entrepreneurs' self-image as the makers of the economic miracle and the bringers of economic prosperity. Or on the other hand, it was nothing but that old tendency to 'cry wolf' whenever political decisions did not go the entrepreneurs' way, something that had manifested itself in their psyche time and again over the years. In any case, the fear has also to be seen in the context and against the background of the Cold War, which intensified again after Khrushchev's Berlin Ultimatum in 1958. This domestic concern about communism, however, contrasts very sharply with industry's attempts to support *Osthandel*, the trade with Eastern Europe, which will be discussed in the next chapter.

8

Osthandel: Trading with the 'Enemy'

This chapter will show that in contrast to their attitudes to communists at home, German industrialists had no hesitation in trading with countries of the Eastern Bloc, in particular the Soviet Union and the GDR. The reason for this lack of reservation (*Berührungsangst*) was due to experiences German businessmen had garnered in the interwar years. The chapter will also explore the work of the famous *Ostausschuß* (Eastern Committee), which was involved in almost all trade with the East. The second part of the chapter examines industrialists' views and impact on West Berlin and the trade with the GDR before arguing that it was differences of opinion on trade with the East that made heavy industry move increasingly away from official government positions before the mid-1960s.

Eastern Europe, and in particular the Soviet Union, had been a significant export market for Germany's interwar economy since at least the 1923 Rapallo Agreement. Bührer estimates that during 1928–33, *Osthandel* on average accounted for 18 per cent of German exports, with another 16 per cent or so going to the Balkan countries and Turkey.[1] Although German exports to Russia before the First World War had amounted to less than 9 per cent of total German exports, German companies had significant sectoral leadership. Siemens and AEG had dominated, either directly or indirectly, the Russian electrical market, holding a share of 85 per cent or more.[2] Although German–Soviet trade after 1918 reached its highest point only in 1940–41, just prior to the German invasion of the Soviet Union, and although the Weimar Republic's total trade with the Soviet Union at its peak was only half of the pre-war trade volume, it remained very important for political reasons. It was part of Germany's strategy to revise the outcome of the First World War and it remained extremely significant for particular sectors of the German economy.[3] Even before the Rapallo Treaty had been signed, the trading house Otto Wolff had paved the way for increased trade between the two countries. The lead sector of Germany's exports to the Soviet Union shifted from the electrical industry towards *Maschinenbau* (mechanical engineering) companies. By 1928, 30 per cent of their total exports went to the Soviet Union and some companies became increasingly dependent on exports to the Soviet Union.[4] After the onset of the Great Depression, Soviet demands for German engineering exports held an even greater significance. Walter Rohland's experience was not untypical. He explained that after 1930, his company, Deutsche Edelstahlwerke, 'kept afloat only because of orders from the Soviet Union' which the company had to take on despite very low profit margins; without these contracts, unfavourable as they may have been, the company would have gone out of business.[5]

Once the Cold War got under way, West German companies were not only faced with losing the Soviet market, but also those areas that under the Potsdam Agreement had been ceded to Poland and to '*Mitteldeutschland*', the area that made up the GDR. Before the Second World War, those inner-German markets had consumed up 36 per cent of West German industrial production; the almost complete loss of those markets was thus a severe blow for West German industry.[6] Until 1949, German exports, not only to the East but also to the West, were controlled by JEIA, the Allied Joint Export-Import Agency, which was loathed by German companies because of its incomprehensible rules and bureaucratic inefficiency. It took the Federal Republic until 1953 to regain full formal sovereignty over its customs, trade and capital exchange policy. By this time West Germany had become a member of the Coordinating Committee for Multilateral Export Controls, or CoCom, and 'a test field for US embargo policies towards the communist East'.[7] In contrast to the Weimar period, however, there would at best be limited support from the new West German government for a revival of German exports to the Eastern Bloc. The outright hostility from some quarters of Adenauer's administration towards eastern trade was also shared by some industrialists, due to their anti-communist convictions.

There had been a number of prominent German business leaders who up to the late 1940s had believed that Germany would eventually play an intermediary role between East and West, amongst them Otto A. Friedrich, Ludwig Vauble and Dietrich Wilhelm von Menges.[8] Although they did change their attitude in the face of political realities, they and with them the majority of German industrialists felt severely discriminated against by the obstructions placed in their path by American authorities, especially between 1949 and 1953. Complaints, such as that lodged by Klöckner in September 1950 that some of their deliveries to Czechoslovakia had been delayed by US troops at the border despite holding valid export licences issued by the Allied High Commission, were commonplace.[9] Partly to circumvent these discriminations, but also in order to prepare for a revival of trade with Eastern Europe, there had been plans to establish a committee for trade with the East since at least February 1950. Its intended task was to co-ordinate the trade with Eastern Europe, but not the GDR.[10] For Cold War political reasons, the FRG saw the GDR as part of its 'domestic' market. The managers realized early on that for political reasons they had to tread quite carefully, and this slowed things down quite considerably. The BDI's foreign trade committee concluded in March 1950 that no new *Ostausschuß* should be established at this point in time 'to avoid misunderstandings on the part of the Allies', but also because Allied decartelization plans ruled out a committee structure that had existed before the war. Instead the Foreign Trade Committee was to set up an '*Ost Referat*' (Eastern department).[11] Concerns about the Allies getting the wrong impression, i.e. one of German embargo violation, remained high, and less than a year later, in January 1951, Fritz Berg had to write to the Allied High Commission in response to newspaper reports in which British High Commissioner Ivone Kirkpatrick had accused the Germans of a seesaw policy between East and West, a claim Berg totally refuted. Later in the year, the BDI compiled extensive statements in preparation for a BDI delegation to the US, with which the delegation wanted to prove that the West German industry was totally opposed to illegal exports with the East, although they insisted on their right to conduct legitimate trade.[12]

Eventually the initiative for the establishment of the *Ostausschuß* came not from industry but from the Economics Ministry.[13] The Ministry's initiative had two main catalysts: first, it was attempting political damage limitation after the Moscow World Economic Conference of April 1952. A small delegation of twenty German businessmen, led by Heinrich Krumm, had defied calls from the government and attended the Moscow conference, returning with contracts to the tune of DM 500 million, which was politically embarrassing for Adenauer's government.[14] Krumm had briefed all relevant authorities about the trip in advance and he claimed that at that stage he had received support from all sides. He was outraged when, after his return, he was heavily criticized, in particular by the government, for participating in the conference. Undeterred, however, he continued to advocate the creation of a new *Ostausschuß*.[15] The Economics Ministry proposed the *Ostausschuß* in order to avoid similarly unpleasant experiences in the future. The expectation was that it would be able to control and influence industrialists' actions in regard to Eastern Europe much more effectively if such a committee were in place. It is therefore ironic that industrialists achieved their aim of a proper committee on Eastern trade not due to their own efforts but rather a political face-saving. The second reason was almost the reverse of the first one: an officially sanctioned *Ostausschuß* could be used for unofficial diplomacy and trade policy with Eastern Bloc countries with which the FRG had no diplomatic relations.[16]

By the time the *Ostausschuß* was set up on 17 December 1952, there were three distinct groups amongst industrialists, and each held a different opinion on the matter.[17] First, there was Fritz Berg, who together with BDI and the BDA officials, was very sceptical, if not outright hostile, to trade with the communist bloc and he stated so repeatedly in public. During the 1950 BDI annual meeting, Berg had pledged to Chancellor Adenauer on behalf of the whole German industry that they were conjoined with the western world and would 'fight until the end to stop the Asiatic deluge'.[18] At the BDI 1951 annual meeting, in reply to an Adenauer speech in which the Chancellor appealed to the industrialists to 'take their place in the inner front against the slavery from the East', Berg promised to do so regardless of the consequences this would have for industry's ideas on trade policy. He condemned all forms of illegal trading with the East and threatened those industrialists who participated in illegal deals with exclusion from their ranks. However, Berg conceded that legitimate trade should be expanded and any discrimination against the FRG be abolished.[19] Berg's speech was a balancing act. On the one side, he was very much in agreement with Adenauer's 'policy of strength' against the East;[20] on the other side, he had to keep his fellow industrialists if not happy, then at least content. This meant acknowledging big industry's complaint about the much more stringent export controls the Federal Republic was facing compared to other Western European countries, while condemning illegal trade with the East, which was still an ongoing problem. In October and November 1951 alone, US military police in Bavaria had stopped over 120 shipments worth more than DM 2.8 million from being shipped illegally to Czechoslovakia. US officials estimated that contraband shipments from Germany to the Eastern Bloc totalled $100 million per year.[21] A very large part of such trade would have involved SME companies and those based in Berlin.[22] The Iron Curtain had cut off their traditional customer base in Central and Eastern Europe, and they had not yet been able to find new customers in the West. At least for the time being, exporting to the East was seen by many of them as the only way their companies could survive.

The second group was the Ruhr's heavy industry and mechanical engineering industries. Still combatting 'reputational issues', they had – more grudgingly than willingly – supported the official BDI line on Eastern trade although they had voiced strong objections to the way Berg had made industry a pawn (*Manöveriermasse*) in Adenauer's foreign policy. During a meeting in April 1952 at the DII, they came up with four key demands, summarized by Karsten Rudolph as:

1. East–West trade was to be defined as being of national interest and therefore had to be expanded;
2. German agreement to the CoCom embargos was made subject to equal treatment of all participants, which meant calling an end to special US controls on German exports;
3. German industry agreed to keep to the embargo list, if German trade with the East and third-party countries was not discriminated against;
4. there was a demand on Great Britain in particular to show solidarity with Western sanctions.

Finally they pleaded that West Germany's special situation in regards to trade with the GDR had to be acknowledged by the Western powers as well.[23] Following their vigorous campaigning behind the scenes, the establishment of the *Ostausschuß der deutschen Industrie* as a committee within the BDI was a victory for those industrialists who wanted to return to their old markets in Eastern Europe.

The third, and by far the smallest, group interested in Eastern trade were industrialists like Heinrich Krumm, who continued the traditional view of Germany being the 'honest broker' between East and West, a Germany that was not attached to either side. Krumm's death in a traffic accident in 1957 while on the way to the Leipzig trade fair, but more so the political realities, meant that this group quickly lost significance.[24]

Adenauer's staunch anti-communism, as well as his intention to show who was determining foreign policy and foreign trade policy in the FRG, caused two early political setbacks for the *Ostausschuß*. In 1954, the Federal Government prevented an *Ostausschuß* trip to Moscow because of foreign policy concerns and some incorrect briefing by Walter Hallstein, the 'hardest of all the anti-Soviet hardliners'.[25] Moreover in 1955, Adenauer did not include *Ostausschuß* members in his delegation when he visited Moscow to establish diplomatic relations between the Soviet Union and the FRG.[26] Irrespective of these hurdles, the committee *was* able to help industry in a significant way. In January 1953, shortly after its creation, it requested from the Ministry of Economics a copy of the secret CoCom embargo lists, so that companies for the first time had a reliable guide of which goods they were not allowed to export, thereby helping them avoid costly delays or even refusal of export altogether as had occurred so often before. However, just one month later, in February 1953, there was a serious complaint from the Economics Ministry. Several press articles about CoCom lists had appeared and while it could not be proven for sure, the ministry assumed that the author was the economics journalist and member of the *Ostausschuß* China group, Herbert Gross. As a consequence, the Ministry considered withholding future lists. The matter seems to have been brought to an agreeable outcome by members of the Eastern Committee themselves who had a serious conversation with Gross. In any case, in April 1954, the Ministry informed the *Ostausschuß* of an upcoming change and liberalization of the embargo list and that a list of exportable goods would now be made public.[27]

The original executive board of the *Ostausschuß* consisted of Ernst Reuter of the civil engineering company DEMAG as chairman and Wilhelm Menne of Hoechst and Hermann Wenhold from the DIHT as first deputies, as well as Hermann Josef Abs of Deutsche Bank.[28] The driving figures for trade with the East, however, were Otto Wolff von Amerongen and Berthold Beitz, and eventually in the 1970s (outside this study's time frame), Ernst Wolf Mommsen, who since the 1950s had been heavy industry's expert on exports to the GDR.[29] At the request of Economics Minister Ludwig Erhard, Wolff von Amerongen was to chair the working party 'USSR'. In 1958, he replaced Reuter, who had been both unlucky and politically insensitive, as *Ostausschuß* chairman.[30] Wolff von Amerongen and Beitz were both 'outsiders' to the Ruhr establishment. Although the former was tolerated as the heir and owner of a steel trading house, in the eyes of the Ruhr elite he had to prove himself for a number of reasons: first, he was not a traditional *Bergassessor*, but had 'only' a commercial training background; second, because of his illegitimate birth; and finally, because of his youth. Born in 1918, he was seen by many as too inexperienced to run both the *Ostausschuß* and his own company. Beitz was even more of an outsider. He had made his post-war name in insurance before Alfried Krupp had made him his plenipotentiary. Beitz, who apparently had never mentioned his humanitarian actions to his fellow industrialists, was declared a 'Righteous Amongst the Nations' by Yad Vashem in 1973 and received the highest Polish civilian order for his wartime rescue of Jewish and Polish workers at the town of Boryslav in Galicia, where he had worked for an oil company. In contrast to most of the other Ruhr industrialists, neither of the two men had had connections with, or sympathies for, the Nazis and they were, at least for top businessmen at the time, rather liberal in their political and social outlook. Wolff von Amerongen's motivation for a revival of German trade with Eastern Europe, and in particular the Soviet Union, had very much to do with his company's history and his father's role as pioneer in trade with the Soviets in the interwar period. As Rudolph states: 'If during the Weimar Republic trade with Russia and China had a name, it was that of Otto Wolff.'[31]

The successful revival of eastern trade would have meant several things for Wolff von Amerongen: that he continued his father's legacy; that he could prove his ability as a manager; and that he could silence his critics amongst other industrialists. Beitz, too, had a tradition to follow in trade with the Soviets, as it had been Krupp that, in 1922, was the first German company to conduct business with the new Soviet state following the Bolshevik revolution.[32]

Although trade with the Eastern Bloc did increase significantly after 1952, with German exports to the Soviet Union reaching DM 50 million in 1954, this remained

Figure 8.1 Otto Wolf von Amerongen (1918–2007), heir to and owner of the steel trading house Otto Wolff. One of the youngest Ruhr industrialists, he was a driving force for trade with the East and a leading figure in and long-time chairman of the *Ostausschuß der deutschen Wirtschaft*, where, together with Berthold Beitz, he conducted an unofficial parallel *Ostpolitik*. © Rheinisch-Westfälisches Wirtschaftsarchiv Köln RWWA 72-F-1597.

insignificant overall compared to total German exports of DM 22 billion; in fact, there was no hope that eastern trade would regain its scale of the 1920s and 1930s, even if this had been wished for politically. Since the Soviet Union paid for its imports with industrial raw materials such as oil, manganese, chrome and timber, trade allowed for 'a structural improvement' of West Germany's foreign trade balance as the country did not need to spend its scant dollar reserves on the world markets. Ultimately, it was the Soviets' overall limited economic capacity which prevented trade expansion. The Soviet Union did not have enough hard currency to pay for German imports so they had to revert to barter, but even those transactions were limited by the Soviet Union's inability to produce more of the goods the West Germans were interested in.[33] By this time, German industry and even the *Ostausschuß* had accepted two things: in eastern trade, political considerations had priority over economic interests; and pre-war trade levels would not be achieved because of the Soviet Union's overall economic weakness and reliance on barter agreements,[34] Despite these limitations, trade with the East did have an impact on German companies, and sometimes this was negative. For example, Krupp's eastern exports by the mid-1960s averaged about 7 to 12 per cent of its total exports. As the Soviet Union did not pay in cash, a liquidity crisis that had hit Krupp in

1967 was exacerbated to such an extent that it brought the company almost to its knees.[35]

All the while *Osthandel* continued at a lower than initially hoped-for but nonetheless stable level, hard-line critics of the trade, especially Fritz Berg, had been silent. He could not speak out too openly against trade with communist states for fear of alienating heavy industry, but Berg's moment would come in another way after Nikita Khrushchev's 1958 Berlin Ultimatum. Before the Second World War, Greater Berlin's industrial capacity had produced a higher GDP output than the Ruhr area and sustained a population of 4.2 million people, more than London or New York at the time.[36] Berlin had been Germany's financial centre, a hub for road, rail and canal transport and home to almost half of Germany's electrical industry, a quarter each of textiles, precision engineering and optics and 20 per cent of the country's mechanical engineering. At the time of the city's surrender to Soviet forces in May 1945, about a quarter of industrial assets had been destroyed in 1,000 air raids and the severe ground fighting. Most of what had survived the war was stripped by Soviet forces as reparations. During the Berlin Blockade (June 1948–May 1949), the Allied airlift was able to sustain the population but not the economy – unemployment in the three western sectors of the city reached higher levels than during the peak of the 1932–33 economic crisis. After the blockade ended joblessness remained stubbornly high at 25 to 30 per cent for years, despite significant work-creation programmes and billions of Deutschmarks of aid that were poured into West Berlin by the Americans and the West German government. Attempts made through the so-called *Berliner Auftragsfinanzierung* (financing of orders to Berlin), in which West German customers received significant loans for their orders to West Berlin's industry, had only a limited effect. Many West German companies had found new suppliers and in general were hesitant to pay for the transport costs to and from the island city, or just shied away from the political risk of a new blockade interrupting their deliveries.[37] By the mid-1950s, even exhibiting at the Berlin Industry Fair was no longer seen as economically beneficial, although it was acknowledged that for political reasons this had to be continued.[38] All this changed on 27 November 1958, when Khrushchev demanded the withdrawal of all Allied troops from West Berlin and the transformation of the three sectors into a 'free city' similar to Danzig in the interwar years. This was Fritz Berg's opportunity to turn his anti-communist rhetoric into action. At the BDI board meeting on 3 December, he called for further investments in the city and an increase in the financing of orders. The board sanctioned his invitation to industrial leaders for a meeting in his hometown of Altena on 19 December, to discuss steps to counter Khrushchev's threat. In a letter to the meeting's participants, Berg emphasized that, although some big companies – amongst them Siemens, AEG, Telefunken and Osram (all of which used to have their headquarters in Berlin before 1945) – had already defied the political risk and invested millions in the city, more had still to be done. Berg suggested to also ask friends abroad to 'buy Berlin'.[39] Yet only two years previously, Berg had condemned as an unnecessary tax burden for businesses and asked for an immediate end to the *Notopfer Berlin* (Berlin emergency contribution), a 2 Pfennig surcharge on all mail posted and a 1 per cent tax surcharge, which had been in place since the Berlin Blockade.[40] Six months after the Altena meeting, on 23 June 1959, the BDI held its annual meeting in West

Berlin, in a sign of defiance to Khrushchev's speech and since 'there was no other city in Germany with which we [the BDI] felt a stronger association than with Berlin'.[41] Berg's Altena initiative, born out of anti-communist sentiment, yielded significant success within a short period of time. A month before the annual meeting, the BDI board could report an increase of 7 per cent in the turnover of the Berlin economy: production output had risen 9 per cent and there had been an overall 6 per cent rise of orders. The comparative figures for West Germany were 0.8, 2.6 and 2 per cent respectively.[42]

West Berlin remained dependent on West German aid in the form of direct budget subsidies, tax breaks and loans for industrial orders until the collapse of the Berlin Wall in 1989. However, the extra boost Berg's initiative brought to the West Berlin economy helped to finally stabilize its overall precarious situation and to keep unemployment below 100,000.[43] The example of West German trade with West Berlin, however, highlights how politics influenced trade with the East, and how quickly the 'unpolitical' managers were involved with economic policy decisions. During the BDI board meeting on 23 September 1960, during which the tone against the East became markedly sharper, Otto Wolff von Amerongen gave a summary of the Federal Republic's trade with West Berlin and the GDR: trade with Berlin was 12 times as large as trade with the GDR, but East Germany still received 12 per cent of its total imports from the FRG and was not able to easily substitute it with trade from other countries. Although this gave West Germany an economic advantage over the GDR, it could not be translated into political leverage to achieve cast-iron guarantees for the free access to Berlin, and thus the GDR continued to hold the FRG to ransom in this regard. A much more successful approach, especially in terms of propaganda, would be 'an absence' from the Leipzig Trade Fair, but this could only happen in agreement with other NATO members and neutral Western European states so that the FRG would not isolate itself, i.e. lose trade to its western competitors. During the discussion that followed Wolff von Amerongen's presentation, it was agreed that if all intra-German trade could be channelled through West Berlin, access to the city would become secured through this shift almost by itself; a boycott of the Leipzig Fair, however, would have only limited effect as other countries would most likely be able to fill the gap West German companies might create through their absence. Nevertheless, the board agreed to support the government's measures concerning the Leipzig Trade Fair and recommended that members should not renew the rental agreements for their fair stalls or, if they had already done so, that they used their right to withdrawal.[44]

There had been previous occasions when worsening German–German relationships had threatened to impact negatively on the trade between the two countries, most notably perhaps in April 1955, when the GDR had increased the toll on the road to Berlin for western haulage companies. In this instance, West German countermeasures beyond the temporary suspension of western steel deliveries to the GDR had been considered, but they had been quickly dismissed because the GDR's stranglehold on West Berlin was regarded as too strong. After one month, Bonn was eventually prepared to pay the higher toll, although for political reasons not 'from one government to another'.[45] In 1960, the situation was different: although the Adenauer government claimed it reacted to a tightening of GDR travel permit regulations, there was another, more serious, reason in the Chancellor's view. For years, West German industry had attended the Leipzig Trade Fair, both in spring and autumn, with up to 1,000 and 1,600 exhibiting companies at the respective fairs, for which they paid a total of DM 500,000 in stall fees,[46] which was a significant hard-currency income stream for the GDR. The stalls of the big West German companies in particular also offered the communist leadership ample opportunity for propaganda; during the 1960 Spring Trade Fair, three such incidences occurred. First, Phoenix Rheinrohr had decorated the outside of their stall with a photograph which showed Nikita Khrushchev and GDR Minister President Otto Grotewohl visiting the company's stall the previous year, which was seen as a breach of etiquette in the western Cold War propaganda battle. Second, following a press report, Ernst Wolf Mommsen was accused of having suggested the creation of an all-German 'steel council' while attending a reception given by East German Economics Minister Rau. Additionally, Phoenix managers at the stall were accused of having listened to anti-western diatribes by Walter Ulbricht without contradicting him, which amounted to 'an outrageous lack of political insight'.[47] The third incident involved Mannesmann managers and the Krupp director Carl Hundhausen, who interrupted a political tirade by Ulbricht with a quick toast 'to peace'. When Berg, after having being briefed by Adenauer about these 'despicable' incidents, wanted to reprimand the managers involved, something extraordinary happened. Berthold Beitz cut him off and told him that he would not be allowed to act as 'the Chancellor's commissar for industry' and Berg retreated in the face of this unprecedented rebuke.[48]

The incident demonstrates that by early 1960, an anti-communist tirade, even if it was initiated by Adenauer himself, was no longer enough to stop the men from the Ruhr trading with the GDR. The GDR's introduction of travel permits in 1960 gave the Adenauer government one last official excuse to ban further visits to the Leipzig fairs, despite protests from the BDI and individual companies and managers.[49] In 1962, the year after the GDR had erected the Berlin Wall, there was little debate among industrialists how they should act in regard to exhibiting at Leipzig. The government had asked industry to boycott the Leipzig Autumn Fair because they thought that suspending inner-German trade altogether was not possible due to the negative consequences this could have for West Berlin. Although West German firms had a share of 20 per cent of all trade contracts agreed at Leipzig, there was no open dissent and the BDI agreed the boycott in order 'to strengthen the solidarity of the whole German people in these serious days'.[50] All of the big companies cancelled their stalls, some rather hesitantly, and some switching to the Brno fair in Czechoslovakia. However, about half of all West German exhibitors, i.e. mainly less prominent SME companies, did attend regardless.[51]

The history of the Leipzig Trade Fair boycott by companies of the iron and steel industry shows a growing unease amongst the Ruhr's top managers about the politically imposed limits to business and first signs of a willingness to no longer following political directives. In July 1962, there was still unanimity that companies should not attend and no senior company representative went to Leipzig, but there was no longer a full boycott of the fair, either. They set up the *Beratungsstelle Stahlverwendung* (Advisory Office for Steel Use), which operated a joint stand for the industry so that orders from Eastern European countries could be taken.[52] One year on, Gerhard

Elkmann of Hoesch formally requested a lifting of the visiting ban since some companies were cheating. He cited the case of Gutehoffnungshütte, where despite Hermann Reusch's clear instructions to all subsidiary companies not to go to Leipzig, Ferrostaal (run by Dietrich Wilhelm von Menges) had allowed its Argentinian subsidiaries to attend and had subsequently bagged all the contracts. Hans Dichgans, the Iron and Steel Association's chief clerk and CDU MP, brought a long discussion on the topic to an end by pointing to the political significance of Elkmann's request and it was declined. This was confirmed just one month later with reference to a BDI meeting which had concluded that: 'Attendance at the fair was a political problem. The decision was therefore one to be taken by each company, who should consider the public reactions their decision would cause.'[53] In other words, the BDI gave a clear warning about the potential damage to a company's image and reputation if they took part. The following year the members of the *Diskussionsabend* had to agree that they were no longer able to find agreement on this political question.[54] By this time the previously solid (if sometimes hesitant) obedience to political decisions had disappeared due to a significant political miscalculation by Adenauer.

It was no accident that it had been Hoesch's Gerhard Elkmann who asked for the boycott to be ended in 1963. Hoesch, together with Mannesmann and Phoenix Rheinrohr, had been hard hit by a NATO embargo of large diameter pipes (19 inch or larger). At the request of European countries, large diameter pipes had been taken off the CoCom embargo list in 1958. Between then and 1962, German companies had exported 660,000 tons of large pipes to the Soviet Union, which paid in part with oil deliveries, so that Soviet oil exports to the FRG increased six-fold from half a million to three million tons by 1962. This in turn alerted American oil companies, which did not like the new competition. For 1963, new deliveries from Mannesmann (120,000 tons), Hoesch (30,000 tons) and Phoenix-Rheinrohr (70,000 tons) had been ordered, which Mannesmann in particular needed to avoid making 600 jobs redundant.[55] On 21 November 1962, under strong American pressure, the NATO council (where in contrast to CoCom decisions could be taken by majority vote) decided to impose an embargo on large diameter pipes, including already existing contracts. One week later, German government officials informed industry about this change in policy – and this time, the political decision was met with open opposition and resistance, including the threat of redundancies by Christmas. There had been no comparable opposition from industry to Adenauer's policy; not even Krumm's 1952 visit to the Moscow trade conference came close. It was only the beginning of a political lobbying of unprecedented scale by the three companies. Mannesmann hired Julius Klein to lobby in the USA and the US Embassy in Bonn, but to no avail. Phoenix-Rheinrohr went even further and risked a direct contravention of the embargo by establishing a new company in Sweden whose sole purpose was the export of pipes to the Soviet Union (not being a NATO member, Sweden was not bound by the embargo).[56] Although they failed to bring significant other parts of industry on their side, domestically the three companies were able to muster not only the support of the economic press but also support from all parties in the Bundestag, including Adenauer's CDU. The aim was to force a vote in Parliament which would have the embargo removed, or at least to allow the companies to fulfil the contracts that had been signed before the embargo's imposition, as other countries had allowed their industry to do. The debate and vote took place on 18 March 1963 and Adenauer avoided defeat only because he was able to hide behind parliamentary rules of procedure – after the debate, he made all his deputies leave the chamber so that the Bundestag was not quorate. A mere six months later, the embargo collapsed because Japanese companies had stepped in and were now delivering the pipes to the Soviet Union.[57]

Never before had there been such an open opposition by industrialists to official government policy and the consequences were significant. In a speech to the BDI board in December 1963, Otto Wolff von Amerongen, in his capacity as *Ostausschuß* chairman, went so far as to altogether question the Hallstein Doctrine.[58] A similar conclusion was drawn by von Menges in 1965 after he had visited the Leipzig Spring Fair. Although a little bit more guarded in his remarks than Wolff von Amerongen, he nevertheless expected that the GDR's economic isolation, and with it the Hallstein Doctrine, could not be maintained for much longer. In a speech given to the CDU's youth organization *Junge Union* and the party's *Wirtschaftsrat* (economic council) in February 1966, he stated two prerequisites for foreign trade: that politics retained primacy over the economy but that the economy could pave the way for politics; and almost as a reward for accepting the first premise, he demanded that the economy should not be used as political leverage in relation to Eastern Europe.[59]

Led by the examples of Berthold Beitz, who had long been nicknamed 'the roaming ambassador' because of his 'economic diplomacy' in Eastern Europe; by Otto Wolff von Amerongen, the long-serving chairman of the *Ostausschuß* who had started out in the tradition of his father's trade with the East; and by Ernst Wolf Mommsen and Dietrich Wilhelm von Menges, the 'new kids on the block', by the mid-1960s West German industrialists had distanced themselves from official trade politics.[60] While they were still prepared to accept the primacy of politics overall, they were no longer prepared to be the stooges of politics or politicians of which Fritz Berg could be seen almost as a prototype.

Eastern trade shows the double standards, if not outright hypocrisy, West German industrialists could display. While they were fearful of German communists, they were happy to conduct lucrative business deals with Eastern European communists. Eastern trade had its origins in two main features, the first being the need to recoup old markets (a cause which became less important with the ongoing export expansion into the rest of the world), and the other the connecting factor of traditional trade with the East by a number of famous companies. This latter point gained increasing traction and was amplified by new men (Beitz, von Menges) in old companies (Krupp and GHH) but they too had to face up to the political and economic limits of trade. The *Osthändler* (eastern traders) had to face up to political limitations and hostility from anti-communist hardliners within industry, most notable Fritz Berg. His anti-communism shone through once more in his reaction to the Berlin Ultimatum, when industrialists yet again rallied to the call. It was events around the Leipzig Trade Fair boycott and even more the 1962 oil pipeline embargo which made industrialists oppose official government policy. In the latter case, it was the inclusion in the embargo of already signed contracts which infuriated the managers because this policy forced them to break signed agreements, something 'a good merchant' would never do, as it was contrary to basic business conduct. While it was in the personal background of Wolff von Amerongen or Berthold Beitz to look for eastern trade, men like von Menges or Elkmann had accepted the political realities of the 1960s and demanded the same from Cold War politicians. When this did not happen, industrialists openly rebelled against the political leadership for the first time. This act by a new generation of managers can be seen as part of West Germany's 'modernization process'.

Conclusion

The post-war reconstruction period was a very special era for German industrialists and businessmen, even more so than the nineteenth-century *Gründerjahre* which peaked around 1869–73 and were then followed by a big slump.[1] For contemporaries, the difference between the ruins of 1945 and the economic recovery, which by the mid-1950s had turned into an economic boom, and a previously unimaginable spread of consumer society must have appeared like a miracle. But contrary to their claim, West Germany's industrialists were not the initiators or creators of the economic miracle as they so often asserted during the reconstruction period. In fact, they were the economic and social beneficiaries; they were in the right place at the right time and proactively took credit for achievements which were not solely of their making. By so doing they confirmed their claim to elite status and reaped societal recognition as a benefit.

Since at least 1943, when the war economy was almost at its peak, German industrialists had begun to consider and secretly implement measures of *Substanzerhaltung* (preservation of substance and assets) within their companies, acts the Nazis would have treated as sabotage of the war effort. Their expectations for the time after the Nazi defeat, which by 1944 most of them saw as inevitable, were carried by the belief of being indispensable for the Allies to keep the German economy going, even under an occupation regime.[2] The re-establishment of the *Industrie- und Handelkammern* was a means of keeping or re-establishing the traditional economic order, both in terms of a preferred political economic system as well as in regard to everyday business. While the arrests of December 1945 and the wider denazification came as a huge shock to most businessmen, the work of the IHK guaranteed the continuity not just of the capitalist system but of the traditional social structures that had been in place since the mid-1800s. The ability of the IHK to thwart trade union demands for labour–capital parity within the Chambers cemented businesses' advantages (in terms of knowledge and influence) and, together with increasing American interference, helped to predetermine (or preserve) the structure of West Germany's post-war economic system. The prompt re-establishment of the Chambers and their relatively successful work (opposite a rather inefficient and overblown bureaucracy) was the first step to claiming elite status but also the first attempt to redeem themselves from their involvement with the Nazi regime.

The changes in the public perception of industrialists from being beneficiaries and outright supporters of the Nazis and in some cases being war criminals, began against the backdrop of the Nuremberg industrialists' trials. Here the industrialists benefitted from a growing feeling amongst the German population that the Allies were applying victors' justice. Industrialists as a group certainly did not look into the question of how or how much they contributed to the collapse of the Weimar Republic and even less into their involvement with the Nazi regime. Instead they portrayed themselves as innocent victims of Allied 'Morgenthau policies' in general, and dismantling in particular. The 1950/51 'Korean Crisis' and the subsequent 1952 *Investitionshilfe Gesetz* heralded a significant turnaround. The IHG has to be understood as the breakthrough of association power and the return to the traditional influence of heavy industry. Not only were the managers able to prevent renewed state intervention in the economy, once they had abandoned their initial utter resistance to the project, they were able to hijack it for their own propaganda, in which they portrayed themselves as making sacrifices for the common good. With the creation of the *Deutsche Industrie Institut*, industrialists had a central propaganda instrument which they used successfully and, in regard to the trade unions, quite aggressively to spread their political views.

It was not least the public relations work of the DII which helped German industrialists to recreate their public image towards one that portrayed them as serving the economic recovery, which they constantly claimed they were responsible for and thus served the public good. In this process, an initially small number of entrepreneurs went beyond their traditional mentality and perception of class antagonism and sought, for example, closer co-operation with the trade unions. This was, however, not a process of Americanization, as Berghahn claimed, but rather one of *modernization* as it was a gradual shift rather than a deliberate strategy. Old attitudes may have changed slowly but they did evolve, in particular when they did not involve sharing power with trade unionists or have a direct benefit for companies, the prime examples being staff and leadership training. This was perhaps the area where German industry in the post-war years made its biggest leap forward. Unsurprisingly, the process started at the highest level, with training for top managers, before it expanded into upper, middle and lower management ranks as well, where the ASU had been a driving force for training. The success of the Bad Harzburger Akademie demonstrates that until the mid-1970s management training in Germany was successful on a large scale only if it was done in what was seen as a 'German', and not an 'American' way. This was regardless of the fact that Reinhard Höhn re-used some US methods and 'Germanized' them by mixing them with features present in German military leadership doctrine that were at the core of his model. In many ways, the Bad Harzburger Akademie was a trailblazer for German management training which helped to pave the way for other, more modern, training institutions. The Academy's fortunes, therefore, reflect to a good degree the modernization process in personnel policy and staff training that went on in the FRG. Carried by an underlying conservative, anti-union thinking, it helped to convince old-school industrialists that they could increase the productivity of their workforce through offering them training. By so doing, staff training became acceptable and actually fashionable, even amongst the most conservative SME companies; this ultimately allowed newer methods of *Menschenführung* to replace the Academy, which was reluctant to modernize its own approach.

Contrary to the claim made by some historians, Germany's particular brand of bourgeoisie, the *Bürgertum*, did not die after the Second World War. The country's industrial and business leadership had been deeply rooted in the mentality and habitus of the middle- and upper-middle class bourgeoisie and they carried this mentality across the 1945 caesura. Bourgeois norms, such as patronage of the arts and sponsorship of sciences, were revived not least because they had the added benefit of improving industrialists' public image. Honour, and in particular 'merchant's honour', remained important for an individual's standing amongst his peers. Nevertheless, as the unflattering events at the *Diskussionsabende* of the early 1960s have shown, the concept of honour underwent significant changes. What is also striking is that honour and honourable conduct was accorded only to the 'insiders'. 'Upstarts', irrespective of their success, could not expect the same treatment as members of long-established companies. When Krupp was faced with Allied obligations to sell off part of his company he was supported by his fellow industrialists who refused to make credible offers for those plants; when there were rumours in 1963 that Krupp was in financial difficulties, those were quashed with a single statement from Hermann Josef Abs, West Germany's dominant banker. When the newcomer Willy Schlicker was in a similar situation, however, no help was forthcoming.[3] The flipside of this tight-knit community was that anyone who broke ranks (as Ernst Wolf Mommsen did in the early 1970s when he accepted the post of State Secretary in the defence ministry under the Social Democrat Helmut Schmidt), risked social ostracism. Unsurprisingly, as a group, German industrialists remained a very solid bloc.

This cohesion was not only one of bourgeois mentality; it also arose out of the tradition of, and membership in, business associations. Despite some Allied reforms, association membership remained crucial for industrialists. Although in the majority of cases, a company owner or manager did not actively get involved in the running of associations, these organizations acted as industry mouthpieces and lobbyists. In the aftermath of the Nazis' system of compulsory association membership, the pressure businesses felt under in the post-war years (threat of socialization, company break-ups and general uncertainty), association membership promised strength through unity. This allowed associations to settle disputes within the sector and act as liaison points to other branches and political decision-makers at all levels. Very few businessmen could dare to ignore the official policy as it had been determined by an association's leadership. The significant expenditure of time association work entailed meant that only extremely committed managers took up these posts and even these men were heavily dependent on the work of their associations' senior chief clerks. It was they who in many cases had been the real hardliners and driving forces behind association policy. The power of associations came also through the parliamentary seats taken up by the chief clerks, as the number of industrialists active in parliament remained relatively low overall. Then again, this did not affect industrialists' political influence. To describe them (or for them to describe themselves) as unpolitical was far from the truth, as Stein's 1952 call for parliamentary candidates testifies. The claim was nothing but the remnants of denazification policy and industrialists' attempts to explain away their role in the collapse of the Weimar Republic and their involvement with the Nazis, a party they said they had joined 'only to prevent worse'. Industry's political influence throughout the 1950s and 1960s remained high because its representatives were able to take important seats on parliamentary working committees where, due to their particular knowledge, they could wield significant influence. It also remained high because of the large donations they gave to the bourgeois parties and because of Fritz Berg's almost unlimited access to Chancellor Adenauer. This influence ended whenever it came into conflict with Adenauer's core policies, in particular European integration, where he was happy to sacrifice industrial interests and advantages, or in 1961 when the Deutschmark was eventually reevaluated. Industrialists in general accepted the supremacy of politics over economic affairs. Grudgingly, they accepted co-determination in the coal and steel industries and, apart from Hermann Reusch, few ever publicly questioned the benefits of European integration. The only real challenge to the supremacy of government policy came in the early to mid-1960s in the form of East–West trade, and here especially concerning trade with the GDR after the building of the Berlin Wall. Many industrialists felt like scapegoats and saw Adenauer's boycott policy, for which they had to foot the bill, as a substitute to a non-existing alternative government policy once the Chancellor's policy of strength had so obviously failed.

It is the area of West German trade with the Eastern Bloc which highlights very clearly that West German industrialists were, despite all political considerations, in the first instance industrialists and businessmen, interested in the bottom line and the economic well-being of their companies. That there had been communist rulers in Moscow had not hindered trade with the Soviet Union in the interwar period; in fact it had saved some companies from bankruptcy after the Wall Street crash. While under Allied control, the eastern European market was heavily restricted for West German companies and with little sympathy from Adenauer on the matter they managed only a limited comeback from the mid-1950s onward. Trade with communist East Germany was perhaps even more delicate. On the one hand, it was limited by Adenauer's policy of not recognizing the GDR; on the other hand, this affected traditional trade with companies which before 1945 had been seen as domestic customers, and old personal contacts existed with some of these firms in the GDR well into the late 1950s. The Leipzig Trade Fair was West Germany's sales window on the East, so boycotting it for a long period after the Berlin Wall had gone up caused significant trade losses for West German companies, as other western countries did not follow the boycott. As an embargo of the Leipzig Trade Fairs did not change political circumstances, it was a mix of commercial interest and political reality which led Beitz, Mommsen and von Menges to increasingly ignore government wishes. Ultimately it is remarkable that while most German industrialists had no *Berührungsängste* (fear of contact) even with the Soviet communist leadership, fear of communism and trade unions at home remained high and almost close to paranoid. Although trade unions had been seen as temporary allies in the struggle against dismantling, they were pushed back into their position as sworn enemies once the co-determination legislation arrived. That the negative rhetoric against the unions did not change despite positive experiences with the *Arbeitsdirektoren* can only be explained by the deep-seated belief that 'only management can manage'. Worker participation in company leadership was a direct challenge not only to entrepreneurs' comprehension of property, but also, especially in the case of the salaried managers, to their claim for elite status, and that only those who were *berufen* were able to successfully run a company.

To conclude: West German industrialists did not create the economic miracle, and they were not the 'miracle-makers' they styled themselves as. They were first and foremost businessmen with a very conservative social outlook and attitude which was paired with 'an irrational belief in entrepreneurial superiority' (Braunthal) who benefitted from and received confirmation out of the global economic boom of the post-war era. Nina Grunenberg has pointed out that in their mentality they often belonged more to the 1930s and 1940s than the 1950s and 1960s. The generation born after 1900 had learned their trade under the Nazi regime but were unwilling to confront their past and compensated for this through their dogged work ethic.[4] In this way they fitted well into West Germany's myth of the economic miracle and, of course, were more than happy to propagate this myth.

Notes

Introduction

1 Werner Abelshauser, *Wirtschaftsgeschichte der Bundesrepublik Deutschland 1945–1980*, Frankfurt/M 1983, pp. 8, 20–24.

2 Ludwig Erhard, *Wohlstand für Alle!*, Düsseldorf 1957, English translation *Prosperity Through Competition*, New York 1958; the English title expressing his neo-liberal economic philosophy much more clearly.

3 Wilhelm Treue, *Die Feuer verlöschen nie. August Thyssen Hütte 1890–1966*, 2 vols, Düsseldorf 1966, 1969; see also Horst A. Wessel, *Kontinuität im Wandel, 100 Jahre Mannesmann 1890–1990*, Düsseldorf 1990, as one of the last books of this genre.

4 Hans Pohl, Stephanie Habeth, Beate Brüninghaus, *Die Daimler-Benz AG in den Jahren 1933 bis 1945. Eine Dokumentation*, Stuttgart 1986; Lothar Gall, Gerald D. Feldman, Harold James, Carl-Ludwig Holtfrerich and Hans E. Büschgen, *Die Deutsche Bank 1870–1995*, München 1995.

5 Volker Berghahn, *Unternehmer und Politik in der Bundesrepublik*, Frankfurt/M 1985; English translation, *The Americanisation of West German Industry 1945–1973*, Leamington Spa 1986.

6 Jonathan Wiesen, *West German Industry and the Challenge of the Nazi Past, 1945–1955*, Chapel Hill 2001; Norbert Frei (ed.), *Hitler's Eliten nach 1945*, München 2001 (5th ed. 2012).

7 Peter Burke, 'Stärken und Schwächen der Mentalitätsgeschichte', in Ulrich Raulff (ed.) *Mentalitäten-Geschichte*, Berlin 1989, pp. 127–145, p. 127.

8 Rainer Schulze, *Unternehmerische Selbstverwaltung und Politik. Die Rolle der Industrie- und Handelskammern in Niedersachsen und Bremen als Vertretungen der Unternehmerinteressen nach dem Zweiten Weltkrieg*, Hildesheim 1988.

9 Alfred Flender, *Die Verantwortung des Unternehmers*, Stuttgart 1961 (ed. Arbeitsgemeinschaft Selbstständiger Unternehmer), p. 164. The ASU had been created in 1949 by owner-entrepreneurs as a lobbying group for SME businesses and as a counter balance to the influence of big industry. The term *beauftragter Unternhemer* (literally: authorized entrepreneur) was used by the ASU to distinguish owner-entrepreneurs from the salaried (top) managers of big industries, originally to allow them to share the prestige of being 'real' entrepreneurs rather than being a 'manager', a term reserved for someone regarded as economic 'travelling bird' with no real interest in a company.

10 Wiesen, *West German Industry*, pp. 7f.

Chapter 1

1 Stiftung Rheinisch Westfälisches Wirtschaftsarchiv zu Köln (henceforth RWWA and file number), 130/40010146/310, letter from Herman Reuscht to Carl Neumann, 16.4. 1953, concerning candidates applying for jobs at the DII.

2 Schulze, *Unternehmerische Selbstverwaltung*, pp. 6–16.
3 Wolfram Fischer, *Unternehmerschaft, Selbstverwaltung und Staat*, Berlin 1964, p. 7, cited in Schulze, *Unternehmerische Selbstverwaltung*, p. 9.
4 The term *Geschäftsführer* can refer to two groups, either the executive manager of a private limited company (in contrast to the managing director of a joint stock company) or the chief clerk of a business association or Chamber of Industry and Commerce, who is rather an administrator than a businessman.
5 Schulze, *Unternehmerische Selbstverwaltung*, pp. 15 f.
6 Schulze, *Unternehmerische Selbstverwaltung*, p. 45.
7 For the reorganization of the Nazi war economy see Adam Tooze, *The Wages of Destruction. The Making and Breaking of the Nazi Economy*, London 2006, ch. 17; and Ludolf Herbst, *Der totale Krieg und die Ordnung der deutschen Wirtschaft. Die Kriegswirtschaft im Spannungsfeld von Politik, Ideologie und Propaganda*, Stuttgart 1982.
8 Rebecca Boehling, *A Question of Priorities. Democratic Reform and Economic Recovery in Postwar Germany. Frankfurt, Munich and Stuttgart under US Occupation, 1945–1949*, Oxford 1996, esp. pp. 156 ff.
9 Schulze, *Unternehmerische Selbstverwaltung*, pp. 39 f.; 163.
10 Schulze, *Unternehmerische Selbstverwaltung*, p.79.
11 Klaus-Dietmar Henke, *Die amerikanische Besetzung Deutschlands*, München 1995, pp. 505 f.
12 Schulze, *Unternehmerische Selbstverwaltung*, pp. 157 f.
13 Henke, *Die amerikanische Besetzung Deutschlands*, p. 510.
14 A point strongly made by Henke, *Die amerikanische Besetzung Deutschlands*, pp. 497, 506 f.; Schulze, *Unternehmerische Selbstverwaltung*, pp. 64 ff for leading players in the reconstruction of North German IHK.
15 Henke, *Die amerikanische Besetzung Deutschlands*, p. 504; RWWA 70-219-21, memo by Josef Wilden on meeting with mayor Fuellenbach, 22.4. 1945.
16 RWWA 1d-12-12, 'Bericht zur augenblicklichen Lage', 19.6. 1945 by Walter Rohland. Rohland, chairman of Vereinigte Stahlwerke, had acquired his nickname 'Panzer Rohland' because of his role as chairman of the tank production committee. See Tooze, *Wages of Destruction*, p.434; and Rohland's rather apologetic autobiography, *Bewegte Zeiten. Erinnerungen eines Eisenhüttenmannes*, Stuttgart 1978, esp. pp. 69 ff.
17 Henke, *Die amerikanische Besetzung Deutschlands*, pp. 497, 511.
18 RWWA 1d-4-3, Proposal for the establishment of the Chamber of Industry and Commerce.
19 Henke, *Die amerikanische Besetzung Deutschlands*, p. 474; also p. 491 for the prevailing optimism amongst industrialists in the summer of 1945.
20 Schulze, *Unternehmerische Selbstverwaltung*, p. 66; Jürgen Weise, *Kammern in Not – zwischen Anpassung und Selbstbehauptung. Die Stellung der Industrie und Handelskammern in der Auseinandersetzung um eine neue politische und wirtschaftliche Ordnung 1945–56. Dargestellt am Beispiel der rheinischen Kammern und ihren Vereinigungen auf Landes-, Zonen- und Bundesebene*, Köln 1989, p. 90. For examples of early Allied–IHK co-operation see RWWA 1-187-3, Niederschrift über die Präsidialsitzung der IHK der Nordrhein Provinz, 23.7. 1946.
21 Weise, *Kammern in Not*, p. 91; RWWA 28-2-4, Report 'Die Entwicklung der Industrie im Kammerbezirk seit dem Zusammenbruch', 17.7. 1947.
22 Henke, *Die amerikanische Besetzung Deutschlands*, p. 530.
23 Schulze, *Unternehmerische Selbstverwaltung*, pp 409–416, p. 454; for denazification, RWWA 1d-7-2, Vertrauliche Notiz zur Geschäftsführerbesprechung, 22.10. 1945.

24 Diethelm Prowe, 'Unternehmer, Gewerkschaften und Staat in der Kammerneuordnung in der britischen Besatzungszone bis 1950', in Dietmar Petzina and Walter Euchner (eds), *Wirtschaftspolitik im britischen Besatzungsgebiet 1945–1949*, Düsseldorf 1985, pp. 238–240; Weise, *Kammern in Not*, p. 66.
25 RWWA, 70-219-21, letter from Wilden to Oberpräsident der Rheinprovinz, 29.6. 1945; RWWA 1d-3-5, Niederschrift über HGF Sitzung der IHK Nordrhein-Westfalen, 19.12. 1946.
26 John Gimbel, 'Amerikanische Besatzungspolitik und deutsche Tradition', in Ludolf Herbst (ed.), *Westdeutschland 1945–1955. Unterwerfung, Kontrolle, Integration*, München 1986, pp. 147–150.
27 Weise, *Kammern in Not*, p. 65; Gimbel, 'Amerikanische Besatzungspolitik', pp. 147–150; Schulze, *Unternehmerische Selbstverwaltung*, p. 158.
28 Schulze, *Unternehmerische Selbstverwaltung*, pp. 11 f.
29 Klara van Eyll et al. (eds), *Die Geschichte der Unternehmerischen Selbstverwaltung in Köln 1914–1997*, Köln 1997, pp. 498 f; http://www.ihk-niederrhein.de/Namhafte-Personen, accessed 6.5. 2015.
30 RWWA 1d-10-3, 'Querschnitt durch die Meinung von Industriellen und Kaufleuten in Köln', 16.7. 1946.
31 Gabriele Teichmann, 'Pferdmenges, Robert' in *Neue Deutsche Biographie 20* (2001), S. 331 f.; Weise, *Kammern in Not*, pp. 102–104.
32 Michael Stürmer, Gabriele Teichmann and Wilhelm Treue, *Striking the Balance. Sal. Oppenheim Jr & Cie. A Family and a Bank*, London 1994, pp. 431, 436.
33 Schulze, *Unternehmerische Selbstverwaltung*, p. 132f.
34 RWWA 28-2-24, memo für Dr Küster für Vortrag am 5. Dezember 1946. The acting senior chief clerk of IHK Essen, Küster, praised his Chamber and its staff for not having interrupted their work in April 1945 for a single day.
35 For the development of the idea of *Wirtschaftsdemokratie* since the Weimar Republic, see Michael Schneider, 'Demokratisierungs-Konsenz zwischen Unternehmern und Gewerkschaften? Zur Debatte um Wirtschaftsdemokratie und Mitbestimmung', in Axel Schildt and Arnold Sywottek (eds), *Modernisierung im Wiederaufbau. Die westdeutsche Gesellschaft der 50er Jahre*, Bonn 1998, pp. 207–222. *Wirtschaftsdemokratie* included in particular the demand for equal trade union participation in all economic policy bodies and supervisory boards of big companies.
36 RWWA 70-169-3, letter from Arbeitsgemeinschaft Bayrische IHK to Arbeitsgemeinschaft IHK in Württemberg-Baden and Greater Hesse, 24.10. 1946.
37 RWWA 70-169-3, letter from IHK München to president Wilden, IHK Düsseldorf, 29.10. 1946.
38 For events and the development of the IHK in the American zone, see representatively Rainer Fuchs, 'Die Bayrischen Industrie- und Handelskammern im Wiederaufbau 1945–1948. Zwischen amerikanischem Demokratisierungswillen und eigener Selbstverwaltungstradition', PhD thesis, München 1988.
39 RWWA 1-186-4, excerpt of Technical Directive no. 49 of 21st Army Group, 30 July 1945; Weise, *Kammern in Not*, p. 127.
40 Schulze, *Unternehmerische Selbstverwaltung*, p. 220; Weise, *Kammern in Not*, p. 157.
41 Here *Mitbestimmung* is meant in its wider sense of 'having a say', in contrast to its narrower, but more frequent, meaning of co-determination, which meant equal representation of capital and labour on the supervisory boards of the coal and iron and steel companies.
42 Weise, *Kammern in Not*, pp. 57 f.

43 Schulze, *Unternehmerische Selbstverwaltung*, pp. 114 ff; IHK Braunschweig (ed.), *150 Jahre IHK Braunschweig. Ehrenamtliches Engagement für die Wirtschaft der Region*, Braunschweig 2014, p. 98–99 at http://braunschweig.ihk.de/fileadmin/v1/media/150jahre/ihk_buch/, accessed 2.5. 2015.
44 RWWA 28-37-3, Sitzungsbericht Präsidialsitzung, 31.1. 1946, also for the following.
45 Schulze, *Unternehmerische Selbstverwaltung und Politik*, p. 5.
46 See Horst W. Schmillinger, 'Die Deutsche Partei', in Richard Stöss (ed.), *Parteien Handbuch: Die Parteien der Bundesrepublik Deutschland, 1945–1980*, vol. 1, Opladen 1983, pp. 1025–1111; Schulze, *Unternehmerische Selbstverwaltung*, pp. 493 ff.
47 Weise, *Kammern in Not*, pp. 109 ff.
48 Weise, *Kammern in Not*, p. 139.
49 Weise, *Kammern in Not*, pp. 140 f.
50 RWWA 1d-10-3, Aktenvermerk 28 June 1946; RWWA 1d-6-3, Niederschrift über Geschäftsführerbesprechung 7 January 1947; Weise, *Kammern in Not*, p. 143.
51 Weise, *Kammern in Not*, pp. 157 f.
52 The plan is reprinted in: Beate Ruhm von Oppen, *Documents on Germany under Allied Occupation, 1945–1954*, London 1955, pp.113–120.
53 Schulze, *Unternehmerische Selbstverwaltung*, pp. 237 f; 243; Weise, *Kammern in Not*, pp. 153 f.
54 RWWA 1-187-3, Niederschrift zur Präsidialsitzung der Vereinigung der IHK Nordrhein-Westfalen, 2.7. 1947; RWWA 28-37-4, Niederschrift zur Präsidialsitzung der Vereinigung der IHK Nordrhein-Westfalen, 10.10. 1947.
55 RWWA 1-186-3, 'Der Standpunkt der rheinischen Kammern', 2.12. 1946.
56 For the Bevin–Byrnes Agreement, see Ruhm von Oppen, *Documents on Germany*, pp. 195–199; for the socialization issue, see Jean Smith (ed.), *The Papers of Lucius D. Clay, Germany 1945–1949*, Bloomington, IN, 1974, pp. 375–377; Schulze, *Unternehmerische Selbstverwaltung*, p. 245. Wolfgang Friedmann was a German trade unionist who spent the Nazi era in exile in Britain and returned to Germany as economic advisor to the British Military Government.
57 RWWA 1-186-3, letter from Hilgermann to Dr von Pohl, IHK Koblenz, 2.12. 1946.
58 Schulze, *Unternehmerische Selbstverwaltung*, pp. 247–249. Prowe, 'Unternehmer, Gewerkschaften und Staat', p. 242. Weise, *Kammern in Not*, p. 190.
59 Rolf Steininger, *Deutsche Geschichte seit 1945. Darstellungen und Dokumente in vier Bänden, Band 1: 1945–1947*, Frankfurt/M 2002, p. 116.
60 Schulze, *Unternehmerische Selbstverwaltung*, pp. 249–263.
61 Weise, *Kammern in Not*, esp. pp. 273 f.
62 The claim of the 'unpolitical' German bourgeois dates back to the late nineteenth century; see David Blackbourn, 'The German Bourgeoisie' in David Blackbourn and Richard J. Evans (eds), *The German Bourgeoisie. Essays on the Social History of the German Middle Class from the Late Eighteenth to the Early Twentieth Century*, London 1991, pp. 1–45, p. 25. It was, however, revived to deflect from their involvement with the Nazis.
63 Hans-Günther Sohl, *Notizen*, private printing 1983, pp. 167 f.
64 Schulze, *Unternehmerische Selbstverwaltung*, pp. 477, 482–483.
65 RWWA 1-185-2, letter from Arbeitsgemeinschaft der IHK des Vereinigten Wirtschaftsgebietes to Mitgliedskammern, 20.5. 1949. The Parliamentary Council was the body tasked with drawing up the West German Constitution; the Economic Council was the pre-parliamentary body the Allies had asked the Germans to set up in preparation for the establishment of the FRG; for details see Wolfgang Benz, *Die*

Gründung der Bundesrepublik, Von der Bizone zum souveränen Staat, München 1989 (3rd ed) and Christoph Weisz et al. (eds), *Akten zur Vorgeschichte der Bundesrepublik Deutschland*, 4 vols. München 1983.

66 Weise, *Kammern in Not*, pp. 94–96; Schulze, *Unternehmerische Selbstverwaltung*, p. 195 f.

67 RWWA 1-185-1 passim.

68 Hanno Sowade, *Wegbereiter des Wiederaufstiegs. Die Industrie- und Handelskammern und die Rekonstruktion der Außenbeziehungen der westdeutschen Wirtschaft 1945–1949/50*, München 1992.

69 Schulze, *Unternehmerische Selbstverwaltung*, pp. 502 ff.; Steininger, *Deutsche Geschichte*, pp. 115 f.

70 Schulze, *Unternehmerische Selbstverwaltung*, pp. 507 f.

Chapter 2

1 Herbst, *Der totale Krieg und die Ordnung der Wirtschaft*, pp. 383 ff.; Henke, *Die amerikanische Besetzung Deutschlands*, pp. 449–468.

2 Dwight D. Eisenhower, *Crusade in Europe*, London 1948.

3 Henke, *Die amerikanische Besetzung Deutschlands*, p. 537.

4 Wiesen, *West German Industry*, pp. 53 f.; Henke, *Die amerikanische Besetzung Deutschlands*, pp. 563 ff. Both Rohland, *Bewegte Zeiten*, p. 123, and Hans-Günther Sohl, *Notizen*, p. 98, make similar claims about how they had expected and prepared for their arrest. Up to 1945 the two men had been chairman and deputy chairman respectively of the managing board of Vereinigte Stahlwerke, Germany's largest steel company.

5 Volker Berghahn, 'Unternehmer in der frühen Bundesrepublik: Selbstverständnis und politischer Einfluß in der Marktwirtschaft', in Thomas Großbölting and Rüdiger Schmidt (eds), *Unternehmerwirtschaft zwischen Markt und Lenkung. Organisationsformen, politischer Einfluß und ökonomisches Verhalten 1930–1960*, München 2002, p. 284.

6 Günter Henle, *Weggenosse des Jahrhunderts. Als Diplomat, Industrieller, Politiker und Freund der Musik*, Stuttgart 1968, p. 80.

7 See, for example, Werner Abelshauser, 'Probleme des Wiederaufbaus der westdeutschen Wirtschaft, 1945–53', in Heinrich August Winkler (ed.), *Politische Weichenstellung im Nachkriegsdeutschland 1945–1953*, Göttingen 1979, pp. 208–243, p. 243.

8 Wiesen, *West German Industry*, p. 54.

9 Dietrich Wilhem von Menges, *Unternehmerentscheide. Ein Leben für die Wirtschaft*, Düsseldorf 1976, pp. 147 f. For Paul Reusch and his work, see Erich Maschke, *Es entsteht ein Konzern. Paul Reusch und die Gutehoffnungshütte*, Tübingen 1969; Peter Langer, *Macht und Verantwortung. Der Ruhrbaron Paul Reusch*, Essen 2012; Christian Marx, *Paul Reusch und die Gutehoffnungshütte. Leitung eines deutschen Großunternehmens*, Göttingen 2013.

10 Ludwig Vaubel of Vereinigte Glanzstoff Fabriken occasionally questions his own moral and political behaviour in his diary; see Ludwig Vaubel, *Zusammenbruch und Wiederaufbau. Ein Tagebuch der Wirtschaft 1945–49* (ed. Wolfgang Benz), München 1984. Wiesen, *West German Industry*, p. 22, gives as an example Siemens, which began to look into their involvement in the 'Jewish question', the use of Jewish workers prior

to their deportation to the extermination camps and the subsequent use of slave labour, and how to best defuse any accusation on the issues.

11 Literally: Persil certificates. The name referred to the washing detergent and a sarcastic modification of Persil's advertisement slogan at the time 'Persil washes the brownest stains away.'

12 RWWA 130/40010145/164, Eidesstattliche Bescheinigung Reusch für Wolfgang Pohle, 7.10. 1946.

13 RWWA 1d-12-12, Niederschrift über die Ereignisse vom 15.3. bis 15.4. 1945 (Rohland's summary on the Nero order); Rohland, *Bewegte Zeiten*, p. 103 also pp. 93; 97; for a critical evaluation of Rohland's work and role in the Nazi war economy, see Henke, *Die amerikanische Besetzung Deutschlands*, esp. pp.513–533; Evelyn Krocker, 'Heinrich Kost: Rationalisierung und Sozialbeziehungen im Bergbau', in Paul Erker and Toni Pierenkemper (eds), *Deutsche Unternehmer zwischen Kriegswirtschaft und Wiederaufbau. Studien zur Erfahrungsbildung von Industrie Eliten*, München 1999, pp. 291–316, esp. pp. 301–304.

14 Hervé Joly, *Großunternehmer in Deutschland. Soziologie einer industriellen Elite, 1933–1989*, Leipzig 1998, pp. 123, 161.

15 RWWA 1d-12-12, 'Hitler und die Ruhrindustriellen'.

16 Rohland, *Bewegte Zeiten*, p. 119, claims that he aided in the memorandum's final drafting.

17 August Heinrichsbauer, *Schwerindustrie und Politik*, Essen 1948. For Heinrichsbauer's background and the origin of the booklet see Wiesen, *West German Industry*, pp. 74 f.

18 RWWA 130/40010145/164, letter from Salewski to Reusch, 15.4. 1947.

19 Among the now buoyant research on Germany's 'coming to terms with the past' – or the lack thereof in the 1950s and 1960s – are Norbert Frei, *Vergangenheitsbewältigung. Die Anfänge der Bundesrepublik und die NS Vergangenheit*, München 1996; Ulrich Brochhagen, *Nach Nürnberg: Vergangenheitsbewältigung und Westintegration in der Ära Adenauer*, Hamburg 1994; and with a specific focus on industry, Wiesen, *West German Industry*.

20 Wirtschaftsvereinigung Stahl Historisches Archiv (henceforth WV Stahl HA and file designation), Sitzungsberichte Eisenkreis, Enger Vorstand 14.3. 1947 – 30.6. 1948 (2), Niederschrift der Sitzung Eisenkreis 20.6. 1947.

21 RWWA 130/40010145/164, Eidesstattliche Erklärung Hermann Reusch, 28.7. 1947.

22 Norbert Frei, Ralf Ahrens, Jörg Osterloh and Tim Schanetzky, *Flick. Der Konzern, die Familie, die Macht*, München 2009, pp. 401 ff.; RWWA 130/400101420/70 various letters expressing shock and promissing support for the relatives; Frei (ed.) *Hitlers Eliten nach 1945*, p. 67.

23 Frei et al., *Flick*, pp. 8, 401, 418.

24 For the opposing historical arguments used by prosecution and defence, see Kim Christian Priemel, 'Der Sonderweg vor Gericht. Angewandte Geschichte im Nürnberger Krupp Prozess', in *Historische Zeitschrift*, vol. 294, no. 2 (April 2012), pp. 391–426.

25 Tilo von Wilmowsky, *Warum wurde Krupp verurteilt? Legende und Justizirrtum*, Stuttgart 1950; Priemel, 'Sonderweg', p. 422, the other two co-authors being the lawyer (and later Basic Law commentator) Ernst-Rudolf Huber and Krupp's leading defence lawyer, Otto Kranzbühler.

26 For a detailed analysis, see Wiesen, *West German Industry*, pp. 73–81; 102.

27 On Krupp's use of company propaganda and image creation before the First World War, see Priemel, 'Sonderweg', p. 394.

28 RWWA 130/400101400/115, Aufzeichnung vom 4.6. 1949, Besprechung bei Henle.
29 WV Stahl HA, D & B, Arbeitskreis Neuordnung, passim, especially letter from Hermann Reusch to Fritz-Aurel Goergen, 15.9. 1949, in which Raul Desvernine suggested a ten-week 'trial period'; Thyssen-Krupp Archiv (henceforth TKA) A 30412 WVESt Diskussionsabend, letter from Ahrens to Sohl, 24.9. 1955, summary of proposals by Julius Klein Public Relations, Chicago.
30 See Ruhm von Oppen, *Documents on Germany*, pp. 335–343; 490–492.
31 See Desvernine's obituary in the *New York Times*, 3 June 1966; WV Stahl HA, Akten aus Sekretariat Dr Ahrens, Arbeitskreis für Fragen der Neuordnung, (bis 10 Mai 1950) minutes of the constituting meeting, 26.9. 1949; memo Ahrens, 31.10. 1949.
32 WV Stahl HA, D & B, Arbeitskreis Neuordnung, letter from Schroeder to Desvernine, 8.2. 1950; letter from Hellwig to Desvernine 4.7. 1950; letter from Staatssekretär Schalfejew to Desvernine, 21.1. 1950; letter from Linz to Hellwig, 7.10. 1950; letter from Schroeder to members of the *Altgesellschaften*, 13.6. 1950.
33 WV Stahl HA, Sitzungsberichte Engerer Vorstand, 9.6. 1949–31.1. 1951 (4), Vermerk über Sitzung Engerer Vorstand, 22.6. 1950. On Hundhausen see Eva-Maria Lehming, *Carl Hundhausen, Sein Leben, Sein Werk, Sein Lebenswerk: Public Relations in Deutschland*, Wiesbaden 1997.
34 For a very good summary of Klein's background and impact, see Jonathan Wiesen, 'Germany's PR Man. Julius Klein and the Making of Transatlantic Memory', in Philipp Gassert and Alan E. Steinweis (eds), *Coping with the Nazi Past. West German Debates on Nazism and Generational Conflict 1955–1975*, Oxford 2006, pp. 294–308, esp. pp. 295–297, also for the following.
35 TKA A 30412, WVESt, Diskussionsabend, letter from Ahrens to Sohl, 24.9. 1955, attachment, summary of Klein's proposals.
36 Archiv der Christlich-Demokratischen Politik (henceforth ACDP), 01-224-221/1, Diskussionsabend 1954–56, Vermerk über DA vom 4.10. 1955. August von Kienriem, *Nürnberg. Rechtliche und menschliche Probleme*, Stuttgart 1953. See also Wiesen, *West German Industry*, pp. 220 ff., for details on the coming about of Louis Lochner's apologetic *Tycoons and Tyrant. German Industry from Hitler to Adenauer*, Chicago 1954.
37 RWWA130/400101400/115, various letters, January 1951 concerning James Stewart Martin's book *All Honorable Men*, Boston 1950, the German translation Hermann Reusch wanted to prevent at all costs. See also Wiesen, *West German Industry*, pp. 215 f.
38 For details see Kim Christian Priemel, 'Gekaufte Geschichte. Der "Freundeskreis Albert Vögler", Gert von Klass und die Entwicklung der historischen Unternehmerforschung nach 1945', in *Zeitschrift für Unternehmensgeschichte*, 52 (2007) 177–202; Wiesen, *West German Industry*, p. 154.
39 Karl Heinrich Herdenröder, *Neue Männer an der Ruhr. Mit einem Vorwort von Wilhelm Zangen*, Düsseldorf 1958.
40 Wiesen, *West German Industry*, p. 156; RWWA; 130/40010146/312, letter Deutsches Industrie Institut to Kuratorium members, 25.1. 1954; RWWA 130/400101411/12, Vortrag Hans-Helmut Kuhnke at the conference 'Public Relations als Aufgabe der Industrie', 5.5. 1959.
41 RWWA 130/40010146/306, letter from Muthesius to Reusch, 17.6. 1949; letter from Heinrichsbauer to Reusch 9.2. 1950, with attached memorandum.
42 Manfred Mansfeld, 'Die Gründung', in Deutsches Industrie Institut (ed.), *Fünfzehn Jahre Deutsches Industrie Institut*, Köln 1966, p. 13, 'Progressives' were Otto A. Friedrich, Ernst Falkenheim and Kurt Pentzlin of the Bahlsen cookie company.

43 RWWA 130/40010146/307, letter Reusch to Neumann, 9.12. 1950. For Neumann, see Beate Battenfeld, 'Neumann, Carl' in *Neue Deutsche Biographie_19* (1999), pp. 154–156
44 ACDP 01-083 212/3 Vorträge 1951, Liste Vortragstätigkeit 1951 Dr. Hellwig.
45 Wiesen, *West German Industry*, pp. 114 ff.
46 RWWA 130/40010146/307, letter from GHH Konzernstelle to various companies, 10.5. 1951, attached the memo 'Warum deutsches Industrie Institut?'
47 See, for example Heinrich Krumm, *Tagebuch eines deutschen Unternehmers, 1937–1947*, Frankfurt/M. 1956 (private printing), p. 28, where Krumm, owner of the renowned Goldpfeil leather goods company, in the introduction to the edition of his personal diary expresses his lasting bitterness at having been barred from his own company for four years.
48 See, for example Bundesverband der Deutschen Industrie, Historisches Archiv (henceforth BDI HA and file designation), SH 509 (Bd 172), letter from Paul Peddinghaus to BDI Steuerabteilung, 21.1. 1952.
49 See Chapter 7.
50 RWWA 130/40010146/309, letter from DII to Reusch, 13.12. 1951, with *Neuer Vorwärts* article of 23.11. 1951; Gabriel A. Almond, 'The Politics of German Business', in Hans Speier and W. Philip Davidson (eds), *West German Leadership and Foreign Policy*, The RAND Corporation, New York 1957, p. 215.
51 RWWA 130/40010146/308, Niederschrift über die Sitzung des Kuratoriums und der Mitgliederversammlung des DII, 11.7. 1952.
52 RWWA 130/40010146/310, letter from Landesvereinigung der industriellen Arbeitgeberverbände Nordrhein-Westfalen to Reusch, 16.12. 1952; Protokoll über Besprechung über DII, 18.1. 1953 RWWA 130/40010146/312, passim.
53 ACDP 01-224-192/1, Streng vertraulicher Vermerk by Ahrens, 19.1. 1955; press cutting *Rheinische Post* 20.1. 1955; BDI HA HGF Pro785 (4/1), Niederschrift Präsidialsitzung, 26.1. 1955.
54 ACDP 01-162-039/2, letter from DII to Becker, 22.10. 1954; 01-162-040/1, letter from Bundesverband Bekleidungsindustrie to Becker, 10.5. 1955; 01-162-015/2, Niederschrift 13. BDI Mitgliederversammlung, 3.4. 1962, TOP 6.
55 RWWA 130/40010146/325, letter from Hans Reischauer to DII Kuratorium, 20.7. 1964.
56 Ernst E. Kunkel, 'Der Aufbau', in DII (ed.), *Fünfzehn Jahre*, p. 29.
57 Wilhelm Weisser, 'Publizisten mit offenem Visier', in DII (ed.), *Fünfzehn Jahre*, p. 38; Günter Triesch, 'Im Kraftfeld der Politik', in DII (ed.), *Fünfzehn Jahre*, p. 64.
58 Fritz Arlt, 'Die Bildungsaufgabe der Wirtschaft', in DII (ed.), *Fünfzehn Jahre* pp. 91 ff; Heinrich Schreiner, 'Das Institut in der sozialpolitischen Diskussion', in DII (ed.), *Fünfzehn Jahre*, pp. 73 ff. For Arlt's considerable role in Nazis' race policies see Götz Aly and Karl Heinz Roth, *The Nazi Census. Identification and Control in the Third Reich*, Philadephia 2004, pp. 75 ff.; and the BBC documentary by Laurence Rees, *The Nazis. A Warning from History*, part 4, 'The first 20 months in Poland', first shown 1 October 1997, BBC 2.
59 Heiner R. Adamsen, *Investitionshilfe für die Ruhr. Wiederaufbau, Verbände und die Soziale Marktwirtschaft*, Wuppertal 1981, pp. 33–41, quote on p. 41.
60 Adamsen, *Investitionshilfe*, p. 45.
61 Werner Abelshauser, 'Ansätze "korporativer Marktwirtschaft" in der Koreakrise der 50er Jahre. Ein Briefwechsel zwischen dem Hohen Kommissar John McCloy und Bundeskanzler Adenauer', in *Vierteljahrshefte für Zeitgeschichte*, vol. 30 (1982), pp. 715–756.

62 Volker Berghahn and Paul J. Friedrich, *Otto A. Friedrich, ein politischer Unternehmer. Sein Leben und seine Zeit, 1902–1975*, Frankfurt/M 1993, pp. 134–160.
63 Berghahn and Friedrich, *Otto A. Friedrich*, pp. 97–133.
64 For the use of counterpart funds for reconstruction investments, see Armin Grünbacher, *Reconstruction and Cold War in Germany. The Kreditanstalt für Wiederaufbau 1948–1961*, Aldershot 2004.
65 Adamsen, *Investitionshilfe*, pp. 133 f; p. 152; for a brief summary see Grünbacher, *Reconstruction and Cold War*, pp. 96–99.
66 BDI HA HGF Pro 786 (Bd 2/1), Niederschrift Präsidiumssitzung, 27.3. 1951.
67 Ibid, Niederschrift Präsidiumssitzung 13.4. 1951.
68 *Bundesgesetzblatt* 1952 I, pp. 7–14, reprinted in Adamsen, *Investitionshilfe*, pp. 276–283.
69 Adamsen, *Investitionshilfe*, pp. 214 ff.
70 WV Stahl HA, Sitzungsberiechte Engere Vorstand, 1.4. 1951–31.12. 1952 (5), Vermerk über Sitzung Engerer Vorstand am 19.10. 1951; Vermerk über Sitzung Engerer Vorstand am 20.12. 1951.
71 Plumpe and Werner, 'Unternehmerverbände und industrielle Interessenpolitik', in Wolfgang Köllmann, Hermann Korte, Dietmar Petzina and Wolfhart Weber (eds), *Das Ruhrgebiet im Industriezeitalter. Geschichte und Entwicklung*, vol. 1 Düsseldorf 1990, pp. 655–727, pp. 725–727.
72 Adamsen, *Investitionshilfe*, pp. 240–242; Abelshauser, 'Ansätze "korporativer Marktwirtschaft"'.

Chapter 3

1 Fritz Berg at the opening ceremony of Haus Biron (seat of the BBUG), 9 March 1957, reprinted in *Mitteilungen des BDI*, no. 3, March 1957, p. 1.
2 Volker Berghahn, *Unternehmer und Politik in der Bundesrepublik*, Frankfurt/M 1985; English translation *The Americanisation of West German Industry 1945–1973.*
3 Alexander von Plato, '"Wirtschaftskapitäne": Biographische Selbstkonstruktionen von Unternehmern in der Nachkriegszeit', in Axel Schildt and Arnold Sywottek (eds), *Modernisierung in Westdeutschland. Die westdeutsche Gesellschaft in den 50er Jahren*, Bonn 1998, pp. 377–391, p. 391.
4 Stefan Unger, '"Die Herren aus dem Westen". Zur Struktur und Semantik der Wirtschaftselite des Ruhrgebiets 1930–1970', in *Westfälische Forschungen*, vol. 50 (2000), pp. 143–162.
5 Paul Erker, 'Einleitung: Industrie-Eliten im 20. Jahrhundert', in Paul Erker and Toni Pierenkemper (eds), *Deutsche Unternehmer zwischen Kriegswirtschaft und Wiederaufbau. Studien zur Erfahrungsbildung von Industrie-Eliten*, München 1999, pp. 1–18.
6 Michael Hartmann, 'Soziale Homogenität und generationelle Muster der deutschen Wirtschaftselite seit 1945', in Volker Berghahn, Stefan Unger and Dieter Ziegler (eds), *Die deutsche Wirtschaftselite im 20. Jahrhundert. Kontinuität und Mentalität*, Essen 2003, pp. 31–50; Hervé Joly, 'Kontinuität und Diskontinuität der industriellen Elite nach 1945', in Dieter Ziegler (ed.), *Großbürger und Unternehmer. Die deutsche Wirtschaftselite im 20. Jahrhundert*, Göttingen 2000, pp. 54–72; Hervé Joly, *Großunternehmer in Deutschland. Soziologie einer industriellen Elite 1933–1989*, Leipzig 1998.
7 Erker, 'Einleitung', pp. 14 ff.

8 RWWA 130/40010146/43, letter from Reusch to Heinrichsbauer, 7.8.1950.

9 For the aristocracy, see Michael Seelig, *Alltagsadel. Der ehemalige ostelbische Adel in der Bundesrepublik Deutschland 1945/49–1975,* Köln 2015; for the military, see Detlef Bald, '"Bürger in Uniform": Tradition und Neuanfang des Militärs in Westdeutschland', in Axel Schildt and Arnold Sywottek (eds), *Modernisierung im Wiederaufbau. Die westdeutsche Gesellschaft der 50er Jahre,* Bonn 1998, pp. 392–402.

10 Bernd Faulenbach, 'Die Preußischen Bergassesoren im Ruhrbergabu. Unternehmermentalität zwischen Obrigkeitsstaat und Privatindustrie', in *Mentalitäten und Lebensverhältnisse. Beispiele aus der Geschichte der Neuzeit. Rudolf Vierhaus zum 60. Geburtstag,* Göttingen 1982, pp. 225–242, *passim,* esp. p. 241.

11 According to trade union chairman Hans Böckler, cited in Faulenbach, 'Preußische Bergassesoren', p. 225.

12 BDI HA HFG Pro786 (2/1), Niederschrift Präsidiumssitzung 20.5.1952.

13 For the founding myth, see Abelshauser, *Wirtschaftsgeschichte der Bundesrepublik Deutschland,* 8f., 10f. and passim.

14 Flender, *Die Verantwortung des Unternehmers,* p. 19.

15 Heinz Hartmann, *Authority and Organization in German Management,* Princeton 1959, pp. 7 f. For the significance of the 'calling', see pp. 28 ff.

16 RWWA 130/400101400/115, note 'Besprechung bei Henle', 4.6.1949, in which Henle had made the proposal for reciprocal asset swaps to prevent further dismantling.

17 On the Industry Plan, see Ruhm von Oppen, *Documents on Germany under Allied Occupation,* p. 239–245; on the Petersberg Protocol, see US Department of State (ed.), *Documents on Germany 1944–1985,* Washington DC, 1985, pp. 310–313.

18 BDI HA HGF Pro 768 (1), Bericht über die Gründung des Ausschusses für Wirtschaftsfragen der industriellen Verbände.

19 Abelshauser, *Wirtschaftsgeschichte der Bundesrepublik Deutschland,* pp. 64 f.

20 Josef Winschuh, *Das neue Unternehmerbild. Grundzüge einer Unternehmerpolitik,* Baden-Baden and Frankfurt/M 1954 (2nd ed.), p. 62.

21 Flender, *Die Verantwortung des Unternehmers,* pp. 14–25; and Winschuh, *Das neue Unternehmerbild,* p. 43, where he lambasts the economic incompetence of politicians.

22 For manager–entrepreneur statements, see for example BDI HA HGF Pro 786 2/1, Speech by Otto Seeling, a SME glass manufacturer from Fürth at the BDI Mitgliederversammlung 25/25.6.1951; RWWA 130/400101402/22, Speech by Hermann Reusch at the MAN annual general meeting 29.5.1953; Speech by ASU president Alfred Flender, November 1955, reprinted in Flender, *Die Verantwortung des Unternehmers,* p. 12; Wiesen, *West German Industry,* pp. 7 f.

23 Ernst-Wolf Mommsen (ed.), *Elitenbildung in der Wirtschaft,* Darmstadt 1955.

24 Ernst-Wolf Mommsen, 'Elitenbildung in der Wirtschaft', in ibid, pp. 7–18.

25 Winschuh, *Das neue Unternehmerbild,* p. 132.

26 Heidrun Abromeit, 'Der Führungsanspruch der Wirtschaft gegenüber der Politik', in *Aus Politik und Zeitgeschichte,* no. 11 (1981), pp. 19–39.

27 Abromeit, 'Der Führungsanspruch der Wirtschaft', p. 26.

28 Abromeit, 'Der Führungsanspruch der Wirtschaft', pp. 20 f., 34 ff.

29 Gustav Stein (ed.), *Unternehmer in der Politik,* Düsseldorf 1954.

30 Ibid, esp. p. 54 ff for criticism of 'mass democracy' and p. 165 for the call for, and tasks of, the new elite. For Gross, see Wiesen, *West German Industry,* p. 108.

31 Morten Reitmayer, '"Unternehmer zur Führung berufen" - durch wen?', in Volker Berghahn, Stefan Unger and Dieter Ziegler (eds), *Die deutsche Wirtschaftselite im 20. Jahrhundert. Kontinuität und Mentalität,* Essen 2003, pp. 317–336, p. 334.

32 RWWA 130/400101402/20, speech for Rotary Club meeting at Bad Mergentheim, 13.7. 1954.
33 Winschuh, *Das neue Unternehmerbild*, pp. 40 f. In 1965, in the so-called 'lex Abs', supervisory board membership was limited to ten. See *Der Spiegel*, no. 45, 1965, p. 49; Lothar Gall, *Der Bankier Hermann Josef Abs*, München 2004.
34 BA N1384/298, letter from Kost to Henle, 30.11. 1950.
35 Helmut Schelsky, 'Die Bedeutung des Schichtbegriffs für die Analyse der gegenwärtigen Deutschen Gesellschaft', in Helmut Schelsky, *Auf der Suche nach Wirklichkeit, Gesammelte Aufsätze*, München 1965, pp. 332–335. While the term *Mittelstand* referred to the economically active part (in the form of independent small and medium firms and businesses) of the bourgeoisie, the meaning of *Mittelschicht* was socially much more encompassing, including parts of the skilled workforce; it was therefore also a move away from the traditional class concept.
36 RWWA 130/400101402/22, Schlußwort zur Kulturkreis Tagung 28.9. 1953; on Ortega y Gasset's influence see also Wiesen, *West German Industry*, p. 170 f.
37 Braunthal, *The Federation of German Industry in Politics*, Ithaca, NY 1965, pp. 56, 58.
38 RWWA 130/40010146/326, *Vortragsreihe des Deutschen Industrie Instituts*, Nr 13, März 1966.
39 Otto A. Friedrich, *Das Selbstbild des Unternehmers wandelt sich*, Stuttgart 1959, pp. 28 ff.
40 Rainer Koehne, *Das Selbstbild deutscher Unternehmer. Legitimation und Leitbild einer Institution*, Berlin 1976, p. 26.
41 See, as a typical example, Herchenröder, *Neue Männer an der Ruhr, passim.*
42 Koehne, *Das Selbstbild deutscher Unternehmer*, pp. 150 f., 155 f.
43 Koehne, *Das Selbstbild deutscher Unternehmer*, p. 50; Rainer Koehne, *Unternehmertum im Wandel. Wie sehen sich die Unternehmer – wie werden sie gesehen? Herausforderungen an eine Institution*, Köln 1975, p. 23.
44 Christian Kleinschmidt, 'Das "1968" der Manager: Fremdwahrnehmung und Selbstreflexion einer sozialen Elite in den 60er Jahren', in Jan-Otmar Hesse, Christian Kleinschmidt and Karl Lauschke (eds), *Kulturalismus. Neue Institutionenökonomik oder Theorievielfalt. Eine Zwischenbilanz der Unternehmensgeschichte*, Essen 2002, pp. 19–31, esp. pp. 21–23, 30f.
45 Hartmut Berghoff, 'Abschied vom klassischen Mittelstand. Kleine und mittlere Unternehmen in der bundesdeutschen Wirtschaft des späten 20. Jahrhunderts', in Volker Berghahn Stefan Unger and Dieter Ziegler (eds), *Die deutsche Wirtschaftselite im 20. Jahrhundert. Kontinuität und Mentalität*, Essen 2003, pp. 93–113, esp. pp. 100–106.
46 Hartmut Berghoff, 'Historisches Relikt oder Zukunftsmodell? Kleine und mittelgroße Unternehmen in der Wirtschafts- und Sozialgeschichte der Bundesrepublik Deutschland', in Dieter Ziegler (ed.), *Großbürger und Unternehmer. Die deutsche Wirtschaftselite im 20. Jahrhundert*, Göttingen 2000, pp. 249–282, p. 267.
47 See for example RWWA 195/B/5/1/15, Niederschrift zur 172. Aufsichtsratssitzung at Vereinigte Glanzstoff Fabriken, 18.2. 1950, in which it was said that the new balances allowed the company higher depreciations for about five years and that for the previous two years since the currency reform, those hoped-for results had been achieved, which had also allowed the payment of a small dividend.
48 Harm G. Schröter, 'Kartellierung und Dekartellierung 1890–1990', in *Vierteljahrsschrift für Sozial- und Wirtschaftsgeschichte*, vol. 81 no. 4 (1994), pp. 457–493, p. 460.
49 Peter Hüttenberger, 'Wirtschaftsordnung und Interessenpolitik in der Kartellgesetzgebung der Bundesrepublik 1949–1957', in *Vierteljahrshefte für*

Zeitgeschichte, vol, 24 no. 3 (July 1976), pp. 287–307. For the debate on the influence the US had on the cartel law, see Lisa Murach-Brand, *Antitrust auf deutsch. Der Einfluß der amerikanischen Alliierten auf das Gesetz gegen Wettbewerbsbeschränkungen (GWB) nach 1945*, Tübingen 2004.

50 BA B102/12679 Heft 2, Vermerk für Herrn Minister, 15.5. 1957.

51 TKA A/30415, letter from Ahrens to Sohl, Entwurf einer Tagesordnung für DA am 2.10. 1957, TOP 2.

52 Werner Abelshauser, 'Kohle und Marktwirtschaft. Ludwig Erhard's Konflikt mit dem Unternehmensverband Ruhrbergbau am Vorabend der Kohlekrise', in *Vierteljahrshefte für Zeitgeschichte*, vol. 33, no. 3 (July 1985), pp. 489–546.

53 Archiv der Ludwig Erhard Stiftung, NE I 4, 36, telex Berg to Erhard, 2.3. 1959; RWWA 130/40010146/187, letter from BDI Hauptgeschäftsführung to Präsiediumsmitglieder, 7.3. 1959.

54 BDI HA HGF Pro 781 (6), Niederschrift Präsidialsitzung 7.4. 1954.

55 ACDP 01-162-357/1, Antrag der CDU Bundestagsfraktion, 23.6. 1959.

56 BA B102/60667, Gesprächsnotiz Adenauer - Allied High Commission, 14.12. 1950.

57 Berghahn and Friedrich, *Otto A. Friedrich*, pp. 55, 70, 113 f.

58 Reinhard Neebe, 'Ludwig Erhard und die Globalisierung: Konzeptionen und Kontroversen deutscher Weltmarktpolitik im 20. Jahrhundert', in Volker Berghahn and Sigurt Vitols (eds), *Gibt es einen deutschen Kapitalismus? Tradition und globale Perspektiven der Sozialen Marktwirtschaft*, Frankfurt/M 2006, pp. 169–185, p. 181. Although Neebe's original idea refers to the foreign policy dispute between 'Atlanticists' and 'Gaullists', the underlying trade interests of the German export industry would have worked in the cartel question in almost the same way.

59 Berghoff, 'Historisches Relikt oder Zukunftsmodell?', p. 275.

60 Jürgen Weise, 'Müller-Wipperfürth, Alfons' in *Neue Deutsche Biographie 18* (1997), S. 513 f.

61 Representative of the three, see Gregor Schöllgen, *Gustav Schickedanz. Biographie eines Revolutionärs*, Berlin 2010.

62 TKA A/30419, letter from Ahrens to Sohl, 2.2. 1959, attached TO for Diskussionsabend, TOP 2.

63 Armin Grünbacher, 'Causes, Response and Effect of the Crisis in the British Petrochemical Industry in the Early 1980s', in *The Journal of Industrial History*, vol. 6 no. 2 (October 2003), pp. 76–89.

64 Almond, 'The Politics of German Business', pp. 195–241, p. 220.

65 Cornelia Rauh-Kühne, 'Zwischen "verantwortlichem Wirkungskreis" und "häuslichem Glanz". Zur Innenansicht wirtschaftsbürgerlicher Familien im 20. Jahrhundert', in Dieter Ziegler (ed.), *Großbürger und Unternehmer. Die deutsche Wirtschaftselite im 20 Jahrhundert*, Göttingen 2000, pp. 215–248, p. 236.

66 Nina Grunenberg, *Die Wundertäter. Netzwerke der deutschen Wirtschaft 1942–1966*, München 2006, p. 125.

67 Rauh-Kühne, 'Zwischen "verantwortlichem Wirkungskreis" und "häuslichem Glanz"', pp. 242 f.

68 Almond, 'The Politics of German Business', p. 206.

69 Bohner, *Der ehrbare Kaufmann*, linked the hard work of previous entrepreneurs to that of the reconstruction period, while Herdenröder, *Neue Männer an der Ruhr*, focussed exclusively on the new generation.

70 Von Plato, 'Wirtschaftskapitäne', p. 388.

71 Koehne, *Das Selbstbild deutscher Unternehmer*, p. 54, p. 238.

72 Berghoff, 'Historisches Relikt oder Zukunftsmodell?', p. 266, p. 271.
73 Berghoff, 'Abschied vom klassischen Mittelstand', pp. 93–95; Berghoff, 'Historisches Relikt oder Zukunftsmodell?', p. 256.
74 On this debate see Gary Herriegel, *Industrial Construction. The Sources of German Industrial Power*, Cambridge 1996; also Berghoff, 'Historisches Relikt oder Zukunftsmodell?'
75 *Der Spiegel*, 1960, no. 45, p. 30; Flender, *Die Verantwortung des Unternehmers*, p. 73.
76 Berghoff, 'Historisches Relikt oder Zukunftsmodell?', pp. 266–271.
77 Vaubel, *Zusammenbruch und Wiederaufbau*, p. 193.
78 Helmuth Uebbing, *Stahl schreibt Geschichte. 125 Jahre Wirtschaftsvereinigung Stahl*, Düsseldorf 1999, pp. 182 f.

Chapter 4

1 See, for example Reiner Pommerin (ed.), *The American Impact on Post-War Germany*, Providence, RI 1995. The more recent works from the business and economic history perspective include Christian Kleinschmidt, *Der Produktive Blick. Wahrnehmung amerikanischer und japanischer Management- und Produktionsmethoden durch deutsche Unternehmer, 1950–1985*, Berlin 2002; Robert R. Locke, *The Collapse of the American Management Mystique*, Oxford 1996; Matthias Kipping and Ove Bjanar (eds), *The Americanisation of European Business. The Marshall Plan and the Transfer of US Management Models*, London 1998; Jonathan Zeitlin and Gary Herrigel (eds), *Americanization and its Limits. Reworking US Technology and Management in Post-War Europe and Japan*, Oxford 2000; Harm G. Schröter, *Americanization of the European Economy. A Compact Survey of American Economic Influence in Europe Since the 1880s*, Dordrecht 2005; Richard Kuisel, 'Americanization for Historians', in *Diplomatic History*, vol. 14 no. 3 (summer 2000), pp. 509–515. For research on Americanization and consumption, see Victoria de Grazia, *Irresistible Empire. America's Advance through 20th Century Europe*, Cambridge 2005. Although Kuisel moves in this direction, research into the link between the Cold War and 'Americanization' is still a desideratum.
2 Berghahn, *The Americanization of West German Industry*; Anselm Doering-Manteuffel, *Wie westlich sind die Deutschen? Amerikanisierung und Westernisierung im 20. Jahrhundert*, Göttingen 1999.
3 Locke, *Management Mystique*, p. 70.
4 Werner Abelshauser, *Kulturkampf. Der deutsche Weg in die Neue Wirtschaft und die Amerikanische Herausforderung*, Berlin 2003.
5 Jacqueline McGlade, 'The big push: the extend of American business education to western Europe after the Second World War', in Lars Engwall and Vera Zamagni (eds), *Management Education in Historical Perspective*, Manchester 1998, pp. 50–65, p. 52. For the German technological perspective, see John Gimbel, *Science, Technology and Reparations: Exploitation and Plunder in Post-War Germany*, Stanford, CA 1990.
6 McGlade, 'The Big Push', pp. 50; 53 f.
7 RWWA 130/400101401/75, Bericht Hanns Voith, undated (summer 1949), also for the following.
8 Christian Kleinschmidt, *Der produktive Blick*, p. 296. Under USTAP, some 1,739 German managers, politicians and trade unionists visited the US over an eight-year period. See Armin Grünbacher, 'The Americanisation that never was? The first

decade of the Baden-Badener Unternehmergespräche, 1954–64 and top management training in 1950s Germany', in *Business History*, vol. 54 no. 2 (April 2012), pp. 245–261, p. 247.

9 Matthias Kipping, '"Operation Impact". Converting European Entrepreneurs to the American Creed', in Matthias Kipping and Ove Bjanar (eds), *Americanisation of European Business. The Marshall Plan and the Transfer of* US *Management Models*, London 1998, pp. 55–73.

10 BDI HA HGF Pro 786/1, Niederschrift BDI Geschäftsführerkonferenz 17.5. 1950.

11 RWWA 130/400101401/85, letter from Berg to Adenauer, 12.10. 1950.

12 Kipping, '"Operation Impact"', p. 69.

13 Grünbacher, 'The Americanisation that never was?', pp. 247 f; RWWA 130/40010146/515, Anmeldeschein Oktober 1955.

14 Ludwig Vaubel, *Unternehmer gehen zur Schule*, Düsseldorf 1952.

15 Vaubel, *Zusammenbruch und Wiederaufbau,* p. 12.

16 Matthias Kipping and Christian Kleinschmidt, 'Ludwig Vaubel and the Renewal of Management Education in Germany after 1945', in Anne-Marie Kuijlaars, Kim Prudon and Joop Visser (eds), *Business and Society. Entrepreneurs, Politics and Networks in Historical Perspective. Proceedings of the 3rd European Business History Association Conference*, Rotterdam 2000, pp. 521–530, p. 523.

17 Jürgen Bertsch and Horst Weitzmann (eds), *Das Netzwerk der Vordenker. Fünfzig Jahre Baden-Badener Unternehmergespräche im Spiegel der Wirtschaftsgeschichte*, Potsdam 2004, p. 91.

18 ACDP, 01-162-055/1, Nachlaß Curt Becker, report 'Förderung des Unternehmernachwuchses in Industriellen Unternehmungen', 20.11. 1953, also for the following. For Kipping's argument, see Matthias Kipping, 'The Hidden Business Schools: Management Training in Germany since 1945', in Engwall and Zamagni (eds), *Management Education*, p. 101.

19 ACDP, 01-162-055/1, Nachlaß Curt Becker, report 'Förderung des Unternehmernachwuchses in Industriellen Unternehmungen', 20.11. 1953.

20 Kipping, 'The Hidden Business Schools', p. 98. In the mid-1950s, only 31 per cent of board members and *Geschäftsführer* had a university degree; by 1990, the figure was 81 per cent.

21 Kipping and Kleinschmidt, 'Ludwig Vaubel', p. 523.

22 Grünbacher, 'The Americanisation that never was?', p. 250.

23 Werner Bührer, 'Zum Wandel der wirtschafts- und sozialpolitischen Zukunftsvorstellungen in der deutschen Industrie zwischen Weltwirtschaftskrise und Wirtschaftswunder', in Matthias Frese and Michael Prinz (eds), *Politische Zäsuren und gesellschaftlicher Wandel im 20. Jahrhundert. Regionale und vergleichende Perspektiven*, Paderborn 1996, p. 102. The attitude described by Bührer was certainly still prevalent during the 1950s.

24 See Faulenbach, 'Die Preußischen Bergassessoren im Ruhrbergbau'.

25 Sohl, *Notizen*, pp. 24 ff.

26 Quoted in Faulenbach, 'Die Preußischen Bergassessoren in Ruhrbergbau', pp. 231 f.

27 RWWA GHH 130/40010146/515, letter from Karl Guth to Hermann Reusch, 13.5. 1955. For the complete list of firms see Bertsch and Weitzmann (eds), *Das Netzwerk der Vordenker*, p. 108. Five of these companies were from heavy industry, eight from the chemical sector and fourteen were from the manufacturing sector, with a majority working in electrical engineering and machine-tool manufacturing. Three companies were part of the food industry.

28 Kleinschmidt, 'An Americanised Company in Germany. The Vereinigte Glanzstoff Fabriken in the 1950s', in Kipping and Bjanar, *Americanisation of European Business*, pp. 171–189, p. 184.
29 Grünbacher, 'The Americanisation that never was?', p. 252. For Merton's role and significance, see Susanne Becker, 'Information and Business at the Turn of the Century: Wilhelm Merton and the Creation and Dissemination of Management Knowledge', in Kuijlaars, Prudon, and Vissen (eds), *Business and Society*, pp. 513–520.
30 Hans Hellwig, 'Die Baden-Badener Unternehmergespräche. Weiterbildung des Unternehmernachwuchses', in Bundesverband deutscher Arbeitgeberverbände and Walter Raymond Stiftung (eds), *Unternehmer und Bildung. Festschrift zum 60. Geburtstag von Ludwig Vaubel*, Köln 1968, pp. 97–105, p. 100.
31 Grünbacher, 'The Americanisation that never was?', p. 252.
32 See also Hans Hellwig and Jürgen Bertsch, 'Ursprung und Werden einer Erfolgsgeschichte', in Jürgen Bertsch and Peter Zürn, *Führen und Gestalten. 100 Unternehmergespräche in Baden-Baden*, Berlin 1997, pp. 13–24, p. 24.
33 Kipping, 'Hidden Business Schools', p. 106.
34 RWWA 130/40010146/516, booklet *Die Baden-Badener Unternehmergespräche* (undated, 1957), Appendix A and B.
35 RWWA 130/40010146/516, 517, 518, 519, Tätigkeitsbericht der GFU, various years.
36 Grünbacher, 'The Americanisation that never was?', pp. 255 f., also for the following.
37 For the high level of university graduates and PhDs amongst bankers, see Dieter Ziegler, 'Strukturwandel und Elitenwechsel im Bankenwesen 1900–1957', in Volker Berghahn, Stefan Unger and Dieter Ziegler (eds), *Die deutsche Wirtschaftselite im 20. Jahrhundert. Kontinuität und Mentalität*, Essen 2003, pp. 187–218, p. 215.
38 Grünbacher, 'The Americanisation that never was?', p. 257. For the significance of *Betriebswirtschaft* to German management, see Robert R. Locke, 'Business Education in Germany: Past Systems and Current Practice', in *Business History Review*, vol. 52, no. 2 (summer 1985), pp. 232–253; in contrast, for the negative attitude of German businessmen at the time, see Schröter, *Americanization of the European Economy*, p. 104.
39 Kleinschmidt, *Der produktive Blick*, p. 299.
40 Kipping, 'Hidden Business Schools', p. 102.
41 Grünbacher, 'The Americanisation that never was?', p. 257.
42 Heinz Hartmann, *Authority and Organization*, pp. 168 f, 196 ff.
43 Ruth Rosenberger, *Experten für Humankapital. Die Entdeckung des Personalmanagements in der Bundesrepublik Deutschland*, München 2008, pp. 19 f.
44 RWWA 195/B/6/12/4, Büro für Wirtschaftsforschung, Protokoll der Zusammenkunft des Arbeitskreises 'Unternehmensführung im Wechsel der Gegebenheiten' am 17.4. 1961. Vaubel had been a participant in these talks.
45 Paul Erker, 'Einleitung: Industrie-Eliten im 20. Jahrhundert', in Paul Erker and Toni Pierenkämper (eds), *Deutsche Unternehmer zwischen Kriegswirtschaft und Wiederaufbau. Studien zur Erfahrungsbildung von Industrie-Eliten*, München 1999, p. 18.
46 ACDP 01-162-177/4, letter from Deutsches Institut zur Förderung des industriellen Führungsnachwuchses to Becker (undated, ca. October 1960).
47 For perhaps the best example, see Robert R. Locke, 'Business Education in Germany', pp. 232–253.
48 For one of the best accounts on the Ruhr coal labour situation, see Mark Roseman, *Recasting the Ruhr. Manpower, Economic Recovery and Labour Relations*, Oxford 1992.
49 See Bernd Weisbrod, 'Der Schein der Modernität. Zur Historisierung der "Volksgemeinschaft"' in Karsten Rudolph and Christel Wickert (eds), *Geschichte als*

Möglichkeit. Über die Chancen von Demokratie. Festschrift für Helga Grebing, Essen 1995, pp. 224–242, p. 233.

50 There is no English equivalent of the German word *Kaderschmiede*. It means an elitist training institution for future leadership.

51 BDI HA HGF Pro 785 (vol. 3), Bericht Beutler zur 4, BDI Mitgliederversammlung, 17.–19.5. 1953.

52 RWWA 195/B/5/1/17, Niederschrift über 191. Aufsichtsratssitzung der VGF, 7.12. 1953, TOP 3; RWWA 195/B/5/1/18, Niederschrift über 197. Aufsichtsratssitzung der VGF, 27.6. 1955, Top 3, Anhang.

53 Rosenberger, *Experten für Humankapital*, p. 291.

54 Vaubel, *Zusammenbruch und Wiederaufbau*, p. 13; for an example of the Circle seen as a training institution see Susanne Hilger, *'Amerikanisierung' deutscher Unternehmen. Wettbewerbsstrategien und Unternehmenspolitik bei Henkel, Siemens und Daimler Benz (1945/49–1975)*, Stuttgart 2004, p. 255.

55 Siegfried Fassbender, '"Wuppertaler Kreis." Die Weiterbildung der unternehmerischen Führungskräfte in der Bundesrepublik', in Bundesverband deutsche Arbeitgeberverbände (ed.), *Unternehmer und Bildung*, pp. 79–96, p. 85; also Rosenberger, *Experten für Humankapital*, p. 339. A critical study of the circle, its work and impact is still a desideratum.

56 RWWA 70-145-9, Kleine Druckschrift 'Die C. Rudolf Poensgen Stiftung e.V. zur Förderung von Führungskräften in der Wirtschaft Düsseldorf 1956'.

57 Fassbender, 'Wuppertaler Kreis', pp. 86–89.

58 RWWA 70-145-9, Kleine Druckschrift; RWWA 70-145-6, Aktenvermerk 16.12. 1955, Besprechung bei Präsident Schneider.

59 RWWA 70-145-6, Aktenvermerk 16.12. 1955, Besprechung bei Präsident Schneider; RWWA 70-145-7, Aufzeichnung Gespräch mit Ernst-Wolff Mommsen, 25.4. 1956.

60 ACDP 01-083-193/2, Protokoll der Mitgliederversammlung der GFU, 13.5. 1959, Bericht von Witzleben.

61 Hartmann, *Authority and Organization*, p. 182; Adelheid von Saldern, 'Das "Harzburger Model." Ein Ordnungssystem für bundesrepublikanische Unternehmen, 1960–1975', in Thomas Etzemüller (ed.), *Die Ordnung der Moderne. Social Engineering im 20. Jahrhundert*, Bielefeld 2009, 303–329, p. 327. Von Saldern also emphasizes the almost complete lack of research into the society.

62 TKA A30515, Deutsche Volkswirtschaftliche Gesellschaft, letter from Höhn to 'members, supporters and friends at Rhine and Ruhr', undated (handwritten date 11.5. 1955).

63 RWWA 28-66-5, brochure 'Aufgaben der Akademie', 5 ff.

64 Hartmann, *Authority and Organization*, p. 176.

65 Reinhard Höhn, 'Der Wandel im Führungsstil der Wirtschaft', in *Führung in der Wirtschaft. Festschrift zum zehnjährigen Bestehen der Akademie für Führungskräfte der Wirtschaft*, Bad Harzburg 1966, pp. 9–87, pp. 9–15.

66 Karl-Friedrich Diedrich, '"Human Relations" als soziales und wirtschaftliches Potential im Betrieb', PhD thesis, Wirtschaftshochschule Mannheim, 1950, p. 47 ff. For a summary of Höhn's management ideas, see Reinhard Höhn, *Führungsbrevier der Wirtschaft*, Bad Harzburg 1966, (and various editions thereafter).

67 Höhn, 'Der Wandel im Führungsstil', p. 50.

68 Ibid, pp. 66 f; p. 59; Höhn, *Führungsbrevier*, pp. 33 f.

69 Von Saldern, 'Das Harzburger Modell', p. 311.

70 Daniel Schmid, '"Quo vadis, homo harzburgiensis?" Aufstieg und Niedergang des "Harzburger Modells"', in *Zeitschrift für Unternehmensgeschichte* vol. 59 no. 1 (April 2014), pp. 73–98, p. 84, table 3.

71 Jean-Jacques Servan-Schreiber, *Die amerikanische Herausforderung*, Hamburg 1968; English ed.: *The American Challenge*, Avon 1971.

72 Rosenberger, *Experten für Humankapital*, p. 407.

73 Heinz Höhne, *Der Orden unter dem Totenkopf. Die Geschichte der* SS, Gütersloh 1967; Engl. translation *The Order of the Death's Head*, London 1969; *Der Spiegel*, 1966 no. 46 to 1967 no. 11. For more recent studies of Höhn's involvement and role in the Nazi period, see Frei (ed.), *Hitler's Eliten nach 1945*; Bernd Rühters, 'Reinhard Höhn, Carl Schmidt und andere - Geschichten und Legenden aus der NS-Zeit', in *Neue juristische Wochenschrift*, Heft 39 (2000), 2866–2871; Michael Wildt, *An Uncompromising Generation. The Nazi Leadership of the Reich Security Main Office*, Madison, WI 2009; Michael Wildt, 'Der Fall Reinhard Höhn. Vom Reichssicherheitshauptamt zur Harzburger Akademie', in Alexander Gallus and Axel Schildt (eds), *Rückblickend in die Zukunft. Politische Öffentlichkeit und intellektuelle Positionen in Deutschland um 1950 und 1930*, Göttingen 2011, pp. 254–271.

74 The post of labour director (*Arbeitsdirektor*) had to be created in each company which was subject to co-determination. It was filled by a worker representative who took a seat on the managing board of those companies with the explicit remit of (or limited to) social affairs.

75 TKA A30413, Diskussionsabend, letter from Ahrens to Sohl, 14.12. 1956 and TKA A 30414, Diskussionsabend, letter from Ahrens to Sohl 4.5. 1957; RWWA 28-66-4, Akademie Terminplan für die Zeit von April bis Juli 1959; Richard Guserl, *Das Harzburger Model. Idee und Wirklichkeit*, Wiesbaden 1973, p. 37.

76 Burkhart Lutz, 'Integration durch Aufstieg. Überlegungen zur Verbürgerlichung der deutschen Facharbeiter in den Jahrzehnten nach dem Zweiten Weltkrieg', in Manfred Hertling and Bernd Ulrich (eds), *Bürgertum nach 1945*, Hamburg 2005, pp. 284–309; von Saldern, 'Das "Harzburger Model"' p. 306.

77 Alfred Flender, *Die Stunde des Unternehmers*, Bonn 1954, p. 10; Alfred Flender, *Die Verantwortung des Unternehmers*, Stuttgart 1961, p. 18; Rosenberger, *Experten für Humankapital*, p. 325.

78 Guserl, *Harzburger Model*, p. 53.

79 Rosenberger, *Experten für Humankapital*, pp. 397; 406 f.

80 Schmid, '"Quo Vadis"', p. 80; Hartmann, *Authority and Organization*, p. 181; for some of the contemporary debates, see Wolfgang Grunwald and Wilmar F. Bernthal, 'Controversy in German Management. The Harzburg Model Experience', in *Academy of Management Review*, vol. 8 no. 2 (1983), pp. 233 f.

81 *Der Spiegel*, no. 35, 1989, p. 85.

82 Volker Berghahn, 'Das "deutsche Kapitalismus Modell" in Geschichte und Geschichtswissenschaft', in Volker Berghahn and Sigurt Vitols (eds), *Gibt es einen deutschen Kapitalismus? Traditionen und globale Perspektiven der sozialen Marktwirtschaft*, Frankfurt/M 2006, pp. 25–43, 39.

83 Kipping and Kleinschmidt, 'Ludwig Vaubel', p. 527; Grünbacher, 'The Americanization that never was?', pp. 245, 257.

84 *Auftragstaktik* meant that a superior gave an objective to his subordinate but left it to the latter's initiative how this was to be achieved. The concept's flexibility is seen as the reason for the tactical successes of the Germany army.

85 Lutz, 'Integration durch Aufstieg', pp. 307 f.

86 Von Menges, *Unternehmensentscheide*, p. 26.
87 RWWA 70-145-12, Gründungsakte der C. Rudolf Poensgen Stiftung, 15.6. 1956, Jubiläumsansprache Wilhelm Zangen.
88 Erker, 'Einleitung', pp. 12 f.
89 For example in a speech to young entrepreneurs in April 1950, see Winschuh, *Das neue Unternehmerbild*, pp. 57 ff.
90 Koehne, *Das Selbstbild deutscher Unternehmer*, p. 55.
91 Dieter Ziegler, 'Die wirtschaftsbürgerliche Elite im 20. Jahrhundert. Eine Bilanz', in Dieter Ziegler (ed.), *Großbürger und Unternehmer. Die deutsche Wirtschaftselite im 20. Jahrhundert*, Göttingen 2000, pp. 7–29, pp. 20 f.
92 For Krupp, see Lothar Gall (ed.), *Krupp im 20. Jahrhundert. Die Geschichte des Unternehmens vom Ersten Weltkrieg bis zur Gründung der Stiftung*, Berlin 2002; for Reusch, see Benjamin Obermüller, 'Hermann Reusch und die Beziehungen zur Eigentümer Familie Haniel', in Susane Hilger and Ulrich S. Soénius (eds), *Familienunternehmen im Rheinland im 19. und 20. Jahrhundert*, Schriften zur rheinisch-westfälischen Wirtschaftsgeschichte, vol. 47, Köln, Stiftung Rheinisch-Westfälisches Wirtschaftsarchiv 2009, pp. 159–174.
93 Sohl, *Notizen*, pp. 26, 33. For the social habitus of the Bergassessoren and their self-perception as social and business elite, see Faulenbach, 'Die Preußischen Bergassessoren im Ruhrbergbau'.
94 Sohl, *Notizen*, p. 29.
95 Martin Fiedler and Bernhard Lorentz, 'Kontinuitäten in den Netzwerkbeziehungen der deutschen Wirtschaftseliten zwischen Weltwirtschaftskrise und 1950. Eine quantitative und qualitative Analyse', in Berghahn, Unger and Ziegler (eds), *Die deutsche Wirtschaftselite*, pp. 51–74.
96 Hartmann, 'Soziale Homogenität und generationelle Muster', pp. 31–50, p. 43 ff.
97 Ziegler, 'Strukturwandel und Elitenwechsel', p. 215; Joly, *Großunternehmer in Deutschland*, p. 48.
98 Hartmann, 'Soziale Homogenität', *passim*.
99 On the significance of the in-house career, see Joly, *Großunternehmer in Deutschland*, pp. 57 ff.
100 See von Menges, *Unternehmensentscheide*.
101 Joly, *Großunternehmer in Deutschland*, shows Beitz (pp. 36, 38) and Sohl (pp. 87 f) as prime examples of managers unable to cede power and emphasizes the age limit for chairmen (p. 92).
102 See Rosenberger, *Experten für Humankapital*.
103 Schröter, *Americanization of the European Economy*, p. 4. A good summary against the uses of the term 'Americanization' is provided by Kuisel, 'Americanization for Historians'.

Chapter 5

1 David Blackbourne, 'The German Bourgeoisie. An Introduction', in David Blackbourne and Richard J. Evans (eds), *The German Bourgeoisie. Essays on the Social History of the German Middle Class from the Late Eighteenth to the Early Twentieth Century*, London 1991, pp. 1–45, p. 23; also p. xvi on the difference to the French bourgeoisie and the British middle class.
2 Hans-Ulrich Wehler, 'Deutsches Bürgertum nach 1945. Exitus oder Phoenix aus der Asche?', in *Geschichte und Gesellschaft*, vol. 27 (2001), pp. 617–634, p. 620; Dieter

Gosewinkel, 'Zivilgesellschaft - Bürgerlichkeit - Zivilität. Konzeptionelle Überlegungen zur Deutung der deutschen Geschichte im 20. Jahrhundert', in Gunilla Budde, Eckhart Conze and Cornelia Rauh (eds) *Bürgertum nach dem bürgerlichen Zeitalter. Leitbilder und Praxis seit 1945*, Göttingen 2010, pp. 29–52, pp. 32 f.

3 Manfred Hettling and Stefan-Ludwig Hoffmann, 'Zur Historisierung bürgerlicher Werte', in Manfred Hettling and Stefan-Ludwig Hoffmann (eds) *Der bürgerliche Wertehimmel. Innenansichten des 19. Jahrhunderts*, Göttingen 2000, pp. 7–21, p. 9.

4 Manfred Riedel, 'Bürger, Staatsbürger, Bürgertum', in Otto Brunner, Werner Conze and Reinhard Koselleck (eds), *Geschichtliche Grundbegriffe*, vol. 1, Stuttgart 1972, pp. 672–725, esp. pp. 712–24.

5 'Einleitung', in Budde, Conze and Rauh (eds), *Bürgertum nach dem bürgerlichen Zeitalter*, pp. 16, 21; Blackbourne, 'The German Bourgeoisie', p. 7.

6 Manfred Hettling, 'Die persönliche Selbstständigkeit. Der archimedische Punkt bürgerlicher Lebensführung', in Hettling and Hoffmann (eds), *Der bürgerliche Wertehimmel*, pp. 57–78, p. 57.

7 Christina von Hodenberg, 'Der Fluch des Geldsacks. Der Aufstieg der Industriellen als Herausforderung bürgerlicher Werte', in Hettling and Hoffmann (eds), *Der bürgerliche Wertehimmel*, pp. 79–103, p. 79.

8 On the debate about 'German capitalism', see Volker Berghahn and Sigurt Vitols (eds), *Gibt es einen deutschen Kapitalismus? Tradition und globale Perspektiven der sozialen Marktwirtschaft*, Frankfurt/M 2006; Robert R. Locke, 'Mistaking a historical phenomenon for a functional one: post-war management training reconsidered', in Lars Engwall and Vera Zamagni (eds) *Management Education in Historical Perspective*, Manchester 1998, pp. 145–156, p. 149.

9 Groundbreaking and representative for the former is Jürgen Kocka (ed.), *Bürger und Bürgerlichkeit im 19. Jahrhundert*, Göttingen 1987; for the latter it is, as its title indicates, Budde, Conze and Rauh (eds), *Bürgertum nach dem bürgerlichen Zeitalter*.

10 Hans Mommsen, 'Die Auflösung des Bürgertums seit dem späten 19. Jahrhundert', in Kocka (ed.), *Bürger und Bürgerlichkeit*, pp. 288–315, cited in Christof Biggeleben, 'Kontinuität von Bürgerlichkeit im Berliner Unternehmertum. Der Verein Berliner Kaufleute und Industrieller (1879–1961)', in Berghahn, Unger and Ziegler (eds), *Die deutsche Wirtschaftselite*, pp. 241–274; Wehler, 'Deutsches Bürgertum nach 1945', p. 625.

11 Cited in Stürmer, Teichmann and Treue, *Striking the Balance*, p. 407.

12 Vaubel, *Zusammenbruch und Wiederaufbau*, p. 190.

13 Gosewinkel, 'Zivilgesellschaft - Bürgerlichkeit - Zivilität', pp. 33 f.

14 Norbert Elias, *The Germans. Power Struggles and the Development of Habitus in the 19th and 20th Century* (ed. Michael Schröter), Cambridge 1996, p. 50.

15 Ziegler, 'Die Wirtschaftsbürgerliche Elite im 20. Jahrhundert', p. 21.

16 Cornelia Rauh-Kühne, 'Zwischen "verantwortlichem Wirkungskreis" und "häuslichem Glanz"', pp. 214, 224.

17 Ibid, p. 216, quoted from a greeting card to Reusch on the occasion of his silver wedding anniversary, May 1952.

18 Berghahn, Friedrich, *Otto A. Friedrich*, passim, esp. pp. 79–84.

19 Cornelia Rauh-Kühne, '"... so weiß ich heute, dass Dein Leben in unserer Familiengeschichte einen wertvolleren Platz haben wird als das Deiner Söhne". Zur Bürgerlichkeit von Unternehmerfamilien der Wiederaufbaugeneration', in Berghahn, Unger and Ziegler (eds), *Die Deutsche Wirtschaftselite*, pp. 443–461, esp. pp. 454–456.

20 RWWA 130/40010146/188, letter from BDI to *Hauptgeschäftsführer* and member associations, 15.2. 1960. The letter contains some criticism about the willingness of some associations to provide their dues.
21 Braunthal, *The Federation of German Industry*, p. 70.
22 Biggeleben, 'Kontinuität von Bürgerlichkeit', pp. 252 ff.
23 Evelyn Kroker, 'Die Gründungsgeschichte der VFKK', in *Der Anschnitt*, vol. 50 (1998), pp. 186–195, also for the following.
24 Werner Bührer, 'Der Kulturkreis im Bundesverband der deutschen Industrie und die "kulturelle Modernisierung" der Bundesrepublik in den 50er Jahren', in Schildt and Sywottek (eds), *Modernisierung im Wiederaufbau*, pp. 583–595, p. 584.
25 RWWA 130/40010146/218, letter from Paul Reusch to Hermann Reusch, 5.2. 1952.
26 TKA A30114, letter from Reusch to Sohl, 1.9. 1951, Appendix 1, speech by Reusch.
27 TKA A 30114, letter from Reusch to Sohl, 1.9.1951, Appendix 2, Reusch's opening speech.
28 Bührer, 'Der Kulturkreis', p. 587.
29 Bührer, 'Der Kulturkreis', pp. 587–589.
30 *Jahresring* 63/64, pp. 369–375, cited in Bührer, 'Der Kulturkreis', p. 591.
31 RWWA 130/40010146/326, letter from DII to members of *Vorstand*, *Beirat* and *Kuratorium*, 14.10.1965.
32 TKA A 30114, letter from Reusch to *Kulturkreis* members, 3.1. 1952.
33 On the political debate, see Günter Schulz, *Wiederaufbau in Deutschland. Die Wohnungsbaupolitik in den Westzonen und der Bundesrepublik von 1945 bis 1957*, Düsseldorf 1994.
34 For some very revealing views on industrialists' perception of workers' style and taste, see Roseman, *Recasting the Ruhr*, esp. pp. 192–197.
35 TKA A30114, letter from the *Kulturkreis* to board members, 9.5. 1953, report on the *Verwaltungsrat* meeting on 29.4. 1953.
36 TKA A 30114, letter from Reusch to Sohl, 1.4. 1952.
37 TKA A 30115, Report on *Verwaltungsrat Sitzung* 23.11. 1955.
38 See, for example RWWA 130/40010146/186
39 RWWA 130/400101402/20, undated address by Hermann Reusch on the occasion of the 1952 BDI *Kulturkreis* awards.
40 RWWA 130/400101402/20, address to the Bad Mergentheim Rotary Club meeting, 13.7. 1954.
41 RWWA 130/40010146/515 letter from Reusch to Karl Guth, 24.8. 1955 and passim.
42 Bührer, 'Der Kulturkreis', pp. 592–595.
43 Wirtschaftsvereinigung Stahl und Stahlinstitut VDEh (eds), *Portraits im Stahlzentrum*, Düsseldorf 2006, p. 31.
44 Henle, *Weggenosse des Jahrhunderts*, pp. 301–353; Berghahn and Friedrich, *Otto A. Friedrich*, pp. 76 ff.
45 Vaubel, *Zusammenbruch und Wiederaufbau*, passim and specifically on the failure of the 'spiritual elite' pp. 88; the involvement with the Nazis p. 185; and criticism of US cultural policy p. 61.
46 Sohl, *Notizen*, pp. 13–21; 219–28.
47 See, for example, Hans-Günther Sohl, *Industrie und Kunst, Vortrag vor den Mitgliedern des Düsseldorfer Industrieclubs*, 5.6. 1978 (no place, no date (1978)).
48 TKA A30338, Niederschrift *Vorstandkreis*, speech Schroeder on the occasion of his leave-taking as WVES chairman, 16.5. 1956.
49 Herdenröder, *Neue Männer an der Ruhr*, passim for the cultural interests and p. 63 for the depreciative quote.

50 Gustav Stein, *Unternehmer als Förderer der Kunst*, Frankfurt/M 1952, p. 8 and *passim.*
51 Werner Bührer, '"... insofern steckt in jedem echten Unternehmer auch ein künstlerisches Element." Die Erneuerung des Bundesverbandes der Deutschen Industrie (BDI) in den 1970er Jahren', in Morten Reitmayer and Ruth Rosenberger (eds), *Unternehmer am Ende des "goldenen Zeitalters". Die 1970er Jahre in unternehmens-und wirtschaftshistorischer Perspektive*, Essen 2008, pp. 233–248, p. 248.
52 Biggeleben, 'Kontinuität von Bürgerlichkeit', p. 259; for Stinnes see Gerald Feldman, *Hugo Stinnes: Biographie eines Industriellen, 1870–1924*, München 1998.
53 Bohner, *Der ehrbare Kaufmann*, pp. vii–viii. It is not a coincidence that the DII supported the reprint of this hagiographic description of the achievements of 'great' German traders and industrialists, it rather confirms that they were still concerned about their reputation.
54 Friedrich Zunkel, 'Ehre', in Brunner, Conze and Koselleck, *Geschichtliche Grundbegriffe*, vol. 2, pp. 1–63, p. 49.
55 Fritz Hellwig, 'Der echte Unternehmer in der Marktwirtschaft.' Vortrag auf der Jahreshauptversammlung der Arbeitsgemeinschaft Selbstständiger Unternehmer, 30.3. 1951 (no date, no place), pp. 7 f; also Alfred Flender, *Die Verantwortung des Unternehmers*, p. 25, where Flender emphasizes that in contrast to a salaried manager, who after a mistake could move to another company, the owner-entrepreneur always had his neck on the line.
56 Wilfried Speitkamp, *Ohrfeige, Duell, Ehrenmord. Eine Geschichte der Ehre*, Stuttgart 2010, pp. 11, 22.
57 Ibid, p. 17.
58 Ute Frevert, *Men of Honour. A Social and Cultural History of the Duel*, Cambridge 1995, pp. 2–4; Ann Goldberg, *Honour, Politics and the Law in Imperial Germany, 1871–1914*, Cambridge 2010, p. 5.
59 James Q. Whitman, 'Civility and Respect: Three Societies', in *The Yale Law Journal*, vol. 109 no. 6 (2000), pp. 1279–1398; Frevert, *Men of Honour*, p. 212.
60 See, for example, Fritz Pudor, *Lebensbilder aus dem Rheinisch-Westfälischen Industriegebiet: Jahrgang 1962–1967*, Baden-Baden 1977.Wirtschaftsvereinigung Stahl und Stahlinstitut VDEh (eds), *Portraits im Stahlzentrum*, *passim.*
61 *Der Spiegel* no. 45, 1960, p. 34.
62 Speitkamp, *Ohrfeige, Duell, Ehrenmord*, p. 176. It can be assumed that the drop in litigation was in part due to the more severe economic situation after the First World War.
63 Henke, *Die amerikanische Besetzung Deutschlands*, pp. 472, 490.
64 Krumm, *Tagebuch eines deutschen Unternehmers*, pp. 247 ff, quote on p. 249.
65 Henle, *Weggenosse des Jahrhunderts*, pp. 80–82.
66 Sohl, *Notizen*, pp. 98–109.
67 Von Menges, *Unternehmensentscheide*, pp. 104–105; for the detail of the case see Armin Grünbacher, '"Honourable Men": West German Industrialists and the Role of Honour and Honour Courts in the Adenauer Era', in *Contemporary European History*, vol. 2 no. 2 (April 2013), pp. 233–252, here pp. 242–243.
68 For board memberships of Gutehoffnungshütte Aktienverein, which was the holding company which included amongst others, the Gutehoffnungshütte steelworks, the manufacturer MAN and Ferrostaal, see Johannes Bähr, Ralf Banken and Thomas Flemming, *Die MAN: eine deutsche Industriegeschichte* (3rd ed.), München 2009, p. 286, and for Kirchfeld's political activities pp. 283–284.

69 Benjamin Obermüller, 'Hermann Reusch und die Beziehungen zur Eigentümerfamilie Haniel', pp. 164 ff. For the Haniel/Carp family tree see Harold James, *Family Capitalism: Wendels, Haniels, Falcks, and the Continental European Model*, Harvard 2006, pp. 390–392.

70 Benjamin Obermüller, '"Auf einen groben Klotz gehört ein grober Keil." Hermann Reuschs Kampf gegen Dr Franz Kirchfeld 1947–1950', in Historische Gesellschaft Oberhausen (ed.), *Ursprünge und Entwicklungen der Stadt Oberhausen*, Band 8, Oberhausen 2009, pp. 119–133, pp. 124–125.

71 Although still unusual, James Whitman points out that the last two duels fought in Europe took place in France in 1958 and 1967; see Whitman, 'Civility and Respect', p. 1360.

72 Grünbacher, 'Honourable Men', p. 242.

73 Grünbacher, 'Honourable Men', pp. 242 f. For the Schlieker-Kirchfeld business and its origins in the war economy see, briefly, Richard Tilly, *Willy H. Schlieker, Aufstieg und Fall eines Unternehmers (1914–1980)*, Berlin 2008, p. 89.

74 For the scale of Nazi party membership amongst Gutehoffnungshütte management see Bähr, Banken and Flemming, *Die MAN*, pp. 283-291.

75 Obermüller, 'Auf einen groben Klotz', p. 122.

76 RWWA 130/400101404/25, *passim*, though there was also criticism from von Menges that Reusch at times put the Haniels before the company; see von Menges, *Unternehmerentscheide*.

77 Grünbacher, 'Honourable Men', p. 243.

78 RWWA 130/400101420/70, various letters on *Demontageausgleich*, December 1949 to January 1950.

79 Goldberg, *Honour, Politics and the Law*, p. 63. For those groups, honour courts meant an emancipation from state authority and at the same time helped to set minimum professional standards.

80 Biggeleben, 'Kontinuität von Bürgerlichkeit', pp. 260 f.

81 Elias, *The Germans*, p. 46.

82 Biggeleben, 'Kontinuität von Bürgerlichkeit', pp. 265 f.

83 Petra Bräutigam, 'Südwestdeutsche Unternehmer der mittelständischen Industrie während des Nationalsozialismus', in Großbölting and Schmidt (eds), *Unternehmerwirtschaft zwischen Markt und Lenkung*, pp. 121–140, pp. 136–140. This was in contrast to big business, where, except for the chemical industry, Jews were expelled from the companies early on; see Ziegler, 'Struktureller Wandel und Elitenwechsel im Bankenwesen 1900–1950', in Berghahn, Unger and Ziegler (eds), *Die deutsche Wirtschaftselite im 20. Jahrhundert*, pp. 187–218; Raymond Stokes, 'From the IG Farben Fusion to the Establishment of BASF AG (1922–1952)', in Werner Abelshauser et al., *German Industry and Global Enterprise. BASF: The History of a Company*, Cambridge 2004, pp. 206–361, esp. pp. 251, 291. Stephan H. Lindner, *Inside IG Farben. Hoechst during the Third Reich*, Cambridge 2008.

84 RWWA 22-643-3, Niederschrift über die Geschäftsführersitzung der IHKn im Regierungsbezirk Düsseldorf, 4.10. 1935, TOP 3; Niederschrift 30.6. 1936 TOP 14; Bericht über die Geschäftsführerbesprechung 22.6. 1937.

85 RWWA 1-144-1, Schiedsgerichtsordnung der IHK Bonn, 15.2. 1946; Schiedsgerichtsordnung der IHK Aachen; Dortmund; Duisburg; Essen; Koblenz; Neuss; Trier; Krefeld; letter from Vereinigung der IHKn der Britischen Besatzungszone to IHK Köln, 4.8. 1948.

86 RWWA 1d-5-4, Memo für Assessor Wellmann, 24.9. 1948

87 RWWA 28-2-4, letter from IHK Essen to Mitglieder der Vollversammlung, 24.1. 1949; RWWA 28-173-5, Ehrengerichtsordnung der IHK Essen.
88 RWWA 28-173-5, Folder 'Ehrengericht, Einzelne Fälle'.
89 ACDP 01-433-K0782, letter from Birrenbach to G.V. Winterhalter, 22.3. 1955.
90 Grünbacher, 'Honourable Men', p. 233, also on the difference between honour courts (which deal with professional misconduct) and honour councils (which act as associational arbitration bodies).
91 TKA A/30413, Diskussionsabend, letter from Ahrens to Sohl, 12.3. 1957, Appendix 13. However, the existence of the guidelines could not be verified.
92 Plumpe, 'Unternehmerverbände und industrielle Interessenpolitik', pp. 655–727; for the following also Grünbacher, 'Honourable Men', pp. 249 f.
93 For industry's response to that challenge see Feldman's monumental work, Gerald D. Feldman, *Army, Industry and Labor in Germany 1914–1918*, Princeton 1966.
94 Bernd Weisbrod, *Schwerindustrie in der Weimarer Republik. Interessenpolitik zwischen Stabilisierung und Krise*, Wuppertal 1978, pp. 415–456.
95 Gerhard Mollin, *Montankonzerne und 'Drittes Reich'. Der Gegensatz zwischen Monopolindustrie und Befehlswirtschaft in der deutschen Rüstung und Expansion, 1936–1944*, Göttingen 1988.
96 TKA, A/30415, letter from Ahrens to Sohl, 30.11. 1957, Appendix 1 c.
97 TKA A/30346, letter from Ahrens to Schroeder, 18.2. 1958.
98 Wolff von Amerongen wrote protocols of the meetings to inform his six most important managers about the event. Although very subjective, the protocols give a very good reflection of the prevailing mood, well beyond the official summaries provided by the WVES's chief clerks. For Wolff von Amerongen and his company see Peter Danylow and Ulrich S. Soénius (eds), *Otto Wolff. Ein Unternehmen zwischen Wirtschaft und Politik*, München 2005. For the meeting see Grünbacher, 'Honourable Men', p. 246.
99 Whitman, 'Civility and Respect', p. 1302. Whitman provides a list of liable insults which is a full page long, see pp. 1305–1306.
100 ACDP 01-224-151/2, Diskussionsabend, memo on the meeting 11.11. 1958, TOP 8.
101 ACDP 01-224-227/1, letter from Köhler to Sohl, 8.5. 1963.
102 ACDP 01-224-227/1, *passim*.
103 RWWA SWB 509, Aktennotiz Wolff von Amerongen, 12.9. 1963 betr. DA vom 10.9. 1963, also for the following.
104 ACDP 01-224-227/1, letter from Ehrenrat to Sohl and Sendler, 16.1. 1964.
105 Grünbacher, 'Honourable Men', p. 248.
106 TKA SWB 510, memo by Wolff von Amerongen on DA on 8.9. 1965.
107 Grünbacher, 'Honourable Men', p. 249.
108 Although a commissioned hagiography celebrating the WVES's anniversary, Uebbing's *Stahl schreibt Geschichte* still gives some good insight into the association's firm discipline up to the 1950s.
109 TKA SWB 510, memo by Wolff von Amerongen on DA 14.6. 1965.
110 Konrad Jarausch, *Die Umkehr. Deutsche Wandlungen 1945–1995*, Bonn 2004, p. 9.
111 Joachim Käppen, *Bertold Beitz. Die Biographie*, Berlin 2010, p. 156. Käppen's book is a commissioned work and highly hagiographic, in particular about Beitz's running of the company. For a more balanced account see Norbert Pötzel, *Beitz. Eine deutsche Geschichte*, München 2011.
112 Joley, *Großunternehmer in Deutschland*, p. 166.
113 See Rohland's euphemistic autobiography, *Bewegte Zeiten*, pp. 45–75; also Gregor Janssen, *Das Ministerium Speer. Deutschlands Rüstung im Krieg*, Frankfurt/M 1968.

114 Rohland, *Bewegte Zeiten*, pp. 61 f.,123; 154;157 f.
115 Sohl, *Notizen*, p. 141.
116 Rohland, *Bewegte Zeiten*, p. 159; Berghahn *Unternehmer und Politik*, pp. 51 f.
117 RWWA 130/400101401/58, Letter from Otto Meyer to Reusch, 21.3. 1950.
118 Joly, 'Kontinuität und Diskontinuität der industriellen Elite nach 1945', in Dieter Ziegler (ed.), *Großbürger und Unternehmer. Die deutsche Wirtschaftselite im 20. Jahrhundert*, Göttingen 2000, pp. 54–72, pp. 86 f.; Joly, *Großunternehmer in Deutschland*, pp. 157 f.
119 Joly, *Großunternehmer in Deutschland*, p. 134.
120 Priemel, 'Gekaufte Geschichte: Der "Freundeskreis Albert Vögler"', pp. 192 f.
121 Vaubel, *Zusammenbruch und Wiederaufbau*, p. 193. See also ch. 3.
122 Henke, *Die amerikanische Besetzung Deutschlands*, pp. 513–520, esp. pp. 514, 519.
123 In 1950, Schlieker had appeard on the cover of *Time Magazine* as 'Wirtschaftswunderknabe no. 1', see Grunenberg, *Die Wundertäter*, p. 210.
124 Frei et al., *Flick*, p. 449.
125 Tilly, *Schlieker. Aufstieg und Fall*, p. 41; pp. 65 f.
126 Ibid, p. 108.
127 *Der Spiegel*, 'Der Lückenschließer', no. 39, 1956, pp. 20–26.
128 Herdenröder, *Neue Männer an der Ruhr*, pp. 128–131.
129 Tilly, *Schlieker. Aufstieg und Fall*, pp. 157–159.
130 Tim Schanetzky, Review of: Tilly, Richard: *Willy H. Schlieker. Aufstieg und Fall eines Unternehmers (1914–1980)*. Berlin 2008, in *H-Soz-Kult*, 17 March 2009, http://www.hsozkult.de/publicationreview/id/rezbuecher-11811. Schanetzky comes to a different conclusion in his review.
131 Sohl, *Notizen*, pp. 231 f.; p. 83.
132 Grunenberg, *Die Wundertäter*, pp. 69 f.
133 See, for example, RWWA 130/400101420/62 letter from Reusch to Henle, 5.5. 1947; 130/400101420/70, letter from Reusch to Janssen, 16.12. 48; and ACDP 01-083 - 147/3, *passim*, where Dinkelbach's denunciation continued well into 1954.
134 John Gillingham, *Coal, Steel and the Rebirth of Europe. The German and French from Ruhr Conflict to Economic Community*, Cambridge 1991, p. 197; Joly, *Großunternehmer in Deutschland*, pp. 148, 156.
135 Henke, *Die amerikanische Besetzung Deutschlands*, p. 461.
136 BBA 76/56, note to Brigadier Gilman, undated, but presumably after 5.1. 1947.
137 Vaubel, *Zusammenbruch und Wiederaufbau*, p. 164.
138 Joly, *Großunternehmer in Deutschland*, p. 141.
139 While not an outright outsider due to his wealth, the size of his industrial conglomerate and widespread company participations, Flick was not seen as an insider either, as he disregarded agreements and had extended his business empire, in particular during the Third Reich, with methods which were seen as objectionable.
140 Uebbing, *Stahl schreibt Geschichte*, p. 27.
141 ACDP, 01-224-222/1, minutes of the Diskussionsabend 6 March 1956.
142 Grünbacher, 'Honourable men', p. 245.
143 Biggeleben, 'Kontinuität von Bürgerlichkeit', pp. 265, 272. For the overall bad economic situation in Berlin see Armin Grünbacher, 'Sustaining the Island: Western Aid to 1950s Berlin', in *Cold War History*, vol. 3 no. 3 (2003), pp. 1–22.
144 Frei et al, *Flick*, p. 555, for media praise for Flick breaking the mould of traditional thinking at the Ruhr.

Chapter 6

1 Hans-Peter Ullmann, *Interessenverbände in Deutschland*, Frankfurt/M. 1988.
2 On Hugenberg see Klaus Werneke and Peter Heller, *Der vergessene Führer. Alfred Hugenberg. Presemacht und Nationalsozialismus*, Hamburg 1987; on Paul Reusch see specifically Erich Maschke, *Es entsteht ein Konzern. Paul Reusch und die Gutehoffnungshütte*, Tübingen 1985 and more recently Peter Langer, *Macht und Verantwortung. Der Ruhrbaron Paul Reusch*, Essen 2012; and Christian Marx, *Paul Reusch und die Gutehoffnungshütte: Leitung eines deutschen Großunternehmens*, Göttingen 2013. On the newspapers' limited political impact see Ziegler, 'Die wirtschaftsbürgerliche Elite im 20. Jahrhundert', p. 25.
3 Blackbourne, 'The German Bourgeoisie', p. 25.
4 Also the title of an influential booklet by the eminent political scientist Theodor Eschenburg, *Herrschaft der Verbände*, Stuttgart 1955.
5 Bräutigam, 'Südwestdeutsche Unternehmer', p. 121.
6 Bräutigam, 'Südwestdeutsche Unternehmer', pp. 124 f.
7 Almond, 'The Politics of German Business', pp. 220 ff., esp. p. 222.
8 Sohl, *Notizen*, pp. 167 f.
9 Almond, 'The Politics of German Business', pp. 196 f, 198, 219.
10 Almond, 'The Politics of German Business', p. 207.
11 ACDP 01-228-002/1, Rede Stein vor BDI Geschäftsführern und Vertreter der Landesverbände (undated, early summer 1952).
12 BDI HA HGF Pro 785 (3), Kundgebung und Mitgliederversammlung des BDI, 17–19.5. 1953, speech by Gustav Stein.
13 RWWA 130/40010146/312, table 'Zusammensetzung des Bundestages' (undated, October 1953).
14 Flender, *Die Verantwortung des Unternehmers*, p. 142; the Statistisches Bundesamt gave the 1961 figure of independent businesses as 205,600, see Statistisches Bundesamt (ed.), *Statistisches Jahrbuch für die Bundesrepublik Deutschland, 1963*, cited in Rainer Koehne, *Das Selbstbild der deutschen Unternehmer. Legitimation und Leitbild einer Institution*, Berlin 1976, p. 49, Statistisches Bundesamt (ed.), *Statistisches Jahrbuch 1965*, p. 34.
15 RWWA 130/40014146/312, *passim*.
16 Rudolf Vierhaus and Ludolf Herbst (eds), *Biographisches Handbuch der Abgeordneten des Deutschen Bundestages, 1949–2002*, München 2002, pp. 325–326; for Hellwig's succession of Erhard see Braunthal, *The Federation of German Industry*, p. 196; ACDP 01-228-004/1, Rede Stein, 'Unternehmer und Parlament' (undated, about 1961). The 'presidential affair' had been caused by Chancellor Adenauer's political shenanigans to find a successor to Federal president Theodor Heuss and ended with the election of a second-rate candidate.
17 ACDP 01-228-004/1, Tonbandnieddrschrift of speech given on 25.6. 1956 to the Institut für die Niedersächsische Wirtschaft.
18 ACDP 01-228-004/1, Rede Stein, 'Unternehmer und Parlament', (undated, about 1961).
19 ACDP 01-228-004/1, Rede Stein, 'Die politische Verantwortung des Unternehmers' 24.5. 1957.
20 Gustav Stein (ed.), *Unternehmer in der Politik*, Düsseldorf 1954, pp. 7–9.
21 See Morten Reitmayer, 'Unternehmer zur Führung berufen – durch wen?', in Berghahn, Unger and Ziegler (eds), *Die deutsche Wirtschaftselite im 20. Jahrhundert*, pp. 317–336.

22 BA NL1384/39, letter from Henle to Adenauer, 27.7. 1953; Henle, *Weggenosse des Jahrhunderts*, pp. 92, 115f.
23 Werner Bührer, *Ruhrstahl und Europa. Die Wirtschaftsvereinigung Eisen und Stahlindustrie und die Anfänge der europäischen Integration, 1945–1952*, München 1986, pp. 126, 133.
24 RWWA 130/400101400/116, memo Reusch to Blank, 14.5. 1953. Between 1922 and 1945, Blank was the head of the GHH liaison office in Berlin and responsible for the company's political contacts, see Bähr, Banke, Flemming, *Die MAN*, p. 258.
25 RWWA 130/400101413/89 letter from Wellhausen to Reusch, 27.5. 1957.
26 Braunthal, *The Federation of German Industry*, p. 102.
27 Karsten Rudolph, *Wirtschaftsdiplomatie im Kalten Krieg. Die Ostpolitik der westdeutschen Großindustrie 1945–1991*, Frankfurt/M 2004, p. 190.
28 Sohl, *Notizen*, p. 170.
29 A list of business interests in Bundestag committees in Hartmann, *Authority and Organization*, p. 241.
30 Almond, 'The Politics of German Business', p. 210.
31 Arnulf Bahring (ed.), *Sehr verehrter Herr Bundeskanzler: Heinrich von Brentano im Briefwechsel mit Konrad Adenauer, 1949–1964*, Hamburg 1974, transl. in Armin Grünbacher, *The Making of German Democracy. West Germany during the Adenauer Era*, Manchester 2010, pp. 296 f.
32 Grünbacher, *Reconstruction and Cold War*, p. 32.
33 Achim Schulte-Goebel, 'Fritz Berg 1901–1979. Unternehmer und Industriepräsident in der Adenauer Ära', PhD Universität Düsseldorf, 1999, p. 155. Surprisingly, despite Berg's prominence in the politics of the Adenauer era, Schulte-Goebel's thesis is to date the only dedicated research into Berg and his role.
34 Schulze-Goebel, 'Fritz Berg', p. 144.
35 ACDP 01-162-015/2, letter from BDI Presseabteilung to Becker, 21.7. 1962.
36 Schulze-Goebel, 'Fritz Berg', pp. 128 f.
37 BDI HA HGF 787 (8), Minutes of the Präsidial- und Vorstandssitzung am 15.3. 1961; Braunthal, *The Federation of German Industry*, pp. 200 f.
38 BDI HA HGF Pro 781 (6), letter from BDI an Präsidiums- und Vorstandsmitglieder, 7.3. 1959.
39 See Hentschel, *Ludwig Erhard. Ein Politikerleben*, München 1996, pp. 326 ff.
40 Almond, 'The Politics of German Business', p. 216. See also Christian L. Glossner, *The Making of the German Post-War Economy. Political Communication and Public Perception of the Social Market Economy after the Second World War*, London, New York 2010, for a good account of the propaganda for the Social Market Economy, particularly pp. 55 f.
41 Translated in Grünbacher, *The Making of German Democracy*, pp. 100 f.
42 See Vierhaus and Herbst (eds), *Biographisches Handbuch der Mitglieder des Deutschen Bundestages, 1949–2002*, vol. 1, p. 187 and more generally on Erhard in Hentschel, *Ludwig Erhard*.
43 See Vierhaus and Herbst (eds), *Biographisches Handbuch der Mitglieder des Deutschen Bundestages, 1949–2002*, vol. 2, pp. 808 f. Seebohm managed to become the FRG's longest serving minister, with seventeen years of continuous ministerial service, from 1949 to 1966.
44 Glossner, *The Making of the German Post-War Economy*, p. 56.
45 ACDP VII-001-050, Niederschrift über die 4. Sitzung des CDU Bundesfinanzausschusses, 14.4.1961.

46 Schulze, *Unternehmerische Selbstverwaltung und Politik*, pp. 456, 477, 493 f.
47 Schulze, *Unternehmerische Selbstverwaltung und Politik*, p. 500; Almond, 'The Politics of German Business', p. 211.
48 ACDP 01-433-K001, letter from Berg to Birrenbach, 18.4. 1957; letter from Birrenbach to Berg, 2.5. 1957.
49 Schulze-Goebel, 'Fritz Berg', p. 60; p. 142, citing *Der Spiegel*, no. 45 (4 November 1959), pp. 22 ff.
50 Hartmann, *Authority and Organization*, p. 218; Braunthal, *The Federation of German Industry*, p. IX
51 Braunthal, *The Federation of German Industry*, p. 41.
52 Ullmann, *Interessenverbände in Deutschland*, pp. 77 f.
53 Ullmann, *Interessenverbände in Deutschland*, pp. 77 f, p. 81.
54 Ullmann, *Interessenverbände in Deutschland*, pp. 133 ff.
55 Ullmann, *Interessenverbände in Deutschland*, p. 143.
56 See Henry Asby Turner, *German Big Business and the Rise of Hitler*, New York 1985; Reinhard Neebe, *Großindustrie, Staat und NSDAP 1930–1933. Paul Silverberg und der Reichsverband der Deutschen Industrie in der Krise der Weimarer Republik*, Göttingen 1981.
57 See Herbst, *Der totale Krieg und die Ordnung der Wirtschaft*; Mollin, *Stahlkonzern im 3. Reich*; Matt Bera, *Lobbying Hitler. Industrial Associations between Democracy and Dictatorship*, New York 2016.
58 WV Stahl HA Vorstandsbericht Eisenkreis/Engerer Vorstand Wirtschaftsvereinigung, 5. 945–13.3. 1947, (1), *passim*.
59 RWWA 70-219-21, Memo by Josef Wilden, 22.4. 1945; Bührer, *Ruhrstahl und Europa*, p. 15.
60 Bührer, *Ruhrstahl und Europa*, p. 18; see for a confusing number of designation and meeting dates WV Stahl HA Vorstandsbericht Eisenkreis/Engerer Vorstand Wirtschaftsvereinigung, 5. 1945–13.3. 1947, (1).
61 Bührer, *Ruhrstahl und Europa*, pp. 41 ff, p. 47.
62 Ullmann, *Interessenverbände in Deutschland*, pp. 239 f.; Braunthal, *The Federation of German Industry*, p. 25.
63 RWWA 72-552-8, Memo by Gasper on meeting 14.6. 1945.
64 BA NL 1384/277, letter from Henle to Rohland, 24.8. 1945; memo from Henle for Karl Jarres, 29.8. 1945.
65 RWWA 130/40010146/154, Memo from GHH Hauptverwaltung to Reusch, 16.2. 1946.
66 RWWA 130/400101400/115, membership list, 4 ½ pp.
67 BA NL 1384/279, letter from Wirtschaftsvereinigung Eisen und Stahl to Henle, 26.6. 1948.
68 Ullmann, *Interessenverbände in Deutschland*, p. 240.
69 Ibid.
70 Bührer, '"... insofern steckt in jedem echten Unternehmer"', p. 234.
71 Schulte-Goebel, 'Fritz Berg', p. 56.
72 Schulte-Goebel, 'Fritz Berg', pp. 10–12; 29 ff; 35 f; 51.
73 Bührer, '"... insofern steckt in jedem echten Unternehmer"', p. 234.
74 Almond, 'The Politics of German Business', p.214.
75 Schulte-Goebel, 'Fritz Berg', pp. 15, 21 ff.
76 Schulte-Goebel, 'Fritz Berg', pp. 24–51.
77 Schulte Goebel, 'Fritz Berg', p. 67.
78 BDI HA HGF Pro 781, Bericht über die Gründung des Ausschusses für Wirtschaftsfragen der Industriellen Verbände, 19 Oktober 1949; Ullmann, *Interessenverbände in Deutschland*, p. 242.

79 BDI HA HGF Pro 781, Bericht über die Gründung des Ausschusses für Wirtschaftsfragen der Industriellen Verbände, 19 Oktober 1949, also for the following. For an example of Reusch's hostility towards the ECSC see RWWA 130/40010146/47, draft letter from Reusch to ECSC vice president Etzel, 19.1. 1955, translated (in part) in Grünbacher, *The Making of German Democracy*, p. 199.
80 Ullmann, *Interessenverbände in Deutschland*, p. 244. On the attitudes and mentality of the Bergassessoren, see Volker Berghahn, 'Die versunkene Welt der Bergassessoren', in *Revier-Kultur*, no. 3 (1986), and Faulenbach, 'Die Preußischen Bergassessoren im Ruhrbergbau'.
81 Braunthal, *The Federation of German Industry*, p. 49.
82 Bührer, '" insofern steckt in jedem Unternehmer"', *passim*; Ullmann, *Interessenverbände in Deutschland*, p. 244.
83 Bührer, '"... insofern steckt in jedem Unternehmer", p. 234, quote on p. 247.
84 Almond, 'The Politics of German Business', p. 203; Braunthal, *The Federation of German Industry*, p. XII.
85 Braunthal, *The Federation of German Industry*, p. 39.
86 TKA A30338, letter from Stein to Sohl, 31.12.1955; letter from Sohl to Stein, 11.1. 1956; letter from Arntzen to Sohl, 25.1. 1956; letter from Dichgans to Arntzen, 21.2. 1956.
87 Grünbacher, *Reconstruction and Cold War*, p. 144; for more details on the crisis see Christoph Nonn, *Die Ruhrbergbaukrise. Entindustrialisierung und Politik 1958–1969*, Göttingen 1999.
88 BDI HA HGF Pro 784 (5/1), Niederschrift Landesverbands-Geschäftsführer Sitzung, 27.6. 1957, TOP 3.
89 Grünbacher, *Reconstruction and Cold War*, pp. 144 f.
90 BDI HA HGF Pro 8784 (5/2), draft minutes for the Präsidiumssitzung on 3.12. 1958; ibid, shorthand notes by BDI clerk Schniewind, 4.12. 1958.
91 BDH HA HGF Pro 781 (6), draft minutes for the Präsidiumssitzung on 4.9. 1959.
92 Flender, *Die Verantwortung des Unternehmers*, pp. 110–112; for the AVI agreement see Matthias Kipping,, 'Inter-Firm Relations and Industrial Policy: The French and German Steel Producers and Users in the Twentieth Century', in *Business History*, vol. 38, no. 1 (1996), pp. 1–25, p. 11.
93 Flender, *Die Verantwortung des Unternehmers*, pp. 124–136. In the German language *Großkapital* insinuated the uncaring, plutocratic capitalist, in contrast to the caring and paternalistic entrepreneur as the 'father of the factory'. 'Functionaries' was the term reserved for full-time trade union representatives or for Soviet officials.
94 Kreditanstalt für Wiederaufbau, *Jahresbericht 1958*, p. 39; Grünbacher, *Reconstruction and Cold War*, p. 93.
95 BDI HA HGF Pro 784 (4/2), Niederschrift Präsidiumssitzung 7.12. 1956, TOP 2, Mittelstandsprogramm.
96 BDI HA HGF Pro 784 (5/1), Opening speech Berg 16.1. 1958.
97 BDI HA HGF Pro 784 (5/2), Niederschrift zur Präsidialsitzung, 2.10. 1958.
98 BDI HA HGF Pro 781 (1), Niederschrift Geschäftsführerkonferenz 8.4. 1960.
99 Berghoff, 'Historisches Relikt oder Zukunftsmodell?', pp. 249 f.
100 *Der Spiegel*, no. 45, 1960, p. 38.
101 TKA A30346, letter from Ahrens and Dichgans to Sohl, 19.2. 1956; TKA PA Mommsen, Ernst Wolff, Vertraulicher Vermerk Kunze an Dr Homburg, 28.4. 1965.
102 Eschenburg, *Herrschaft der Verbände*. It is only on p. 82 of this eighty-seven-page book that the 'BDI president' has his first mention, and the ASU is criticized for calling for a minister's resignation.

103 Wilhem Beutler, Gustav Stein and Hellmuth Wagner (eds), *Der Staat und die Verbände. Gespräch veranstaltet vom Bundesverband der deutschen Industrie in Köln am 27 März 1957*, Heidelberg 1957.

104 Some of them documented in an article in *Der Spiegel*, no. 45, 1960 (2 November), pp. 24–41, after which Berg banned any visits from *Der Spiegel* journalists at the BDI, threatening 'severest consequences' to those who 'disrespected his wish'; see BDI HA PI 685/157, Vermerk Presseabteilung 18.1.1961. Perhaps Berg's most outrageous outburst -which became known as the 'Berg Affair' - came in 1969, when he had already passed the zenith of his influence. After a wildcat strike at Hoesch steel plant, he stated that one of the strikers should have been shot dead to restore order, see *Der Spiegel*, nos. 38, 39, 1969 (15 and 22 September) pp. 99 f. and 67 f. respectively. The affair and media outrage contributed to Berg's eventual replacement as BDI president.

105 See Wirtschaftsvereinigung Stahl (ed.), *Portraits im Stahlzentrum*, passim; Herbert W. Köhler, *30 Jahre Stahlpolitik aus der Sicht eines Verbandsmanagers. Erinnerungen*, 2 vols., Düsseldorf 1997. I wish to express my gratitude to Prof Manfred Rasch for providing me with a copy of the book.

106 See *Der Spiegel*, no. 25, 1963, pp. 30–33, and *Der Spiegel*, no. 46, 1966, p. 82.

107 Hartmann, *Authority and Organization*, p. 221.

108 Hartmann, *Authority and Organization*, pp 226 f.

109 Hartmann, *Authority and Organization*, p. 226. Friedrich's quote 'wer die Leidenschaft hat, konstruktiv und selbstständig zu wirtschaften', as cited by Günther Schlicht at the opening of the 15th *Baden-Badener Unternehmergespräche* 19.6. 1960, see ACDP 01-083 - 193/2.

110 Winschuh, *Das neue Unternehmerbild*, p. 23.

111 Flender, *Die Verantwortung des Unternehmers*, p. 143; Hartmann, *Authority and Organization*, p. 24. Hartmann's figure for ASU membership refers to 1952.

112 See Isable Warner, *Steel and Sovereignty. The Deconcentration of the German Steel Industry 1949–54*, Mainz 1996.

113 TKA A30336, passim.

114 *Der Spiegel*, no. 18, 1960 (24 April), pp. 28–31.

115 ACDP 01-224 - 128/1, letter from Dichgans to Sohl, 14.7. 1960.

116 ACDP 01-224 - 152/3, Vermerk zum DA 19.8.1960.

117 ACDP 01-224 - 151/1

118 Köhler, *30 Jahre Stahlpolitik*, vol. 1, pp. 13–17. For the Ruhrlade see Henry Ashby Turner, 'The Ruhrlade, Secret Cabinet of Heavy Industry in the Weimar Republic', in *Central European History*, 3, no. 3 (1970), pp.195–228.

119 Uebbing, *Stahl schrebit Geschichte*, p. 185. However, Uebbing's account of the DA contains some inaccuracies, for example an agenda for the meetings existed right from the beginning.

120 For a list of members and some (recurring) DA topics see Köhler, *30 Jahre Stahlpolitik*, vol. 2, Anlage 5; Anlage 6, pp. 65–72.

121 Invitations and agendas for the DA can be found in TKA A30412 - A 30419; TKA A 30428- A 30433; summaries of the meetings written by Otto Wolff von Amerongen for his top managers can be found in TKA SWB 508–512, and in Köhler's papers at the ACDP.

122 Plumpe, 'Unternehmerverbände und industrielle Interessenpolitik'.

123 Kipping, 'Inter-Firm Relations and Industrial Policy', pp. 18 f.

124 Wyn Grant, *Business and Politics in Britain*, Basingstoke 1993 (2nd ed.), p. 104.

125 Hartmann, *Authority and Organization*, p. 223.
126 Uebbing, *Stahl schreibt Geschichte*, p. 185.
127 Köhler, *30 Jahre Stahlpolitik*, p. 17.
128 The 1957 pension reform raised pensions but more importantly it introduced a 'dynamic' pension, i.e. one that rose in line with wages, thus helping to end old age poverty. It was opposed both by Erhard (because in his opinion it destroyed personal responsibility) and by businesses (which were opposed to the rising costs the scheme would cause). As the reform was enacted shortly before the 1957 general election, it was seen as an election gift and credited with providing the CDU with an absolute majority in parliament.

Chapter 7

1 Stephen J. Silvia, *Holding the Shop Together: German Industrial Relations in the Postwar Era*, Ithaca and London, 2013, pp. 43 ff.
2 Gerald Feldman and Irmgard Steinisch, 'The Origins of the Stinnes-Legien-Abkommen. A Documentation', in *IWK Internationale wissenschaftliche Korrespondenz zur Geschichte der deutschen Arbeiterbewegung* Heft 19/20 (1973) S. 45–103.
3 Feldman, *Army, Industry and Labor*, pp. 241, 538; Schneider, 'Demokratisierungs-Konsenz', p. 208.
4 Bührer, 'Zum Wandel der wirtschafts- und sozialpolitischen Zukunftsvorstellungen', pp. 81–104, p. 82.
5 Silvia, *Holding the Shop Together*, ch. 1.
6 Bührer, 'Zum Wandel der wirtschafts- und sozialpolitischen Zukunftsvorstellungen', pp. 83 f., p. 86 f.
7 See, for example, Matthias Freese, *Betriebspolitik im 'Dritten Reich'. Deutsche Arbeitsfront, Unternehmer und Staatsbürokratie in der westdeutschen Großindustrie, 1933–1939*, Paderborn 1991.
8 Reitmayer, 'Unternehmer zur Führung berufen', p. 328.
9 Diedrich, *'Human Relations'*, p. 6, p.52. DINTA, the *Deutsches Institut für technische Arbeitsschulung*, was a training and rationalization institute sponsored by heavy industry and infamous for its militaristic approach to work processes and labour discipline.
10 See, for example, Bernd Weisbrod, 'Der Schein der Modernität', p. 233; Lutz, 'Integration durch Aufstieg'.
11 WV Stahl HA Sitzungsberichte Engerer Vorstand & Vorstand, 9.6. 1949 - 31.3. 1951 (4), English language pamphlet 'Dismantling against Humanity'. There were also very outspoken trade union publications against Allied decartelization plans; see Viktor Agartz and Heinrich Deist (eds), *Gesetz No. 75 und Ruhrstatut*, Köln 1949.
12 Almond, 'The Politics of German Business', p. 200.
13 RWWA 130/400101400/115, 'Wichtige politische und wirtschaftliche Ereignisse in der Doppelzone', August 1949.
14 This organization, established in March 1945 in Aachen, was not able to survive due to Allied restrictions but has to be seen as the precursor to the *Deutsche Gewerkschaftsbund*. It should not be confused with the East German trade union organization of the same name.
15 RWWA 130/40010146/36, letter from Reusch to FDGB (Jochen), 12.10.1946.

16 WV Stahl HA Vorstandsbericht Eisenkreis, 5/1945–13.3.1947 (1), Niederschrift zur Eisenkreis Sitzung am 18.1.1946.
17 WV Stahl HA Vorstandsbericht Eisenkreis, 5/1945 - 13.3.1947 (1), Niederschrift zur Eisenkreis Sitzung am 9.1.1947.
18 WV Stahl HA Vorstandsbericht Eisenkreis, 14.3.1947 - 30.6.1948 (2), Niederschrift zur Eisenkreis Sitzung am 3.4.1947.
19 WV Stahl HA Sitzungsbericht Engerer Vorstand, 1.7.1948 - 30.6.1949 (3), Vermerk zur Sitzung Engerer Vorstand 10.2.1949.
20 See Chapter 1.
21 Berghoff, 'Historisches Relikt oder Zukunftsmodell?', pp. 277 f, p. 280.
22 Bührer, 'Zum Wandel der wirtschafts- und sozialpolitischen Zukunftsvorstellungen', p. 99.
23 Bührer, *Ruhrstahl und Europa*, p. 51.
24 Kroker, 'Heinrich Kost', pp. 312 f.
25 Berg, *Die westdeutsche Wirtschaft in der Bewährung*, p. 253.
26 See Horst Thum, *Mitbestimmung in der Montanindustrie. Der Mythos vom Sieg der Gewerkschaften*, Stuttgart 1982.
27 Lochner, *Tycoons and Tyrant*, p. 261.
28 Berghahn and Friedrich, *Otto A. Friedrich*, p. 310, p. 339.
29 Schneider, 'Demokratisierings-Konsenz', p. 219.
30 Obermüller, 'Hermann Reusch und die Beziehungen zur Eigentümer Familie', p. 163.
31 ACDP 01-224-192/1, letter from Pohle to Sohl, 9.3.1955; letter from BDI to member associations, 28.1.1954; letter from Ahrens to Sendler, 22.8.1955.
32 Sohl, *Notizen*, p. 142. Sohl seemed almost to have pitied Agartz, who had to step down from all his posts in 1957 following trumped-up charges of high treason, of which he was acquitted. He nevertheless was expelled from both the SPD and the trade unions.
33 Toni Pierenkemper, 'Hans-Günther Sohl: Funktionale Effizienz und autoritäre Harmonie in der Eisen- und Stahlindustrie', in Paul Erker and Toni Pierenkemper (eds), *Deutsche Unternehmer zwischen Kriegswirtschaft und Wiederaufbau. Studien zur Erfahrungsbildung von Industriellen*, München 1999, pp. 53–107 pp. 101 f.
34 Sohl, *Notizen*, p. 139; article 13 of the co-determination law, translated in Grünbacher, *The Making of German Democracy*, p. 257. My thanks to Manfred Zilt of the Thyssen Krupp Archive who made me aware of the good working relationship of the two men.
35 ACDP 01-224-151/2 notes on DA meeting on 11.11.1958 (outside TO).
36 ACDP 01-224-171/3, letter from Ahrens to Sohl, 14.1.1957.
37 ACDP 01-224-152/3, Appendix 1e for DA meeting on 12.7.1960.
38 Vaubel, *Zusammenbruch und Wiederaufbau*, p. 181; p. 194.
39 Winschuh, *Das neue Unternehmerbild*, p. 33, p. 42.
40 Winschuh, *Das neue Unternehmerbild*, pp. 137 f, p. 154.
41 Heidrun Edelmann, 'Heinrich Nordhoff: ein deutscher Manager in der Automobilindustrie', in Erker and Pierenkemper (eds), *Deutsche Unternehmer zwischen Kriegswirtschaft und Wiederaufbau*, pp. 19–52, p. 51.
42 Berg, *Die westdeutsche Wirtschaft*, p. 19; Schulte-Goebel, *Fritz Berg*, p. 13.
43 Berghahn and Friedrich, *Otto A. Friedrich*, p. 226. On the topic of social norms in an international comparison, see Whitman, 'Enforcing Civility and Respect: Three Societies'.
44 Winschuh, *Das neue Unternehmerbild*, pp. 117 f, 135.
45 Flender, *Die Verantwortung des Unternehmers*, p. 40. 'Human factor' refers to the input of labour into the production process.
46 Flender, *Die Verantwortung des Unternehmers*, p. 19.

47 RWWA 130/40010146/39, letter from IG Metall to Reusch, 26.4. 1949; letter from Hilbert to Reusch, 30.4. 1949.
48 RWWA 130/40010146/39, letter from Reusch to Herr Mross, IG Metall, 4.5. 1949.
49 Cornelia Rauh-Kühne, 'Hans-Constantin Paulssen: Sozialpartnerschaft aus dem Geiste der Kriegskameradschaft', in Erker and Pierenkemper (eds), *Deutsche Unternehmer*, pp. 109–192, esp. pp. 113 ff.
50 Krumm, *Tagebuch eines deutschen Unternehmers*, p. 14, p. 45.
51 Rauh-Kühne, Cornelia, 'Paulssen, Hans Constantin', in *Neue Deutsche Biographie 20* (2001), S. 131.
52 Rauh-Kühne, 'Hans-Constantin Paulssen', pp. 118 f. Other than the famous example of the 'Krupp works family', these attitudes can also be seen at Vereinigte Glanzstoff Fabriken which was trying from March 1945 onward to keep the core workforce, the so-called *'Glanzstoff Familie'* together. See Henke, *Die amerikanische Besetzung Deutschlands*, p. 464, and Vaubel, *Zusammenbruch und Wiederaufbau*, p. 39.
53 Rauh-Kühne, 'Hans-Constantin Paulssen', pp. 185 f.
54 Rauh-Kühne, 'Hans-Constantin Paulssen', pp. 189 f.
55 See above, ch. 2.
56 Berghahn and Friedrich, *Otto A. Friedrich*, p. 232 f.; on the DII's involvement see ACDP 01-224-192/1 *passim*.
57 Berghahn, *Americanisation of West German Industry*, p. 258.
58 Rauh-Kühne, 'Hans-Constantin Paulssen', pp. 189 ff; and Rau-Kühne, 'Paulssen, Hans-Constantin', p. 131.
59 Rauh-Kühne, 'Hans-Constantin Paulssen', pp. 119; 121 f; 176.
60 Berghahn, Friedrich, *Otto A. Friedrich*, pp. 238f.
61 Schneider, 'Demokratisierungs-Konsenz', p. 221.
62 See Eberhard Kolb, *The Weimar Republic*, London 2005 (2nd ed.), pp. 224 f. for the election results and pp. 45–49 for the suppression of communist uprisings.
63 RWWA 130/4001016/14, Denkschrift Rohland, 2 June 1945, cited in Henke, *Die amerikanische Besetzung Deutschlands*, p. 523. For Lübsen, see Bähr, Banken and Flemming, *Die MAN*, pp. 250, 283, 286.
64 Gerhard A. Ritter and Merith Niehuss, *Wahlen in Deutschland, 1946–1991*, München 1991, pp. 100, 147, 166.
65 Gabriele Müller-List, 'Eine neue Moral für Deutschland? Die Bewegung für Moralische Aufrüstung und ihre Bedeutung beim Wiederaufbau 1947–1952', in *Aus Politik und Zeitgeschichte*, no. 44 (1981), pp. 11–23. See also TKA A30502, letter from Moral Rearmament to Sohl, 9.10. 1952, with a report on the successes at Gelsenkirchenrer Bergbwerks AG, although Sohl apparently neither attended nor joined the movement.
66 RWWA 130/40010146/39, letter from DII to Reusch, 20.12. 1955.
67 ACDP 01-224-192/1, note for Dr Ernst Schroeder, 15.2. 1956.
68 RWWA 130/40010146/40, DII Bericht 2/58; DII Bericht 4/59 'Die kommunistische Betriebsagitation'; ACDP 01-224-153/1, Vermerk zum DA 12.1. 1961, TOP 14.
69 ACDP 01-224-171/3, letter from Röchling to Ahrens, 8.7. 1960.
70 Ritter and Niehus, *Wahlen in Deutschland*, p. 176.

Chapter 8

1 Werner Bührer, 'Der Bundesverband der deutschen Industrie und Adenauers Außenpolitik in den fünfziger Jahren', in *Vierteljahrshefte für Zeitgeschichte*, vol. 40 no. 2

(1992), pp. 241–261, p. 253; Herbert Gross, *Deutschland und der Weltmarkt. Gedanken zur zukünftigen deutschen Handelspolitik*, Hamburg 1948, p. 50.
2 Hartmut Pogge von Strandmann, 'Großindustrie und Realpolitik. Deutsch-Sowjetische Handelsbeziehungen in der Weimarer Republik', in *Historische Zeitschrift*, vol. 222, no. 2 (April 1976), pp. 265–341, pp. 270 f.
3 Pogge von Strandmann, 'Großindustrie und Realpolitik', pp. 333; 274; 334.
4 Pogge von Strandmann, 'Großindustrie und Realpolitik', pp. 313; 325 f. Other than Otto Wolff, DEMAG, and Krupp, it was Gutehoffnungshütte, which in 1932 sent 46 per cent of its total exports to the Soviet Union; see p. 334.
5 Rohland, *Bewegte Zeiten*, p. 50.
6 Wilhelm Hankel, *Die zweite Kapitalverteilung. Ein marktwirtschaftlicher Weg langfristiger Finanzierungspolitik*, Frankfurt/M. 1961, pp. 23, 25.
7 Rudolph, *Wirtschaftsdiplomatie im Kalten Krieg*, pp. 15 f. Except for Tor Egil Førland's *Cold Economic Warfare: CoCom and the Forging of Strategic Export Controls*, Dordrecht 2009, which looks at Norway's role in the embargos, literature on CoCom is mainly concerned with US policies and politics. Literature on CoCom's activities in the 1980s is practically non-existent, despite CoCom files now being freely available at the Archives Diplomatique in Paris.
8 Rudolph, *Wirtschaftsdiplomatie im Kalten Krieg*, pp. 24 f.
9 BA, N 1384/2, letter from Klöckner & Co to Economics Minister Erhard, 29.9. 1950.
10 BA N1384/283, letter from Wirtschaftsvereinigung Eisen und Stahl to Engerer Vorstand, 26.1. 1950.
11 RWWA 130/400101401/85, confidential report by BDI Foreign Trade Committee, 3.3. 1950.
12 RWWA 130/400101401/40, letter from Berg to Kirkpatrick, 31.1. 1951; letter from BDI Hauptgeschäftsführung to BDI Präsidium und Vorstand, 17.7. 1951.
13 RWWA 130/400101401/40, letter from Bundeswirtschaftsministerium to BDI and DIHT, 3.7. 1952.
14 Rudolph, *Wirtschaftsdiplomatie im Kalten Krieg*, pp. 36–38.
15 Krumm, *Tagebuch eines deutschen Unternehmers*, pp. 267 f.
16 Braunthal, *The Federation of German Industry*, p. 310; Rudolph, *Wirtschaftsdiplomatie im Kalten Krieg*, p. 55.
17 Rudolph, *Wirtschaftsdiplomatie in Kalten Krieg*, p. 54.
18 Rudolph, *Wirtschaftsdiplomatie im Kalten Krieg*, p. 31.
19 BDI HA HGF Pro 768 2/1, Kundgebung und Mitgliederversammlung des BDI 25–26.5. 1951.
20 See Bührer, 'Der Bundesverband und Adenauer's Außenpolitik'.
21 Robert Mark Spaulding, *Osthandel und Ostpolitik. German Foreign Trade in Eastern Europe from Bismarck to Adenauer*, Oxford 1997, p. 357; Rudolph, *Wirtschafts-diplomatie im Kalten Krieg*, p. 30. A critical appraisal of the ban on eastern trade is still outstanding.
22 Bundesarchiv Filmarchiv, Berlin (BA FA) Neue Deutsche Wochenschau, NDW 90, 1951, reporting on a Berlin trial against steel industrialists accused of illegal eastern trade.
23 Rudolph, *Wirtschaftsdiplomatie im Kalten Krieg*, pp. 40, 42.
24 Hugo Eberhardt, 'Krumm, Heinrich' in *Neue Deutsche Biographie 13* (1982), S. 121 f.
25 Spaulding, *Osthandel und Ostpolitik*, p. 395.
26 Jochen Thies, 'Otto Wolf von Amerongen: Kundschafter der Marktwirtschaft', in Peter Danylow and Ulrich S. Soénius (eds), *Otto Wolff. Ein Unternehmen zwischen Wirtschaft und Politik*, München 2005, pp. 385–435, p. 406.

27 BA B102/57788, letter from *Ostausschuß* to Economics Ministry (Kroll), 8.1. 1953; Vermerk by Abteilung V, 4.2. 1953 and subsequent correspondence; letter from Economics Ministry, Referat V to *Ostausschuß*, 23.4. 1954.
28 BA B 102/57788, newsletter by Arbeitsgemeinschaft Außenhandel, 5.1. 1953.
29 Rudolph, *Wirtschaftsdiplomatie im Kalten Krieg*, pp. 231 ff. For Mommsen's role in the steel industry see WV Stahl HA Sitzungsbericht Vorstand, 1.1. 1955–31.12. 1957 (7).
30 Thies, 'Wolff von Amerongen', p. 406; Rudolph, *Wirtschaftsdiplomatie im Kalten Krieg*, p. 231 and also for the following, ch 9.
31 Rudolph, *Wirtschaftsdiplomatie im Kalten Krieg*, p. 233.
32 Rudolph, *Wirtschaftsdiplomatie in Kalten Krieg*, p. 246.
33 BA B102/57786, joint record by Economics Ministry and Auswärtigem Amt on a German–Russian trade agreement, 10.8. 1955.
34 Spaulding, *Osthandel and Ostpolitik*, pp. 372; 387 f.
35 Rudolph, *Wirtschaftsdiplomatie im Kalten Krieg*, pp. 245; 252, with one unconfirmed source claiming a record year with a share of 23 per cent.
36 Wolfgang Benz, *Die Gründung der Bundesrepublik*, p. 9.
37 See Grünbacher, 'Sustaining the Island', pp. 1–22.
38 BDI HA HGF Pro 785 (4/1), Niederschrift Präsidiumssitzung 8.6. 1955, TOP 6, statement of Wilhelm Menne.
39 BDI HA HGF Pro 784 (5/2), draft minutes for Präsidialsitzung 3.12. 1959, outside TO; RWWA 130/40010146/187, letter from BDI to participants of the Berlin discussion, 19.12. 1958.
40 Grünbacher, 'Sustaining the Island', pp. 3, 11 f.
41 BDI HA HGF Pro 781 (6), Berg's opening speech, appendix 2 to the tenth annual members' meeting, 23.6. 1959.
42 BDI HA HGF Pro 781 (6), minutes for Präsidialsitzung 13.5. 1959.
43 Grünbacher, 'Sustaining the Island', pp. 15, 17.
44 BDI HA HGF Pro 781 (7), draft minutes of Präsidialsitzung 23.9. 1960.
45 Friedrich von Heyl, *Der innerdeutsche Handel mit Eisen und Stahl 1945–1972. Deutsch-deutsche Beziehungen im Kalten Krieg*, Köln 1997, pp. 92–94. Von Heyl provides a very good overview of the underlying economic disequilibrium between the two countries as well as the political machinations on the part of the FRG to maintain the impression that no negotiations with the GDR were being conducted.
46 BDI HA HGF Pro 787 (8), minutes Präsidiumssitzung 17.8. 1961, statement by Wolff von Amerongen.
47 TKA A30312, Vermerk Dr Kunze for Sohl (undated, presumably 4.3. 1960); letter from Berg to Sohl, 11. 3. 1960 and *passim* for a furious correspondence over a three-week period.
48 *Der Spiegel*, 1960, no. 45, p. 38; TKA A30312, joint letter from Berg and Winkhaus to BDI board members, 6.4. 1960.
49 RWWA 130/40010141/84, letter from Reusch to Kuhlmann, 25.9. 1960; letter from Kuhlmann to Reusch, 29.9. 1960.
50 BDI HA HGF Pro 787 (8), minutes Präsidiumssitzung 17.8. 1961, and statement by Wolff von Amerongen.
51 Rudolph, *Wirtschaftsdiplomatie im Kalten Krieg*, p. 161.
52 TKA SWB 509, Aktennotiz Wolff von Amerongen 13.7. 1962.
53 TKA SWB 509, Aktennotiz Wolff von Amerongen, 11.7. 1963; TKA A30432, Papers for Diskussionsabend on 6.8. 1963.
54 TKA SWB509, Aktennotiz Wolff von Amerongen, 13.5. 1964.

55 Rudolph, *Wirtschaftsdiplomatie im Kalten Krieg*, pp. 156,158, 166, 169, 171–172.
56 Rudolph, *Wirtschaftsdiplomatie im Kalten Krieg*, pp. 182 f.
57 Rudolph, *Wirtschaftsdiplomatie im Kalten Krieg*, pp. 185–193.
58 BDI HA HGF Pro 782 (10) Niederschrift Präsidial- und Vorstandssitzung, 6.12. 1963.
59 RWWA 130/400101400/37 Bericht von Menges 23.3. 1965; RWWA 130/400101400/38 Rede von Menges to Junge Union and CDU Wirtschaftsrat, 3.2. 1966.
60 See Rudolph, *Wirtschaftsdiplomatie im Kalten Krieg*, ch 8.

Conclusion

1 *Gabler Wirtschaftslexikon*, Wiesbaden (12th ed), 1988, p. 2227.
2 See especially Henke, *Die amerikanische Besetzung Deutschlands*.
3 *Der Spiegel*, no. 45, 1965, p. 60.
4 Grunenberg, *Die Wundertäter*, pp. 263 ff.

Bibliography

Archival sources

Archiv der Christlich Demokratischen Politik (ACDP), St Augustin

CDU Bundesschatzmeister
Nachlass Curt Becker
Nachlass Kurt Birrenbach
Nachlass Fritz Hellwig
Nachlass Herbert Köhler
Nachlass Gustav Stein

Bundesarchiv Koblenz (BA)

B102 Bundeswirtschaftsministerium
N 1384 Nachlass Henle

Bundesarchiv Filmarchiv, Berlin (BAFA)

Neue Deutsche Wochenschau, 1951

Bergbau Archiv Bochum (BBA)

Nachlass Ernst Hellmut Vits

Bundesverband der deutschen Industrie, Historisches Archiv (BDI HA)

Bestand HGF
Bestand PA

Stiftung Rheinisch-Westfälisches Wirtschaftsarchiv zu Köln (RWWA)

Abteilung 1, IHK Köln
Abteilung 1d, Nachlass Hilgermann
Abteilung 28, IHK Essen
Abteilung 70, IHK Düsseldorf
Abteilung 130, Gutehoffnungshütte
Abteilung 72, Nachlass Otto Wolff von Amerongen
Abteilung 195, Vereinigte Glanzstoff Fabriken

Thyssen-Krupp Archiv (TKA)

Bestand A Thyssen
Bestand SWB (Stahlwerke Bochum)

Wirtschaftsvereinigung Stahl (WVStahl HA)

Sekretariat Dr Ahrens
Handakte Salewski
WV Vorstand
Registratur

Printed sources

Bundesgesetzblatt, 1952 (I)
Gabler Wirtschaftslexikon, 12th ed., Wiesbaden 1988.
Kreditanstalt für Wiederaufbau, *Jahresberichte* (various years).
Ruhm von Oppen, Beate, *Documents on Germany under Allied Occupation, 1945–1954*, London 1955.
Statistisches Bundesamt (ed.), *Statistisches Jahrbuch für die Bundesrepublik Deutschland*, Wiesbaden (various years).
US Department of State (ed.), *Documents on Germany 1944–1985.*
Weisz, Christoph, et al. (eds), *Akten zur Vorgeschichte der Bundesrepublik Deutschland*, 4 vols. München 1983.

Periodicals

Der Anschnitt
Der Spiegel
Jahresring
Neuer Vorwärts
Rheinische Post
The New York Times

Videos

Rees, Laurence, *The Nazis. A Warning from History*, part 4, 'The first 20 month in Poland', first shown 1 October 1997, BBC 2.

Secondary reading

Abelshauser, Werner, 'Probleme des Wiederaufbaus der westdeutschen Wirtschaft, 1945–53', in Heinrich August Winkler (ed.), *Politische Weichenstellung im Nachkriegsdeutschland 1945–1953*, Göttingen 1979, pp. 208–43.

Abelshauser, Werner, 'Ansätze "korporativer Marktwirtschaft" in der Koreakrise der 50er Jahre. Ein Briefwechsel zwischen dem Hohen Kommissar John McCloy und Bundeskanzler Adenauer', in *Vierteljahrshefte für Zeitgeschichte*, vol. 30 (1982), pp. 715–56.

Abelshauser, Werner, *Wirtschaftsgeschichte der Bundesrepublik Deutschland 1945–1980*, Frankfurt/M 1983.

Abelshauser, Werner, 'Kohle und Marktwirtschaft. Ludwig Erhard's Konflikt mit dem Unternehmensverband Ruhrbergbau am Vorabend der Kohlekrise', in *Vierteljahrshefte für Zeitgeschichte*, vol. 33, no. 3 (July 1985), pp. 489–546.

Abelshauser, Werner, *Kulturkampf. Der deutsche Weg in die Neue Wirtschaft und die Amerikanische Herausforderung*, Berlin 2003.

Abelshauser, Werner, von Hippel, Wolfgang, Johnson, Jeffrey Allan and Stokes, Raymond, *German Industry and Global Enterprise. BASF: The History of a Company*, Cambridge 2004.

Abromeit, Heidrun, 'Der Führungsanspruch der Wirtschaft gegenüber der Politik', in *Aus Politik und Zeitgeschichte*, no. 11 (1981), pp. 19–39.

Adamsen, Heiner R., *Investitionshilfe für die Ruhr. Wiederaufbau, Verbände und die Soziale Marktwirtschaft*, Wuppertal 1981, pp. 33–41.

Agartz, Viktor and Deist, Heinrich (eds), *Gesetz No. 75 und Ruhrstatut*, Köln 1949.

Almond, Gabriel A., 'The Politics of German Business', in Hans Speier and W. Philip Davidson (eds), *West German Leadership and Foreign Policy*, The RAND Corporation, New York 1957, pp. 195–241.

Aly, Götz and Roth, Karl Heinz, *The Nazi Census. Identification and Control in the Third Reich*, Philadephia 2004.

Arlt, Fritz, 'Die Bildungsaufgabe der Wirtschaft', in Deutsches Industrie Institut (ed.), *Fünfzehn Jahre Deutsches Industrie Institut*, Köln 1966, pp. 91–97.

Bähr, Johannes, Banken, Ralf and Flemming, Thomas, *Die MAN: eine deutsche Industriegeschichte*, 3rd ed., München 2009.

Bahring, Arnulf (ed.), *Sehr verehrter Herr Bundeskanzler: Heinrich von Brentano im Briefwechsel mit Konrad Adenauer, 1949–1964*, Hamburg 1974.

Bald, Detlef, '"Bürger in Uniform": Tradition und Neuanfang des Militärs in Westdeutschland', in Axel Schildt and Arnold Sywottek (eds), *Modernisierung im Wiederaufbau. Die Westdeutsche Gesellschaft der 50er Jahre*, Bonn 1998, pp. 392–402.

Battenfeld, Beate. 'Neumann, Carl' in *Neue Deutsche Biographie 19* (1999), pp. 154–56.

Becker, Susanne, 'Information and Business at the Turn of the Century: Wilhelm Merton and the Creation and dissemination of Management Knowledge', in Anne-Marie Kuijlaars, Kim Prudon and Joop Vissen (eds), *Business and Society*, Rotterdam 2000, pp. 513–20.

Benz, Wolfgang, *Die Gründung der Bundesrepublik, Von der Bizone zum souvärenen Staat*, 3rd ed., München 1989.

Berg, Fritz, *Die westdeutsche Wirtschaft in der Bewährung. Ausgewählte Reden aus den Jahren 1950 bis 1965*, Hagen 1966.

Berghahn, Volker, *Unternehmer und Politik in der Bundesrepublik*, Frankfurt/M 1985, English translation *The Americanisation of West German Industry 1945–1973*, Leamington Spa 1986.

Berghahn, Volker, 'Die versunkene Welt der Bergassessoren', in *Revier-Kultur*, no 3, 1986.

Berghahn, Volker and Friedrich, Paul J., *Otto A. Friedrich, ein politischer Unternehmer. Sein Leben und seine Zeit,1902–1975*, Frankfurt/M 1993,

Berghahn, Volker, 'Unternehmer in der frühen Bundesrepublik: Selbstverständnis und politischer Einfluß in der Marktwirtschaft', in Thomas Großbölting and

Rüdiger Schmidt (eds), *Unternehmerwirtschaft zwischen Markt und Lenkung. Organisationsformen, politischer Einfluß und ökonomisches Verhalten 1930–1960*, München 2002.

Berghahn, Volker, 'Das "deutsche Kapitalismus Modell" in Geschichte und Geschichtswissenschaft', in Volker Berghahn and Sigurt Vitols (eds), *Gibt es einen deutschen Kapitalismus? Traditionen und globale Perspektiven der sozialen Marktwirtschaft*, Frankfurt/M 2006, pp. 25–43.

Berghahn, Volker, Unger, Stefan and Ziegler, Dieter (eds), *Die deutsche Wirtschaftselite im 20. Jahrhundert. Kontinuität und Mentalität*, Essen 2003, pp. 93–113.

Berghahn, Volker and Vitols, Sigurt (eds), *Gibt es einen deutschen Kapitalismus? Tradition und globale Perspektiven der sozialen Marktwirtschaft*, Frankfurt/M 2006.

Berghoff, Hartmut, 'Historisches Relikt oder Zukunftsmodell? Kleine und mittelgroße Unternehmen in der Wirtschafts- und Sozialgeschichte der Bundesrepublik Deutschland', in Dieter Ziegler (ed.), *Großbürger und Unternehmer. Die deutsche Wirtschaftselite in 20. Jahrhundert*, Göttingen 2000, pp. 249–82.

Berghoff, Hartmut, 'Abschied vom klassischen Mittelstand. Kleine und mittlere Unternehmen in der bundesdeutschen Wirtschaft des späten 20. Jahrhunderts', in Volker Berghahn, Stefan Unger and Dieter Ziegler (eds), *Die deutsche Wirtschaftselite im 20. Jahrhundert. Kontinuität und Mentalität*, Essen 2003, pp. 93–113

Bertsch, Jürgen and Weitzmann, Horst (eds), *Das Netzwerk der Vordenker. Fünfzig Jahre Baden-Badener Unternehmergespräche im Spiegel der Wirtschaftsgeschichte*, Potsdam 2004.

Beutler, Wilhem, Stein, Gustav and Wagner, Hellmuth (eds), *Der Staat und die Verbände. Gespräch veranstaltet vom Bundesverband der deutschen Industrie in Köln am 27 März 1957*, Heidelberg 1957.

Biggeleben, Christof, 'Kontinuität von Bürgerlichkeit im Berliner Unternehmertum. Der Verein Berliner Kaufleute und Industrieller (1879-1961)', in Volker Berghahn, Stefan Unger and Dieter Ziegler (eds), *Die deutsche Wirtschaftselite*, pp. 241–74.

Boehling, Rebecca, *A Question of Priorities. Democratic Reform and Economic Recovery in Postwar Germany. Frankfurt, Munich and Stuttgart under US Occupation, 1945–1949*, Oxford 1996.

Bohner, Theodor, *Der ehrbare Kaufmann: Vom Werden und Wirken deutscher Wirtschaft*, Hamburg 1956.

Braunthal, Gerard, *The Federation of German Industry in Politics*, Ithaca, NY 1965.

Bräutigam, Petra, 'Südwestdeutsche Unternehmer der mittelständischen Industrie während des Nationalsozialismus', in Großbölting and Schmidt (eds), *Unternehmerwirtschaft zwischen Markt und Lenkung*, pp. 121–40.

Brochhagen, Ulrich, *Nach Nürnberg: Vergangenheitsbewältigung und Westintegration in der Ära Adenauer*, Hamburg 1994.

Bührer, Werner, *Ruhrstahl und Europa. Die Wirtschaftsvereinigung Eisen und Stahlindustrie und die Anfänge der europäischen Integration, 1945–1952*, München 1986.

Bührer, Werner, 'Der Bundesverband der deutschen Industrie und Adenauers Außenpolitik in den fünfziger Jahren', in *Vierteljahrshefte für Zeitgeschichte*, vol. 40 no. 2 (1992), pp. 241–61.

Bührer, Werner, 'Zum Wandel der wirtschafts- und sozialpolitischen Zukunftsvorstellungen in der deutschen Industrie zwischen Weltwirtschaftskrise und Wirtschaftswunder', in Matthias Frese and Michael Prinz (eds), *Politische Zäsuren und gesellschaftlicher Wandel im 20 Jahrhundert. Regionale und vergleichende Perspektiven*, Paderborn 1996.

Bührer, Werner, 'Der Kulturkreis im Bundesverband der deutschen Industrie und die "kulturelle Modernisierung" der Bundesrepublik in den 50er Jahren', in Axel Schildt and Arnold Sywottek (eds), *Modernisierung im Wiederaufbau. Die westdeutsche Gesellschaft in den 50er Jahren*, Bonn 1998.

Bührer, Werner, '"... insofern steckt in jedem echten Unternehmer auch ein künstlerisches Element." Die Erneuerung des Bundesverbandes der Deutschen Industrie (BDI) in den 1970er Jahren', in Morten Reitmayer and Ruth Rosenberger (eds), *Unternehmer am Ende des "goldenen Zeitalters". Die 1970er Jahre in unternehmens-und wirtschaftshistorischer Perspektive*, Essen 2008, pp. 233–48.

Burke, Peter, 'Stärken und Schwächen der Mentalitätsgeschichte', in Ulrich Raulff (ed.), *Mentalitäten-Geschichte*, Berlin 1989, pp. 127–45

Danylow, Peter and Soénius, Ulrich S. (eds), *Otto Wolff. Ein Unternehmen zwischen Wirtschaft und Politik*, München 2005.

De Grazia, Victoria, *Irresistible Empire. America's Advance through 20th Century Europe*, Cambridge 2005.

Diedrich, Karl-Friedrich, '"Human Relations" als soziales und wirtschaftliches Potential im Betrieb', PhD thesis, Wirtschaftshochschule Mannheim, 1950.

Doering-Manteuffel, Anselm, *Wie westlich sind die Deutschen? Amerikanisierung und Westernisierung im 20. Jahrhundert*, Göttingen 1999.

Eberhardt, Hugo, 'Krumm, Heinrich' in *Neue Deutsche Biographie 13* (1982), p. 121 f.

Edelmann, Heidrun, 'Heinrich Nordhoff: ein deutscher Manager in der Automobilindustrie', in Paul Erker and Toni Pierenkemper (eds), *Deutsche Unternehmer zwischen Kriegswirtschaft und Wiederaufbau. Studien zur Erfahrungsbildung von Industriellen*, München 1999, pp. 19–52.

'Einleitung', in Gunilla Budde, Eckhart Conze and Cornelia Rauh (eds), *Bürgertum nach dem bürgerlichen Zeitalter. Leitbilder und Praxis seit 1945*, Göttingen 2010, pp. 7–25.

Eisenhower, Dwight D., *Crusade in Europe*, London 1948.

Elias, Norbert, *The Germans. Power Struggles and the Development of Habitus in the 19th and 20th Century* (ed. Michael Schröter), Cambridge 1996.

Erhard, Ludwig, *Wohlstand für Alle!*, Düsseldorf 1957, English translation *Prosperity Through Competition*, New York 1958.

Erker, Paul, 'Einleitung: Industrie-Eliten im 20. Jahrhundert', in Paul Erker and Toni Pierenkämper (eds), *Deutsche Unternehmer zwischen Kriegswirtschaft und Wiederaufbau. Studien zur Erfahrungsbildung von Industrie-Eliten*, München 1999.

Eschenburg, Theodor, *Herrschaft der Verbände*, Stuttgart 1955.

Fassbender, Siegfried, '"Wuppertaler Kreis." Die Weiterbildung der unternehmerischen Führungskräfte in der Bundesrepublik', in Bundesverband deutsche Arbeitgeberverbände (ed.), *Unternehmer und Bildung*, pp. 79–96.

Faulenbach, Bernd, 'Die Preußischen Bergassessoren im Ruhrbergbau: Unternehmermentalität zwischen Obrigkeitsstaat und Privatindustrie', in *Mentalitäten und Lebensverhältnisse. Beispiele aus der Geschichte der Neuzeit. Rudolf Vierhaus zum 60. Geburtstag*, Göttingen 1982.

Feldman, Gerald D., *Army, Industry and Labor in Germany 1914–1918*, Princeton 1966.

Feldman, Gerald D., *Hugo Stinnes: Biographie eines Industriellen, 1870–1924*, München 1998.

Feldman, Gerald D. and Steinisch, Irmgard, 'The Origins of the Stinnes-Legien-Abkommen. A Documentation', in *IWK Internationale wissenschaftliche Korrespondenz zur Geschichte der deutschen Arbeiterbewegung* Heft 19/20 (1973), pp. 45–103.

Fiedler, Martin and Lorentz, Bernhard, 'Kontinuitäten in den Netzwerkbeziehungen der deutschen Wirtschaftseliten zwischen Weltwirtschaftskrise und 1950. Eine quantitative und qualitative Analyse', in Volker Berghahn, Stefan Unger and Dieter Ziegler (eds), *Die deutsche Wirtschaftselite*, pp. 51–74.

Fischer, Wolfram, *Unternehmerschaft, Selbstverwaltung und Staat*, Berlin 1964.

Flender, Alfred, *Die Stunde des Unternehmers*, Bonn 1954.

Flender, Alfred, *Die Verantwortung des Unternehmers*, Stuttgart 1961 (ed. Arbeitsgemeinschaft Selbstständiger Unternehmer).

Førland, Tor Egil, *Cold Economic Warfare: CoCom and the Forging of Strategic Export Controls*, Dordrecht 2009.

Freese, Matthias, *Betriebspolitik im 'Dritten Reich'. Deutsche Arbeitsfront, Unternehmer und Staatsbürokratie in der westdeutschen Großindustrie, 1933–1939*, Paderborn 1991.

Frei, Norbert, *Vergangenheitsbewältigung. Die Anfänge der Bundesrepublik und die NS Vergangenheit*, München 1996.

Frei, Norbert, Ahrens, Ralf, Osterloh, Jörg and Schanetzky, Tim, *Flick. Der Konzern, die Familie, die Macht*, München 2009.

Frei, Norbert (ed.), *Hitler's Eliten nach 1945*, 5th ed., München 2012.

Frevert, Ute, *Men of Honour. A Social and Cultural History of the Duel*, Cambridge 1995.

Friedrich, Otto A., *Das Selbstbild des Unternehmers wandelt sich*, Stuttgart 1959.

Fuchs, Rainer, 'Die Bayrischen Industrie- und Handelskammern im Wiederaufbau 1945–1948. Zwischen amerikanischem Demokratisierungswillen und eigener Selbstverwaltungstradition', PhD thesis, Munich 1988.

Gall, Lothar, Feldman, Gerald D., James, Harold, Holtfrerich, Carl-Ludwig and Büschgen, Hans E., *Die Deutsche Bank 1870–1995*, München 1995.

Gall, Lothar (ed.), *Krupp im 20. Jahrhundert. Die Geschichte des Unternehmens vom Ersten Weltkrieg bis zur Gründung der Stiftung*, Berlin 2002.

Gall, Lothar, *Der Bankier Hermann Josef Abs*, München 2004.

Gillingham, John, *Coal, Steel and the Rebirth of Europe. The German and French from Ruhr Conflict to Economic Community*, Cambridge 1991.

Gimbel, John, 'Amerikanische Besatzungspolitik und deutsche Tradition', in Ludolf Herbst (ed.), *Westdeutschland 1945–1955. Unterwerfung, Kontrolle, Integration*, München 1986, pp. 147–150.

Gimbel, John, *Science, Technology and Reparations: Exploitation and Plunder in Post-War Germany*, Stanford 1990.

Glossner, Christian L., *The Making of the German Post-War Economy. Political Communication and Public Perception of the Social Market Economy after Second World War*, London, New York 2010.

Goldberg, Ann, *Honour, Politics and the Law in Imperial Germany, 1871–1914*, Cambridge 2010.

Goswinkel, Dieter, 'Zivilgesellschaft – Bürgerlichkeit – Zivilität. Konzeptionelle Überlegungen zur Deutung der deutschen Geschichte im 20. Jahrhundert', in Gunilla Budde, Eckhart Conze and Cornelia Rauh (eds), *Bürgertum nach dem bürgerlichen Zeitalter. Leitbilder und Praxis seit 1945*, Göttingen 2010, pp. 29–52.

Grant, Wyn, *Business and Politics in Britain*, 2nd ed., Basingstoke 1993.

Gross, Herbert, *Deutschaland und der Weltmarkt. Gedanken zur zukünftigen deutschen Handelspolitik*, Hamburg 1948.

Grünbacher, Armin, 'Sustaining the Island: Western Aid to 1950s Berlin', in *Cold War History*, vol. 3 no. 3 (2003), pp. 1–22.

Grünbacher, Armin, 'Causes, Response and Effect of the Crisis in the British Petrochemical Industry in the Early 1980s', in *The Journal of Industrial History*, vol. 6 no. 2 (October 2003), pp. 76–89.
Grünbacher, Armin, *Reconstruction and Cold War in Germany. The Kreditanstalt für Wiederaufbau 1948–1961*, Aldershot 2004.
Grünbacher, Armin, *The Making of German Democracy. West Germany during the Adenauer Era*, Manchester 2010.
Grünbacher, Armin, 'The Americanisation that never was? The first decade of the Baden-Badener Unternehmergespräche, 1954–64 and top management training in 1950s Germany', in *Business History*, vol. 54 no. 2 (April 2012), pp. 245–61, p. 247.
Grünbacher, Armin, '"Honourable Men": West German Industrialists and the Role of Honour and Honour Courts in the Adenauer Era', in *Contemporary European History*, vol. 2, no. 2 (April 2013), pp. 233–52.
Grunenberg, Nina, *Die Wundertäter. Netzwerke der deutschen Wirtschaft 1942–1966*, München 2006.
Grunwald, Wolfgang and Bernthal, Wilmar F., 'Controversy in German Management. The Harzburg Model Experience', in *Academy of Management Review*, vol. 8 no. 2 (1983), pp. 233–34.
Guserl, Richard, *Das Harzburger Model. Idee und Wirklichkeit*, Wiesbaden 1973.
Hankel, Wilhelm, *Die zweite Kapitalverteilung. Ein marktwirtschaftlicher Weg langfristiger Finanzierungspolitik*, Frankfurt/M. 1961.
Hartmann, Heinz, *Authority and Organization in German Management*, Princeton 1959.
Hartmann, Michael, 'Soziale Homogenität und generationelle Muster der deutschen Wirtschaftselite seit 1945', in Volker Berghahn, Stefan Unger and Dieter Ziegler (eds) *Die deutsche Wirtschaftselite*, pp. 31–50.
Heinrichsbauer, August, *Schwerindustrielle und Politik*, Essen 1948.
Hellwig, Fritz, 'Der echte Unternehmer in der Marktwirtschaft'. *Vortrag auf der Jahreshauptversammlung der Arbeitsgemeinschaft Selbstständiger Unternehmer, 30.3. 1951* (no place or year of publication).
Hellwig, Hans, 'Die Baden-Badener Unternehmergespräche. Weiterbildung des Unternehmernachwuchses', in Bundesverband deutscher Arbeitgeberverbände and Walter Raymond Stiftung (eds), *Unternehmer und Bildung. Festschrift zum 60. Geburtstag von Ludwig Vaubel*, Köln 1968, pp. 97–105.
Hellwig, Hans and Bertsch, Jürgen, 'Ursprung und Werden einer Erfolgsgeschichte', in Jürgen Bertsch, Peter Zürn, *Führen und Gestalten. 100 Unternehmergespräche in Baden-Baden*, Berlin 1997, pp. 13–24.
Henke, Klaus-Dietmar, *Die Amerikanische Besetzung Deutschlands*, München 1995.
Henle, Günter, *Weggenosse des Jahrhunderts. Als Diplomat, Industrieller, Politiker und Freund der Musik*, Stuttgart 1968.
Hentschel, Volker, *Ludwig Erhard. Ein Politikerleben*, München 1996.
Herbst, Ludolf, *Der totale Krieg und die Ordnung der deutschen Wirtschaft. Die Kriegswirtschaft im Spannungsfeld von Politik, Ideologie und Propaganda*, Stuttgart 1982.
Herdenröder, Karl Heinrich, *Neue Männer an der Ruhr. Mit einem Vorwort von Wilhelm Zangen*, Düsseldorf 1958.
Herriegel, Gary, *Industrial Construction. The Sources of German Industrial Power*, Cambridge 1996.
Hettling, Manfred, 'Die persönliche Selbstständigkeit. Der archimedische Punkt bürgerlicher Lebensführung', in Manfred Hettling and Stefan-Ludwig Hoffmann (eds), *Der bürgerliche Wertehimmel. Innenansichten des 19. Jahrhunderts*, Göttingen 2000, pp. 57–78.

Hilger, Susanne, '*Amerikanisierung' deutscher Unternehmen. Wettbewerbsstrategien und Unternehmenspolitik bei Henkel, Siemens und Daimler Benz (1945/49–1975)*, Stuttgart 2004.

Höhn, Reinhard, 'Der Wandel im Führungsstil der Wirtschaft', in *Führung in der Wirtschaft. Festschrift zum zehnjährigen Bestehen der Akademie für Führungskräfte der Wirtschaft*, Bad Harzburg 1966, pp. 9–87.

Höhn, Reinhard, *Führungsbrevier der Wirtschaft*, Bad Harzburg 1966.

Höhne, Heinz, *Der Orden unter dem Totenkopf. Die Geschichte der SS*, Gütersloh 1967; Engl. translation, *The Order of the Death's Head*, London 1969.

Hüttenberger, Peter, 'Wirtschaftsordnung und Interessenpolitik in der Kartellgesetzgebung der Bundesrepublik 1949–1957', in *Vierteljahrshefte für Zeitgeschichte*, vol, 24 no. 3 (July 1976), pp. 287–307.

IHK Braunschweig (ed.), *150 Jahre IHK Braunschweig. Ehrenamtliches Engagement für die Wirtschaft der Region*, Braunschweig 2014, p. 98–99 at http://braunschweig.ihk.de/fileadmin/v1/media/150jahre/ihk_buch/, accessed 2 May 2015.

James, Harold, *Family Capitalism: Wendels, Haniels, Falcks, and the Continental European Model*, Harvard 2006.

Janssen, Gregor, *Das Ministerium Speer. Deutschlands Rüstung im Krieg*, Frankfurt/M 1968.

Jarausch, Konrad, *Die Umkehr. Deutsche Wandlungen 1945–1995*, Bonn 2004.

Joly, Hervé, *Großunternehmer in Deutschland. Soziologie einer industriellen Elite 1933–1989*, Leipzig 1998.

Joly, Hervé, 'Kontinuität und Diskontinuität der industriellen Elite nach 1945', in Dieter Ziegler (ed.), *Großbürger und Unternehmer. Die deutsche Wirtschaftselite im 20. Jahrhundert*, Göttingen 2000, pp. 54–72

Käppen, Joachim, *Berthold Beitz. Die Biographie*, Berlin 2010.

Kipping, Matthias, 'Inter-Firm Relations and Industrial Policy: The French and German Steel Producers and Users in the Twentieth Century', in *Business History*, vol. 38 no. 1 (1996), pp. 1–25.

Kipping, Matthias, '"Operation Impact". Converting European Entrepreneurs to the American Creed', in Kipping and Bjanar (eds), *Americanisation of European Business*, pp. 55–73.

Kipping, Matthias and Bjanar, Ove (eds), *The Americanisation of European Business. The Marshall Plan and the Transfer of US Management Models*, London 1998.

Kipping, Matthias, 'The Hidden Business Schools: Management Training in Germany since 1945', in Lars Engwall and Vera Zamagni (eds), *Management Education*, p 101.

Kipping, Matthias and Kleinschmidt, Christian, 'Ludwig Vaubel and the Renewal of Management Education in Germany after 1945', in Anne-Marie Kuijlaars, Kim Prudon and Joop Visser (eds), *Business and Society. Entrepreneurs, Politics and Networks in Historical Perspective. Proceedings of the 3rd European Business History Association Conference*, Rotterdam 2000, pp. 521–30.

Kleinschmidt, Christian, 'An Americanised Company in Germany. The Vereinigte Glanzstoff Fabriken in the 1950s', in Matthias Kipping and Ove Bjanar, *Americanisation of European Business*, pp. 171–89.

Kleinschmidt, Christian, 'Das "1968" der Manager: Fremdwahrnehmung und Selbstreflexion einer sozialen Elite in den 60er Jahren', in Jan-Otmar Hesse, Christian Kleinschmidt and Karl Lauschke (eds), *Kulturalismus. Neue Institutionenökonomik oder Theorievielfalt. Eine Zwischenbilanz der Unternehmensgeschichte*, Essen 2002, pp. 19–31

Kleinschmidt, Christian, *Der Produktive Blick, Wahrnehmung amerikanischer und japanischer Management- und Produktionsmethoden durch deutsche Unternehmer, 1950–1985*, Berlin 2002.

Kocka, Jürgen (ed.), *Bürger und Bürgerlichkeit im 19. Jahrhundert*, Göttingen 1987.

Koehne, Rainer, *Unternehmertum im Wandel. Wie sehen sich die Unternehmer - wie werden sie gesehen? Herausforderungen an eine Institution*, Köln 1975.

Koehne, Rainer, *Das Selbstbild der deutschen Unternehmer. Legitimation und Leitbild einer Institution*, Berlin 1976.

Köhler, Herbert W., *30 Jahre Stahlpolitik aus der Sicht eines Verbandsmanagers. Erinnerungen*, 2 vols., Düsseldorf 1997.

Kolb, Eberhard, *The Weimar Republic*, 2nd ed., London 2005.

Kroker, Evelyn, 'Die Gründungsgeschichte der VFKK', in *Der Anschnitt*, vol. 50 (1998), pp. 186–95.

Krocker, Evelyn, 'Heinrich Kost: Rationalisierung und Sozialbeziehungen im Bergbau', in Paul Erker, Toni Pierenkemper (eds), *Deutsche Unternehmer zwischen Kriegswirtschaft und Wiederaufbau. Studien zur Erfahrungsbildung von Industrie Eliten*, München 1999, pp. 291–316.

Krumm, Heinrich, *Tagebuch eines deutschen Unternehmers 1937–1947*, Frankfurt/M 1956, (private printing).

Kuisel, Richard, 'Americanization for Historians', in *Diplomatic History*, vol. 14 no. 3 (summer 2000), pp. 509–15.

Kunkel, Ernst E., 'Der Aufbau', in Deutsches Industrie Institut (ed.), *Fünfzehn Jahre Deutsches Industrie Institut*, Köln 1966.

Langer, Peter, *Macht und Verantwortung. Der Ruhrbaron Paul Reusch*, Essen 2012.

Lehming, Eva-Maria, *Carl Hundhausen, Sein Leben Sein Werk, sein Lebenswerk: Public Relations in Deutschland*, Wiesbaden 1997.

Lindner, Stephan H., *Inside IG Farben. Hoechst during the Third Reich*, Cambridge 2008.

Lochner Louis, *Tycoons and Tyrant. German Industry from Hitler to Adenauer*, Chicago 1954.

Locke, Robert R., 'Business Education in Germany: Past Systems and Current Practice', in *Business History Review*, vol. 52, no. 2 (summer 1985), pp. 232–53.

Locke, Robert R., *The Collapse of the American Management Mystique*, Oxford 1996.

Locke, Robert R., 'Mistaking a historical phenomenon for a functional one: post-war management training reconsidered', in Lars Engwall and Vera Zamagni (eds), *Management Education in Historical Perspective*, Manchester 1998, pp. 145–56.

Lutz, Burkhart, 'Integration durch Aufstieg. Überlegungen zur Verbürgerlichung der deutschen Facharbeiter in den Jahrzehnten nach dem Zweiten Weltkrieg', in Manfred Hertling and Bernd Ulrich (eds), *Bürgertum nach 1945*, Hamburg 2005, pp. 284–309.

Mansfeld, Manfred, 'Die Gründung', in Deutsches Industrie Institut (ed.), *Fünfzehn Jahre Deutsches Industrie Institut*, Köln 1966.

Martin, James Stewart, *All Honorable Men*, Boston 1950

Marx, Christian, *Paul Reusch und die Gutehoffnungshütte. Leitung eines deutschen Großunternehmens*, Göttingen 2013.

Maschke, Erich, *Es entsteht ein Konzern. Paul Reusch und die Gutehoffnungshütte*, Tübingen 1969.

McGlade, Jacqueline, 'The big push: the extend of American business education to western Europe after the Second World War', in Lars Engwall and Vera Zamagni (eds), *Management Education in Historical Perspective*, Manchester 1998, pp. 50–65, p. 52.

Mollin, Gerhard, *Montankonzerne und 'Drittes Reich'. Der Gegensatz zwischen Monopolindustrie und Befehlswirtschaft in der deutschen Rüstung und Expansion, 1936–1944*, Göttingen 1988.

Mommsen, Ernst-Wolf (ed.), *Elitenbildung in der Wirtschaft*, Darmstadt 1955.

Mommsen, Hans, 'Die Auflösung des Bürgertums seit dem späten 19. Jahrhundert', in Kocka (ed.), *Bürger und Bürgerlichkeit*, pp. 288–315.

Müller-List, Gabriele, 'Eine neue Moral für Deutschland? Die Bewegung für Moralische Aufrüstung und ihre Bedeutung beim Wiederaufbau 1947–1952', in *Aus Politik und Zeitgeschichte*, no. 44 (1981), pp. 11–23.

Neebe, Reinhard, *Großindustrie, Staat und NSDAP 1930–1933. Paul Silverberg und der Reichsverband der Deutschen Industrie in der Krise der Weimarer Republik*, Göttingen 1981.

Neebe, Reinhard, 'Ludwig Erhard und die Globalisierung: Konzeptionen und Kontroversen deutscher Weltmarktpolitik im 20. Jahrhundert', in Volker Berghahn and Sigurt Vitols (eds), *Gibt es einen deutschen Kapitalismus? Tradition und globale Perspektiven der Sozialen Marktwirtschaft*, Frankfurt/M 2006, pp. 169–185.

Nonn, Christoph, *Die Ruhrbergbaukrise. Entindustrialisierung und Politik 1958–1969*, Göttingen 1999.

Obermüller, Benjamin, 'Hermann Reusch und die Beziehungen zur Eigentümer Familie Haniel', in Susane Hilger and Ulrich S. Soénius (eds) *Familienunternehmen im Rheinland im 19. und 20 Jahrhundert*, Schriften zur rheinisch-westfälischen Wirtschaftsgeschichte, vol. 47, Köln, Stiftung Rheinisch-Westfälisches Wirtschaftsarchiv 2009, pp. 159–74.

Obermüller, Benjamin, '"Auf einen groben Klotz gehört ein grober Keil." Hermann Reuschs Kampf gegen Dr Franz Kirchfeld 1947–1950', in Historische Gesellschaft Oberhausen (ed.), *Ursprünge und Entwicklungen der Stadt Oberhausen*, Band 8, Oberhausen 2009, pp. 119–33.

Pierenkemper, Toni, 'Hans-Günther Sohl: Funktionale Effizienz und autoritäre Harmonie in der Eisen- und Stahlindustrie', in Paul Erker and Toni Pierenkemper (eds), *Deutsche Unternehmer zwischen Kriegswirtschaft und Wiederaufbau. Studien zur Erfahrungsbildung von Industriellen*, München 1999, pp. 53–107.

Plumpe, Werner, 'Unternehmerverbände und industrielle Interessenpolitik', in Wolfgang Köllmann, Hermann Korte, Dietmar Petzina and Wolfhart Weber (eds), *Das Ruhrgebiet im Industriezeitalter. Geschichte und Entwicklung*, vol. 1 Düsseldorf 1990, pp. 655–727.

Pogge von Strandmann, Hartmut, 'Großindustrie und Realpolitik. Deutsch-Sowjetische Handelsbeziehungen in der Weimarer Republik', in: *Historische Zeitschrift*, vol. 222, no. 2 (April 1976), pp. 265–341.

Pohl, Hans, Habeth, Stephanie and Brüninghaus, Beate, *Die Daimler-Benz AG in den Jahren 1933 bis 1945. Eine Dokumentation*, Stuttgart 1986.

Pötzel, Norbert, *Beitz. Eine deutsche Geschichte*, München 2011.

Priemel, Kim Christian, 'Der Sonderweg vor Gericht. Angewandte Geschichte im Nürnberger Krupp Prozess', in *Historische Zeitschrift* vol. 294, no. 2 (April 2012) pp 391–426.

Priemel, Kim Christian, 'Gekaufte Geschichte: Der "Freundeskreis Albert Vögler", Gert von Klass und die Entwicklung der historischen Unternehmensforschung nach 1945', in *Zeitschrift für Unternehmensgeschichte*, vol. 52 (2009), pp. 177–202.

Prowe, Diethelm, 'Unternehmer, Gewerkschaften und Staat in der Kammerneuordnung in der britischen Besatzungszone bis 1950, in Dietmar Petzina and Walter Euchner (eds), *Wirtschaftspolitik im britischen Besatzungsgebiet 1945–1949*, Düsseldorf 1985, pp. 238–40.

Pudor, Fritz, *Lebensbilder aus dem Rheinisch-Westfälischen Industriegebiet: Jahrgang 1962–1967*, Baden-Baden 1977.

Rauh-Kühne, Cornelia, 'Hans-Constantin Paulssen: Sozialpartnerschaft aus dem Geiste der Kriegskameradschaft', in Paul Erker and Toni Pierenkemper (eds), *Deutsche Unternehmer zwischen Kriegswirtschaft und Wiederaufbau. Studien zur Erfahrungsbildung von Industriellen*, München 1999, pp. 109–92.

Rauh-Kühne, Cornelia, 'Paulssen, Hans Constantin', in *Neue Deutsche Biographie 20* (2001), p. 131.

Rauh-Kühne, Cornelia, 'Zwischen "verantwortlichem Wirkungskreis" und "häuslichem Glanz". Zur Innenansicht wirtschaftsbürgerlicher Familien im 20. Jahrhundert', in Dieter Ziegler (ed.), *Großbürger und Unternehmer*, pp. 215–48.

Rauh-Kühne, Cornelia, '"... so weiß ich heute, dass Dein Leben in unserer Familiengeschichte einen wertvolleren Platz haben wird als das Deiner Söhne." Zur Bürgerlichkeit von Unternehmerfamilien der Wiederaufbaugeneration', in Volker Berghahn, Stefan Unger and Dieter Ziegler (eds), *Die Deutsche Wirtschaftselite im 20. Jahrhundert*, pp. 443–46.

Reitmayer, Morten, 'Unternehmer zur Führung berufen – durch wen?', in Volker Berghahn, Stefan Unger and Dieter Ziegler (eds) *Die deutsche Wirtschaftselite im 20. Jahrhundert*, pp. 317–36.

Riedel, Manfred, 'Bürger, Staatsbürger, Bürgertum', in Otto Brunner, Werner Conze and Reinhard Koselleck (eds), *Geschichtliche Grundbegriffe*, vol. 1, Stuttgart 1972, pp. 672–725, esp. pp.712–24.

Ritter, Gerhard A. and Niehuss, Merith, *Wahlen in Deutschland, 1946–1991*, München 1991.

Rohland, Walter, *Bewegte Zeiten. Erinnerungen eines Eisenhüttenmannes*, Stuttgart 1978.

Roseman, Mark, *Recasting the Ruhr. Manpower, Economic Recovery and Labour Relations*, Oxford 1992.

Rosenberger, Ruth, *Experten für Humankapital. Die Entdeckung des Personalmanagements in der Bundesrepublik Deutschland*, München 2008.

Rudolph, Karsten, *Wirtschaftsdiplomatie im Kalten Krieg. Die Ostpolitik der westdeutschen Großindustrie 1945–1991*, Frankfurt /M 2004.

Rühters, Bernd, 'Reinhard Höhn, Carl Schmidt und andere – Geschichten und Legenden aus der NS-Zeit', in *Neue juristische Wochenschrift*, Heft 39 (2000), 2866–2871.

Schanetzky, Tim, Review of Tilly, Richard: *Willy H. Schlieker. Aufstieg und Fall eines Unternehmers (1914–1980)*. Berlin 2008, in *H-Soz-Kult*, 17 March 2009, http://www.hsozkult.de/publicationreview/id/rezbuecher-11811.

Schelsky, Helmut, 'Die Bedeutung des Schichtbegriffs für die Analyse der gegenwärtigen Deutschen Gesellschaft', in Helmut Schelsky, *Auf der Suche nach Wirklichkeit, Gesammelte Aufsätze*, München 1965, pp. 332–35.

Schmid, Daniel, '"Quo vadis, homo harzburgiensis?" Aufstieg und Niedergang des "Harzburger Modells"', in *Zeitschrift für Unternehmensgeschichte* vol. 59 no. 1 (April 2014), pp. 73–98.

Schmillinger, Horst W., 'Die Deutsche Partei', in Richard Stöss (ed.), *Parteien Handbuch: Die Parteien der Bundesrepublik Deutschland, 1945–1980*, vol. 1, Opladen 1983, pp. 1025–1111.

Schneider, Michael, 'Demokratisierungs-Konsenz zwischen Unternehmern und Gewerkschaften? Zur Debatte um Wirtschaftsdemokratie und Mitbestimmung', in Axel Schildt and Arnold Sywottek (eds), *Modernisierung im Wiederaufbau. Die westdeutsche Gesellschaft der 50er Jahre*, Bonn 1998, pp. 207–22.

Schöllgen, Gregor, *Gustav Schickedanz. Biographie eines Revolutionärs*, Berlin 2010.

Schreiner, Heinrich, 'Das Institut in der sozialpolitischen Diskussion', in Deutsches Industrie Institut (ed.), *Fünfzehn Jahre Deutsches Industrie Institut*, Köln 1966.

Schröter, Harm G., 'Kartellierung und Dekartellierung 1890–1990', in *Vierteljahrsschrift für Sozial- und Wirtschaftsgeschichte*, vol. 81 no. 4 (1994), pp. 457–93.

Schröter, Harm G., *Americanization of the European Economy. A compact survey of American economic influence in Europe since the 1880s*, Dordrecht 2005.

Schulte Goebel, Achim, 'Fritz Berg 1901–1979. Unternehmer und Industriepräsident in der Adenauer Ära', unpublished PhD thesis, University of Düsseldorf.

Schulz, Günter, *Wiederaufbau in Deutschland. Die Wohnungsbaupolitik in den Westzonen und der Bundesrepublik von 1945 bis 1957*, Düsseldorf 1994.

Schulze, Rainer, *Unternehmerische Selbstverwaltung und Politik. Die Rolle der Industrie- und Handelskammern in Niedersachsen und Bremen als Vertretungen der Unternehmerinteressen nach dem Zweiten Weltkrieg*, Hildesheim 1988,

Seelig, Michael, *Alltagsadel. Der ehemalige ostelbische Adel in der Bundesrepublik Deutschland 1945/49–1975*, Köln 2015.

Servan-Schreiber, Jean-Jacques, *Die amerikanische Herausforderung*, Hamburg 1968, English ed.: *The American Challenge*, Avon 1971.

Silvia, Stephen J., *Holding the Shop Together: German Industrial Relations in the Postwar Era*, Ithaca and London, 2013.

Smith, Jean (ed.), *The Papers of Lucius D. Clay, Germany 1945–1949*, Bloomington 1974.

Sohl, Hans-Günther, *Industrie und Kunst, Vortrag vor den Mitgliedern des Düsseldorfer Industrieclubs*, no place of publication, 1978.

Sohl, Hans-Günther, *Notizen*, private printing 1983.

Sowade, Hanno, *Wegbereiter des Wiederaufstiegs. Die Industrie- und Handelskammern und die Rekonstruktion der Außenbeziehungen der westdeutschen Wirtschaft 1945–1949/50*, München 1992.

Spaulding, Robert Mark, *Osthandel und Ostpolitik. German Foreign Trade in Eastern Europe from Bismarck to Adenauer*, Oxford 1997.

Speitkamp, Wilfried, *Ohrfeige, Duell, Ehrenmord: Eine Geschichte der Ehre*, Stuttgart 2010.

Statistisches Bundesamt (ed.), *Statistisches Jahrbuch für die Bundesrepublik Deutschland*, Stuttgart (various years).

Stein, Gustav, *Unternehmer als Förderer der Kunst*, Frankfurt/M 1952.

Stein, Gustav (ed.), *Unternehmer in der Politik*, Düsseldorf 1954.

Steininger, Rolf, *Deutsche Geschichte seit 1945. Darstellungen und Dokumente in vier Bänden, Band 1: 1945–1947*, Frankfurt/M 2002.

Stokes, Raymond, 'From the IG Farben Fusion to the Establishment of BASF AG, (1922–1952)', in Werner Abelshauser et al., *German Industry and Global Enterprise. BASF: The History of a Company*, Cambridge 2004.

Stürmer, Michael, Teichmann, Gabriele and Treue, Wilhelm, *Striking the Balance. Sal. Oppenheim jr & Cie. A Family and a Bank*, London 1994.

Teichmann, Gabriele, 'Pferdmenges, Robert' in: *Neue Deutsche Biographie 20* (2001), p. 331 f.

Thies, Jochen, 'Otto Wolf von Amerongen: Kundschafter der Marktwirtschaft', in Peter Danylow and Ulrich S. Soénius (eds), *Otto Wolff. Ein Unternehmen zwischen Wirtschaft und Politik*, München 2005, pp. 385–435.

Thum, Horst, *Mitbestimmung in der Montanindustrie. Der Mythos vom Sieg der Gewerkschaften*, Stuttgart 1982.

Tilly, Richard, *Willy H. Schlieker, Aufstieg und Fall eines Unternehmers (1914–1980)*, Berlin 2008.

Tooze, Adam, *The Wages of Destruction. The Making and Breaking of the Nazi Economy*, London 2006.

Treue, Wilhelm, *Die Feuer verlöschen nie. August Thyssen Hütte 1890–1966*, 2 vols, Düsseldorf 1966, 1969.

Triesch, Günter, 'Im Kraftfeld der Politik', in Deutsches Industrie Institut (ed.), *Fünfzehn Jahre Deutsches Industrie Institut*, Köln 1966, pp. 63–71.

Turner, Henry Ashby, 'The Ruhrlade, Secret Cabinet of Heavy Industry in the Weimar Republic', in *Central European History*, 3, no. 3 (1970), pp. 195–228.

Turner, Henry Ashby, *German Big Business and the Rise of Hitler*, New York 1985.

Uebbing, Helmut, *Stahl schreibt Geschichte. 125 Jahre Wirtschaftsvereinigung Stahl*, Düsseldorf 1999.

Ullmann, Hans-Peter, *Interessenverbände in Deutschland*, Frankfurt 1988.

Unger, Stefan, '"Die Herren aus dem Westen." Zur Struktur und Semantik der Wirtschaftselite des Ruhrgebiets 1930–1970', in *Westfälische Forschungen*, vol. 50 (2000), pp. 143–62.

Van Eyll, Klara, et al (eds), *Die Geschichte der Unternehmerischen Selbstverwaltung in Köln 1914–1997*, Köln 1997. http://www.ihk-niederrhein.de/Namhafte-Personen, accessed 6 May 2015.

Vaubel, Ludwig, *Unternehmer gehen zur Schule*, Düsseldorf 1952.

Vaubel, Ludwig, *Zusammenbruch und Wiederaufbau. Ein Tagebuch der Wirtschaft 1945–49* (ed. Wolfgang Benz), München 1984.

Vierhaus, Rudolf and Herbst, Ludolf (eds), *Biographisches Handbuch der Abgeordneten des Deutschen Bundestages, 1949–2002*, München 2002.

Von Heyl, Friedrich, *Der innerdeutsche Handel mit Eisen und Stahl 1945–1972. Deutsch-deutsche Beziehungen im Kalten Krieg*, Köln 1997.

Von Hodenberg, Christina, 'Der Fluch des Geldsacks. Der Aufstieg der Industriellen als Herausforderung bürgerlicher Werte', in Hettling and Hoffmann (eds), *Der bürgerliche Wertehimmel*, pp. 79–103.

Von Kienriem, August, *Nürnberg. Rechtliche und menschliche Probleme*, Stuttgart 1953.

Von Menges, Dietrich Wilhem, *Unternehmerentscheide. Ein Leben für die Wirtschaft*, Düsseldorf 1976.

Von Plato, Alexander, '"Wirtschaftskapitäne": Biographische Selbstkonstruktionen von Unternehmern in der Nachkriegszeit', in, Axel Schildt and Arnold Sywottek (eds), *Modernisierung in Westdeutschland. Die westdeutsche Gesellschaft in den 50er Jahren*, Bonn 1998, pp. 377–91.

Von Saldern, Adelheid, 'Das "Harzburger Model." Ein Ordnungssystem für bundesrepublikanische Unternehmen, 1960–1975', in Thomas Etzemüller (ed.), *Die Ordnung der Moderne. Social Engineering im 20 Jahrhundert*, Bielefeld 2009, pp. 303–29.

Von Wilmowsky, Tilo, *Warum wurde Krupp verurteilt? Legende und Justizirrtum*, Stuttgart 1950.

Warner, Isable, *Steel and Sovereignty. The Deconcentration of the German Steel Industry 1949–54*, Mainz 1996.

Wehler, Hans-Ulrich, 'Deutsches Bürgertum nach 1945. Exitus oder Phoenix aus der Asche?', in *Geschichte und Gesellschaft*, vol. 27 (2001), pp. 617–34.

Weisbrod, Bernd, 'Der Schein der Modernität. Zur Historisierung der "Volksgemeinschaft", in Karsten Rudolph and Christel Wickert (eds), *Geschichte als Möglichkeit. Über die Chancen von Demokratie. Festschrift für Helga Grebing*, Essen 1995, pp. 234–42.

Weisbrod, Bernd, *Schwerindustrie in der Weimarer Republik. Interessenpolitik zwischen Stabilisierung und Krise*, Wuppertal 1978.

Weise, Jürgen, *Kammern in Not - zwischen Anpassung und Selbstbehauptung. Die Stellung der Industrie- und Handelskammern in der Auseinandersetzung um eine neue politische und wirtschaftliche Ordnung 1945–56. Dargestellt am Beispiel der rheinischen Kammern und ihren Vereinigungen auf Landes-, Zonen- und Bundesebene*, Köln 1989.

Weise, Jürgen, 'Müller-Wipperfürth, Alfons', in *Neue Deutsche Biographie 18* (1997), pp. 513 f.

Weisser, Wilhelm, 'Publizisten mit offenem Visier', in Deutsches Industrie Institut (ed.), *Fünfzehn Jahre Deutsches Industrie Institut*, Köln 1966.

Werneke, Klaus and Heller, Peter, *Der vergessene Führer. Alfred Hugenberg. Presemacht und Nationalsozialismus*, Hamburg 1987.

Wessel, Horst A., *Kontinuität im Wandel, 100 Jahre Mannesmann 1890–1990*, Düsseldorf 1990.

Whitman, James Q., 'Civility and Respect: Three Societies', in *The Yale Law Journal*, vol. 109 no. 6 (2000), pp. 1279–1398.

Wiesen, Jonathan, 'Germany's PR Man. Julius Klein and the Making of Transatlantic Memory', in Philipp Gassert and Alan E, Steinweis (eds), *Coping with the Nazi Past. West German Debates on Nazism and Generational Conflict 1955–1975*, Oxford 2006, pp. 294–308.

Wiesen, Jonathan, *West German Industry and the Challenge of the Nazi Past, 1945–1955*, Chapel Hill 2001.

Wildt, Michael, 'Der Fall Reinhard Höhn. Vom Reichssicherheitshauptamt zur Harzburger Akademie', in Alexander Gallus and Axel Schildt (eds), *Rückblickend in die Zukunft. Politische Öffentlichkeit und intellektuelle Positionen in Deutschland um 1950 und 1930*, Göttigen 2011, pp. 254–71.

Wildt, Michael, *An Uncompromising Generation. The Nazi Leadership of the Reich Security Main Office*, Madison 2009.

Winschuh, Josef, *Das neue Unternehmerbild. Grundzüge einer Unternehmerpolitik*, 2nd ed., Baden-Baden/Frankfurt 1954.

Wirtschaftsvereinigung Stahl und Stahlinstitut VDEh (eds), *Portraits im Stahlzentrum*, Düsseldorf 2006.

Zeitlin, Jonathan and Herrigel, Gary (eds), *Americanization and its Limits. Reworking US Technology and Management in Post-War Europe and Japan*, Oxford 2000.

Ziegler, Dieter, ' Strukturwandel und Elitenwechsel im Bankenwesen 1900–1957', in Volker Berghahn, Stefan Unger and Dieter Ziegler (eds), *Die deutsche Wirtschaftselite im 20. Jahrhundert. Kontinuität und Mentalität*, Essen 2003, pp. 187–218.

Ziegler, Dieter, 'Die wirtschaftsbürgerliche Elite im 20. Jahrhundert. Eine Bilanz', in Dieter Ziegler (ed.), *Großbürger und Unternehmer. Die deutsche Wirtschaftselite im 20. Jahrhundert*, Göttingen 2000, pp. 7–29.

Zunkel, Friedrich, 'Ehre', in Otto Brunner, Werner Conze and Reinhard Koselleck, *Geschichtliche Grundbegriffe*, vol. 2.

Index